Oh My Goddess!

ああっ女神さまっ

38

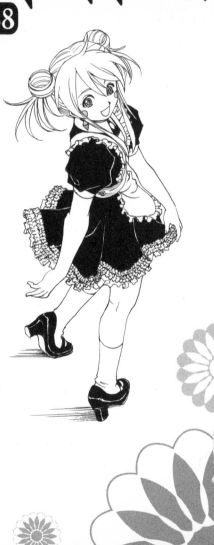

STORY AND ART BY
Kosuke Fujishima

TRANSLATION BY
Dana Lewis and Christopher Lewis

LETTERING AND TOUCHUP BY
Susie Lee and Betty Dong
WITH Tom2K

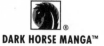

DARK HORSE MANGA™

CHAPTER 237

Where the Main Theme Fled To

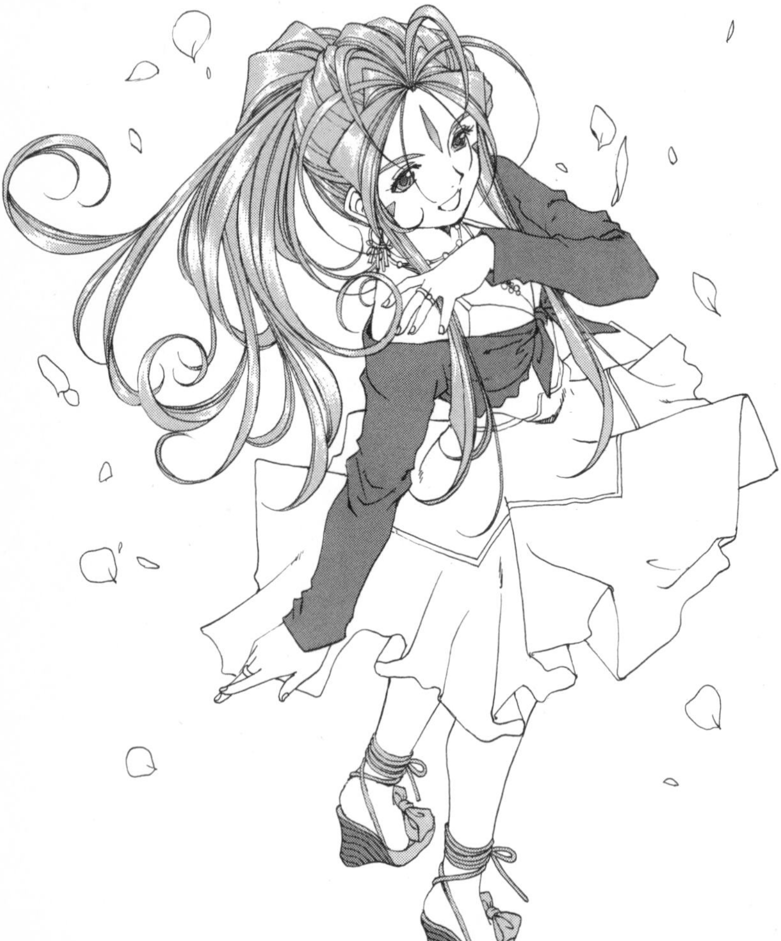

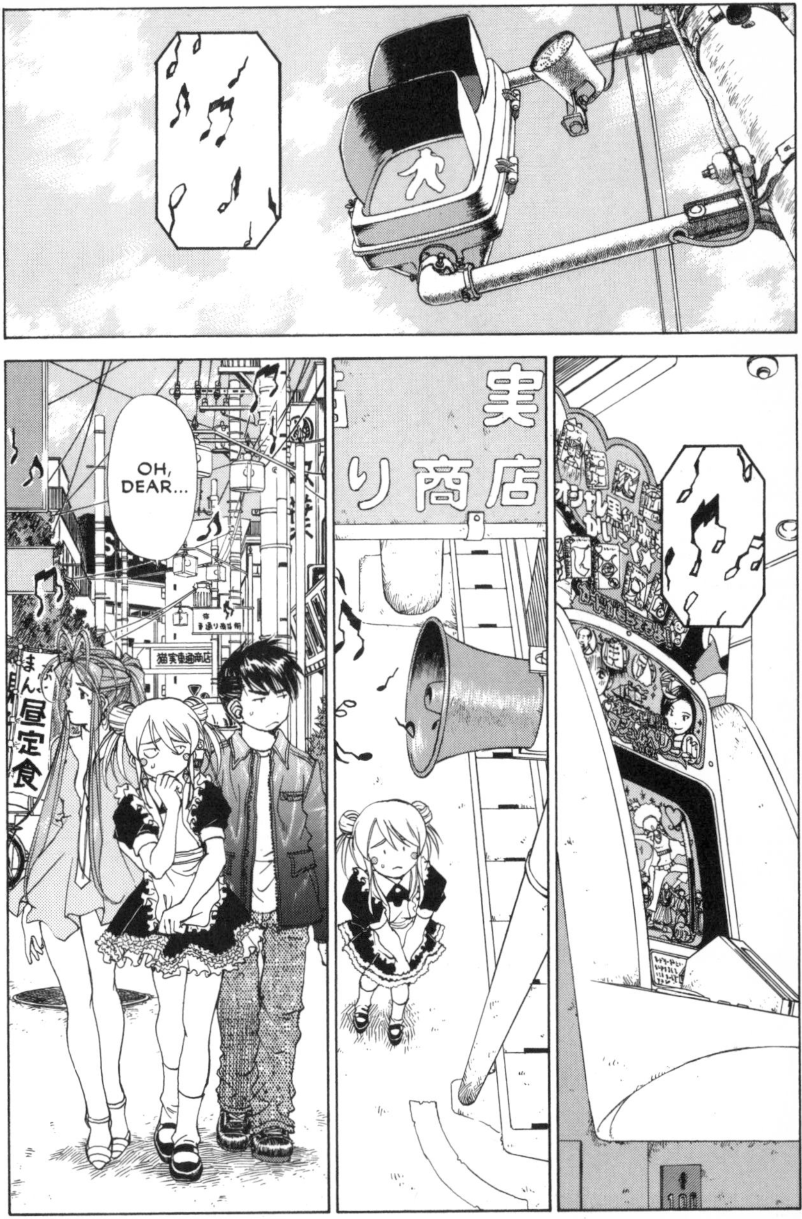
実
り商店
OH, DEAR...
昼定食

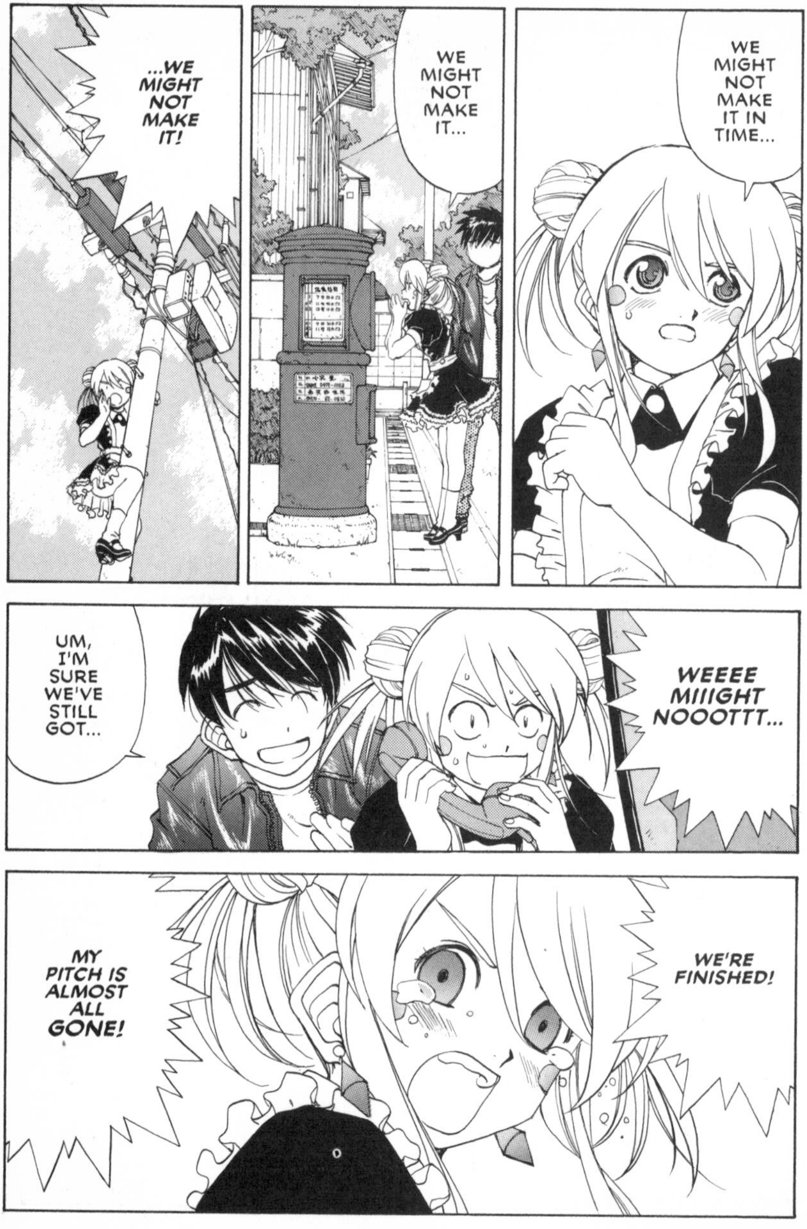
WE MIGHT NOT MAKE IT IN TIME...
WE MIGHT NOT MAKE IT...
...WE MIGHT NOT MAKE IT!
WEEEE MIIIGHT NOOOTTT...
UM, I'M SURE WE'VE STILL GOT...
WE'RE FINISHED!
MY PITCH IS ALMOST ALL GONE!

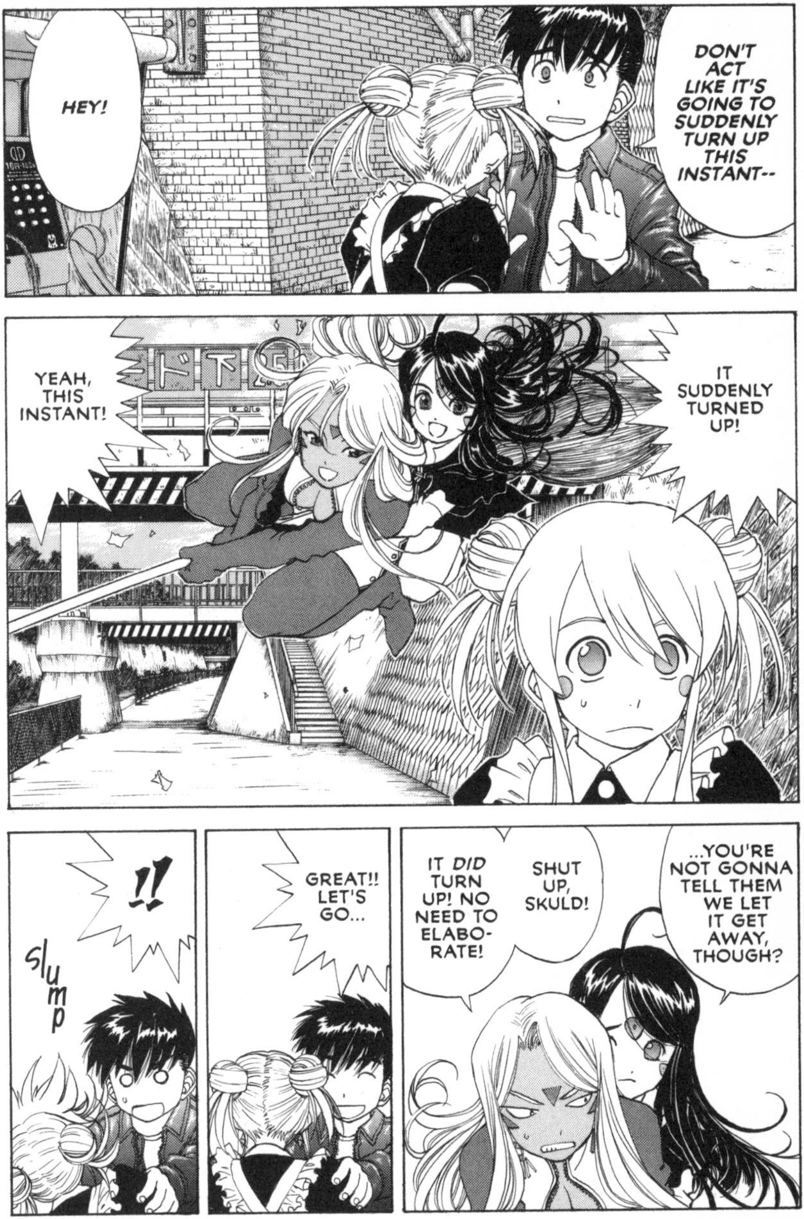
DON'T ACT LIKE IT'S GOING TO SUDDENLY TURN UP THIS INSTANT--
HEY!
IT SUDDENLY TURNED UP!
YEAH, THIS INSTANT!
...YOU'RE NOT GONNA TELL THEM WE LET IT GET AWAY, THOUGH?
SHUT UP, SKULD!
IT *DID* TURN UP! NO NEED TO ELABO-RATE!
GREAT!! LET'S GO...
!!
slump

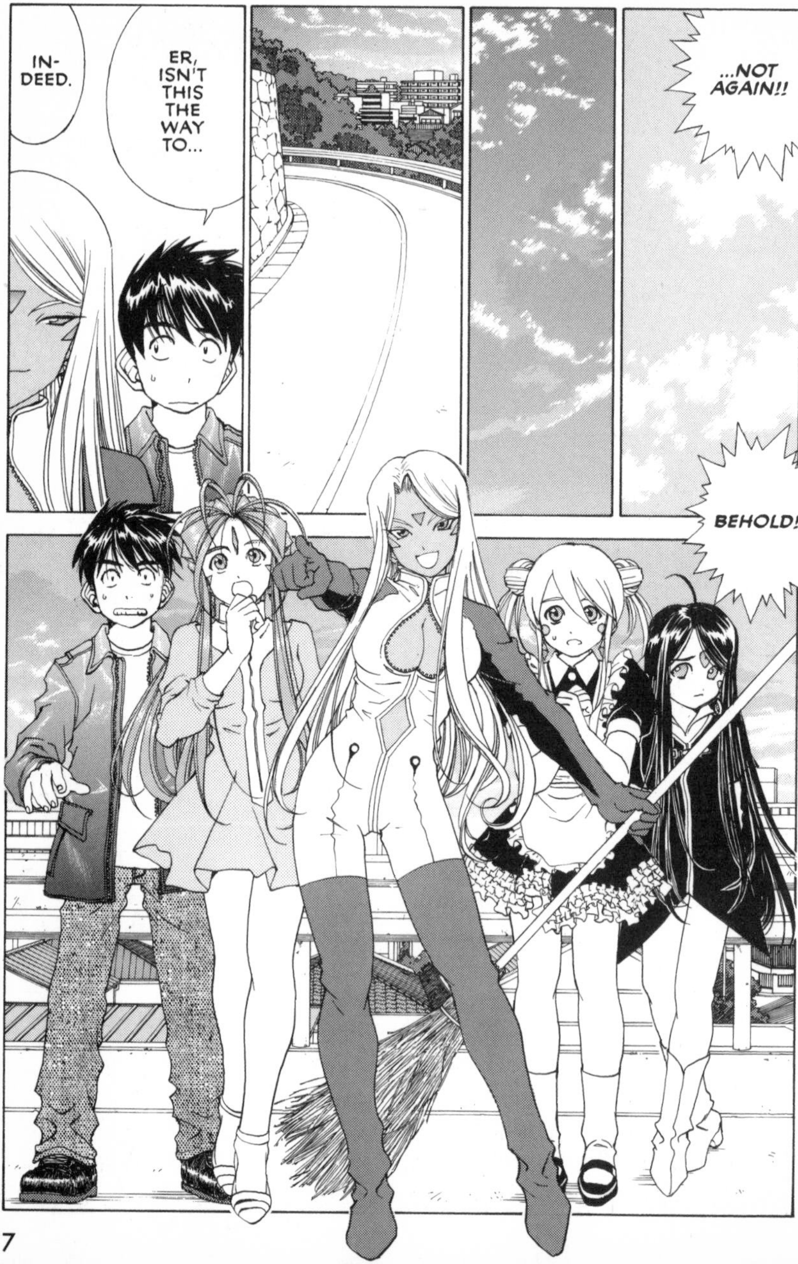
...NOT AGAIN!!
ER, ISN'T THIS THE WAY TO...
IN-DEED.
BEHOLD!

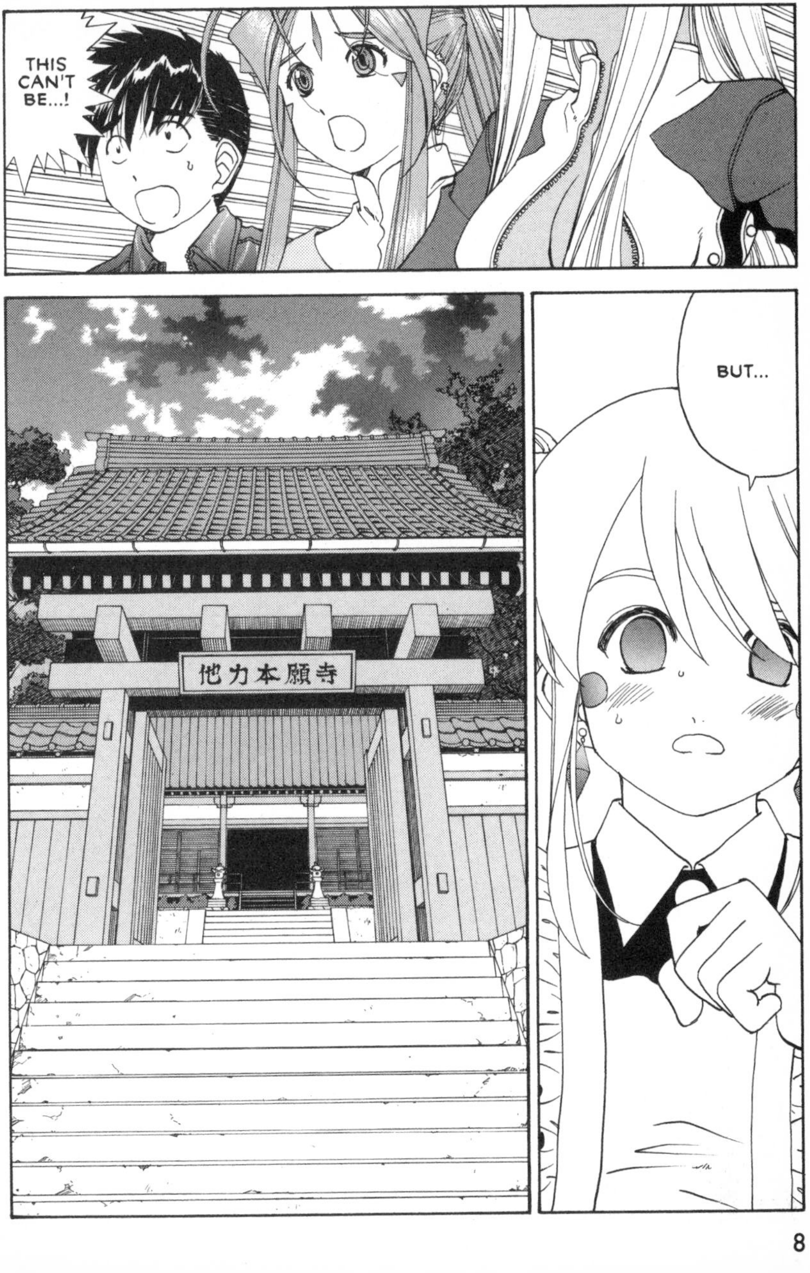
THIS CAN'T BE...!
BUT...
他力本願寺

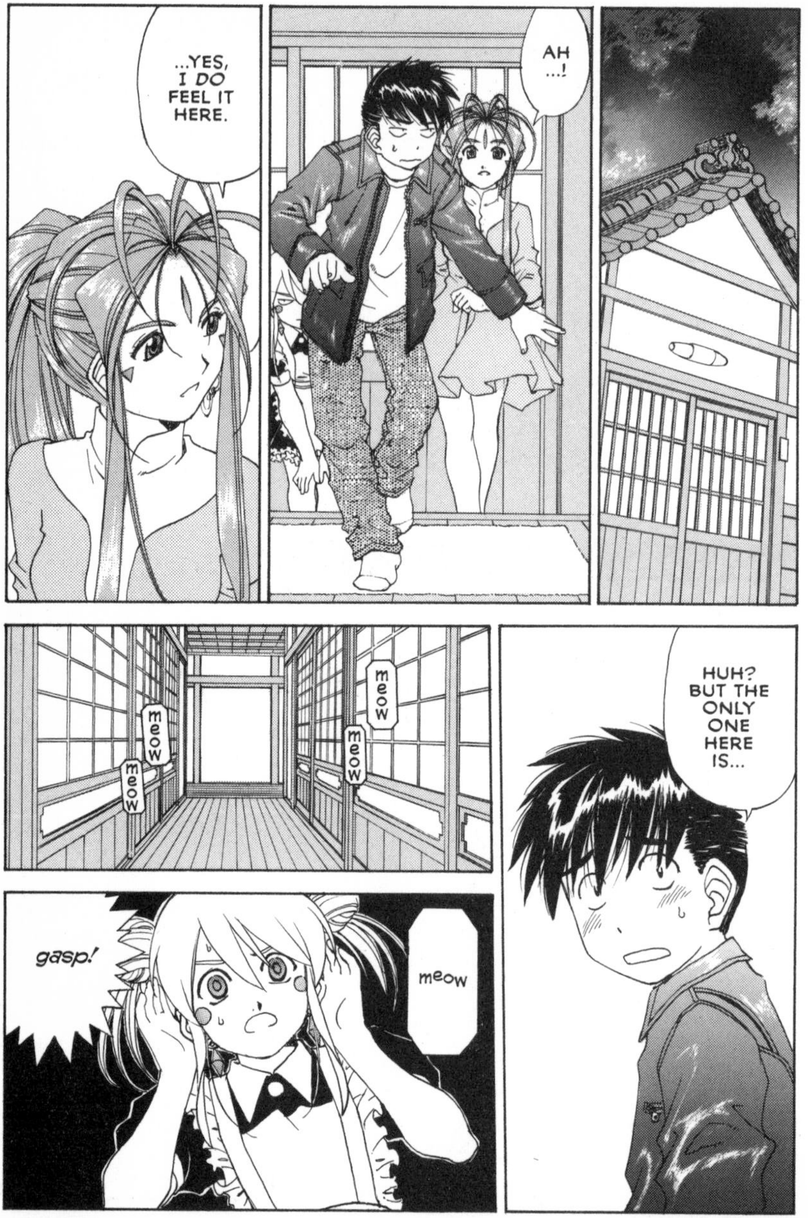
AH ...!
...YES, I *DO* FEEL IT HERE.
HUH? BUT THE ONLY ONE HERE IS...
meow
meow
meow
meow
meow
gasp!

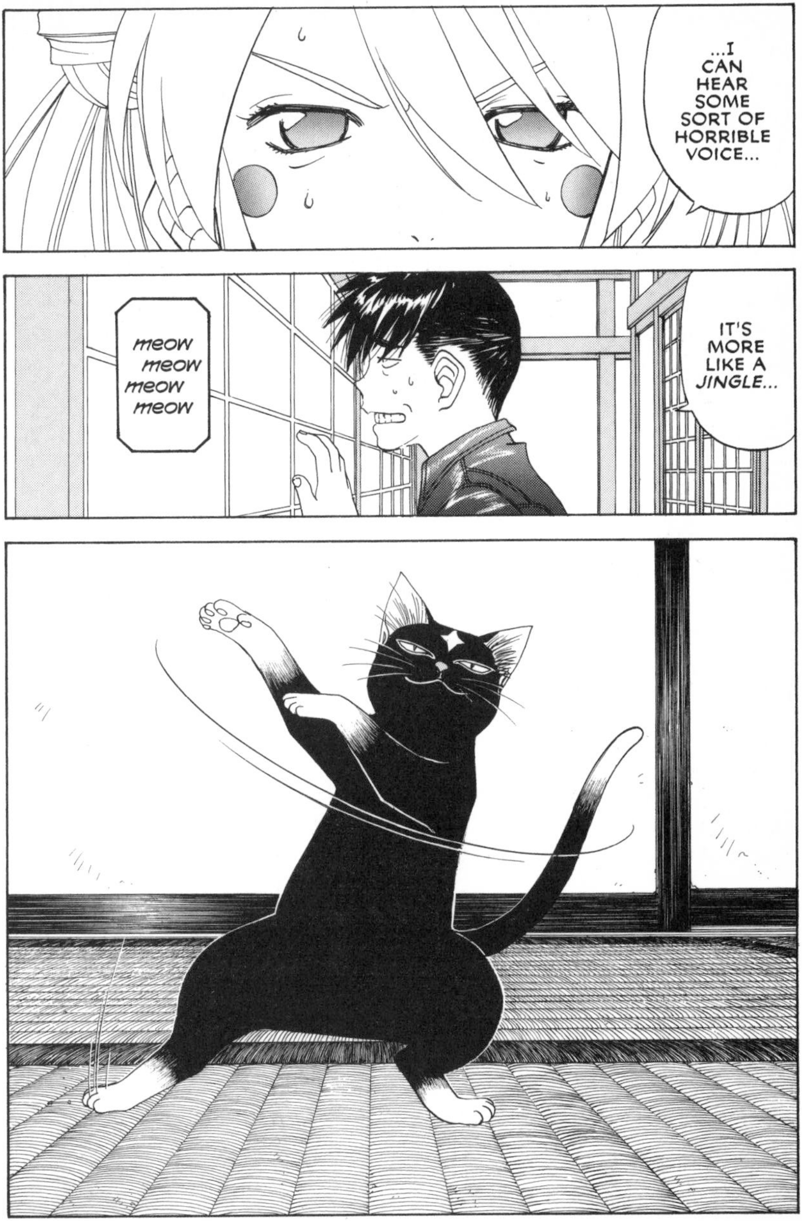
...I CAN HEAR SOME SORT OF HORRIBLE VOICE...
IT'S MORE LIKE A *JINGLE*...
meow meow meow meow

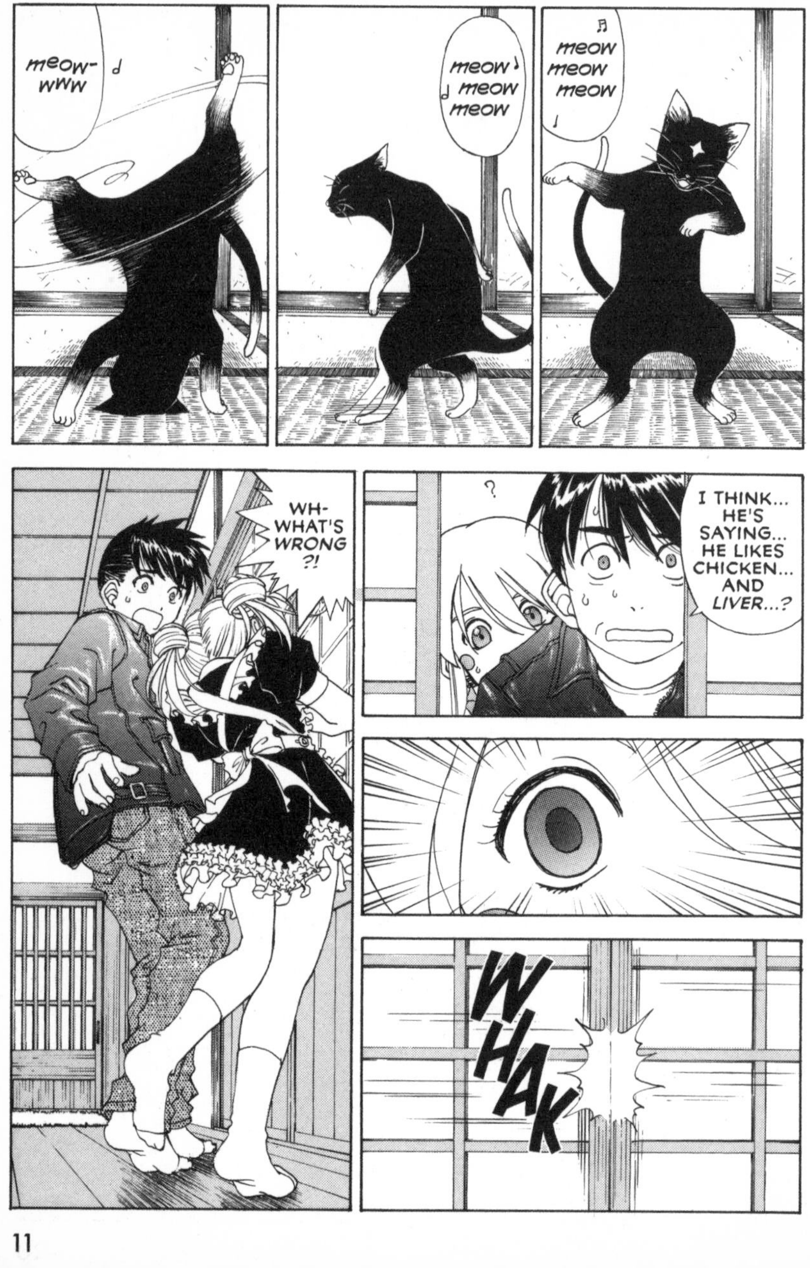
meow meow meow
meow meow meow
meow-www
I THINK... HE'S SAYING... HE LIKES CHICKEN... AND LIVER...?
WHAK
WH-WHAT'S WRONG?!

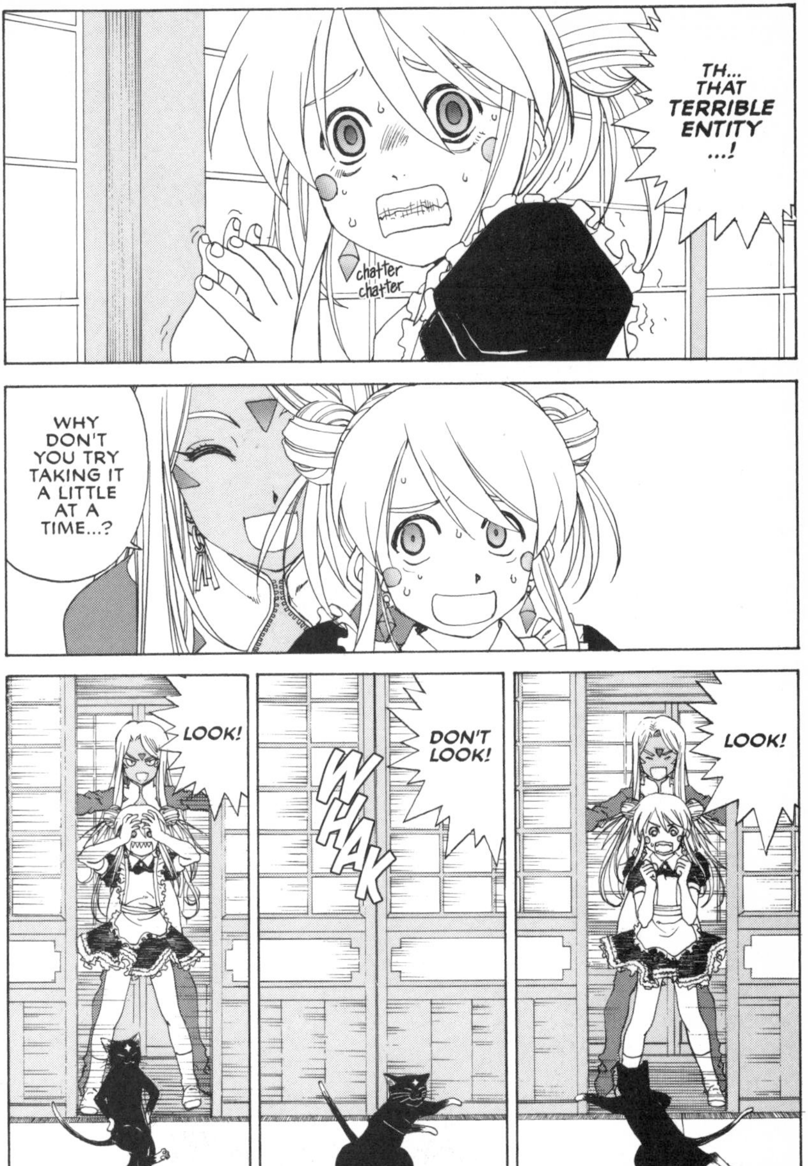
TH... THAT TERRIBLE ENTITY ...!
chatter chatter
WHY DON'T YOU TRY TAKING IT A LITTLE AT A TIME...?
LOOK!
DON'T LOOK!
WHAK
LOOK!

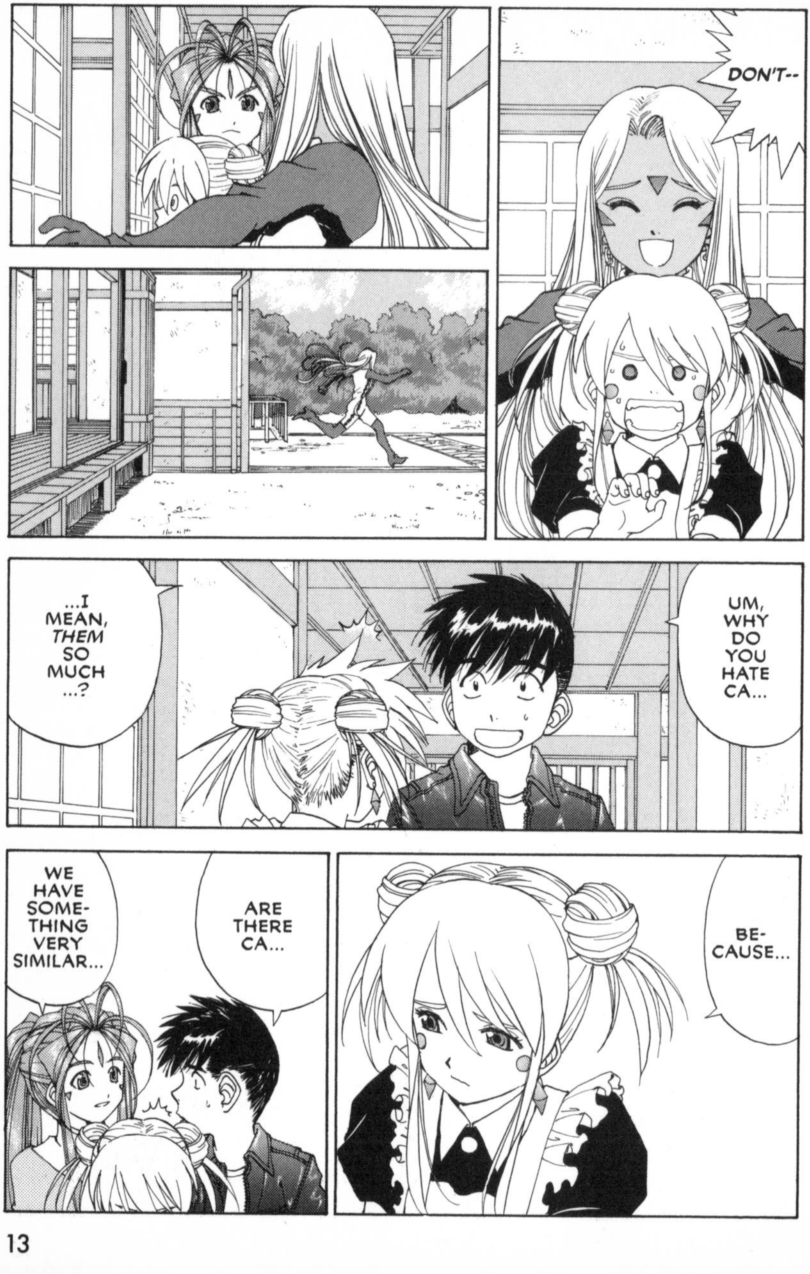
DON'T--
UM, WHY DO YOU HATE CA...
...I MEAN, *THEM* SO MUCH ...?
BE-CAUSE...
ARE THERE CA...
WE HAVE SOME-THING VERY SIMILAR...

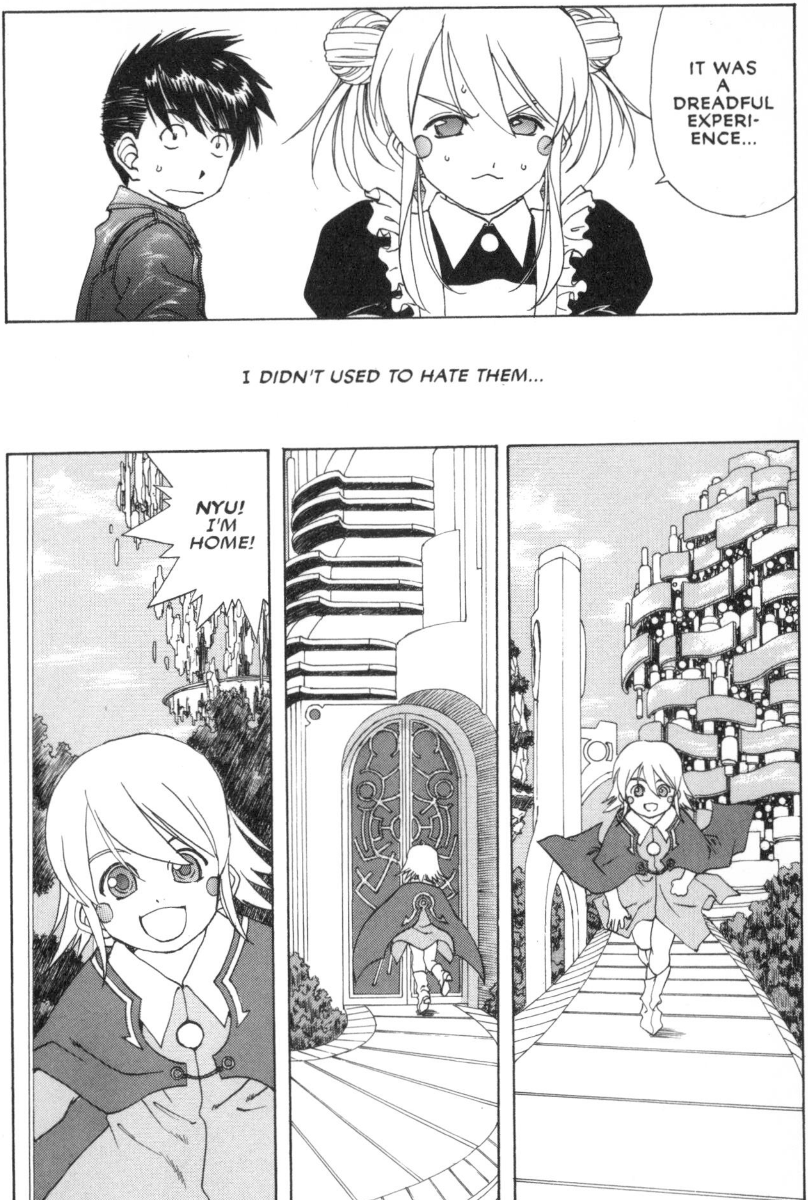
IT WAS A DREADFUL EXPERIENCE...
I DIDN'T USED TO HATE THEM...
NYU! I'M HOME!

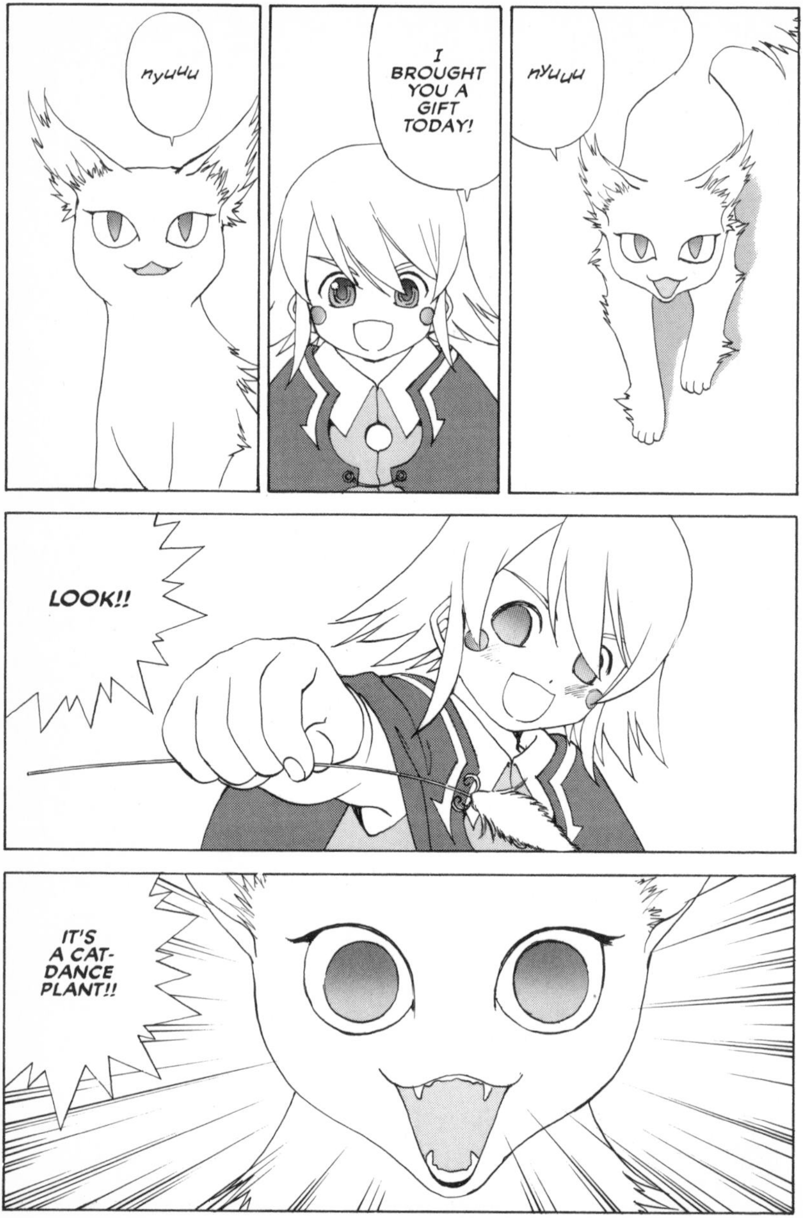
nyuuu
I BROUGHT YOU A GIFT TODAY!
nyuuu
LOOK!!
IT'S A CAT-DANCE PLANT!!

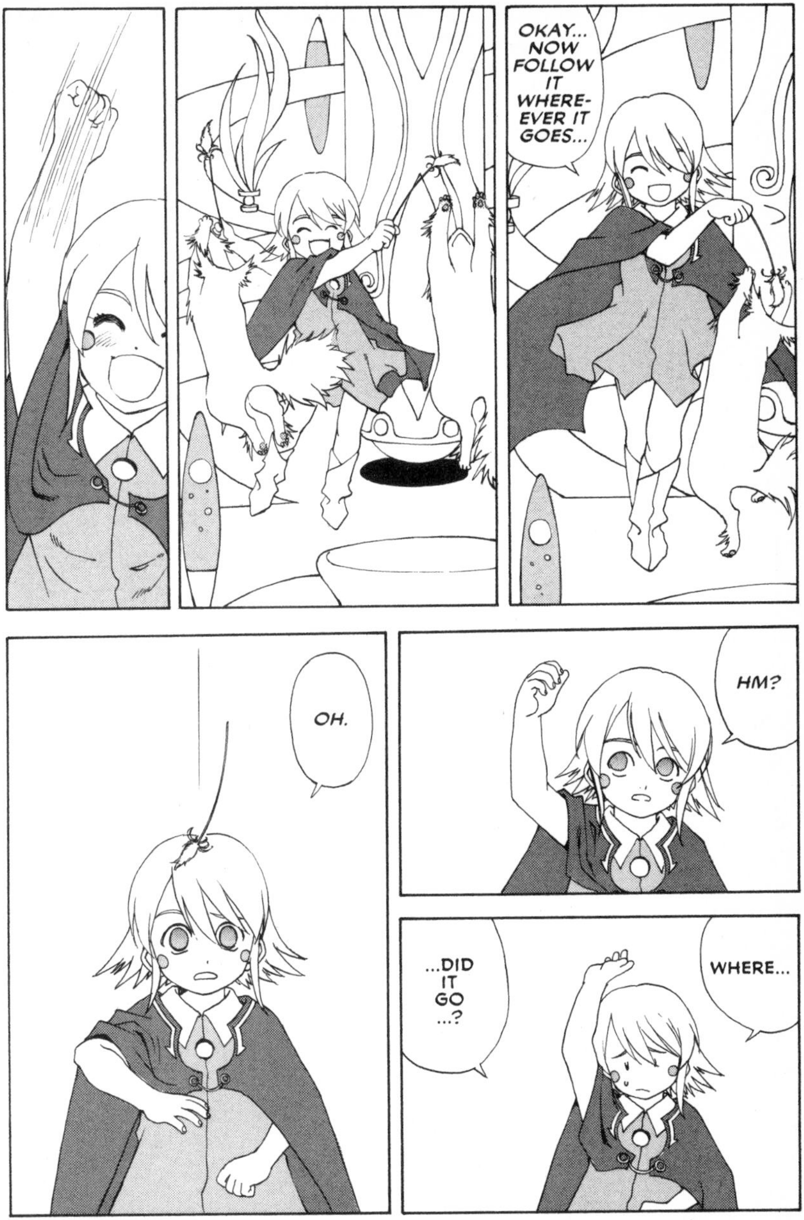
OKAY... NOW FOLLOW IT WHERE-EVER IT GOES...
HM?
WHERE...
...DID IT GO ...?
OH.

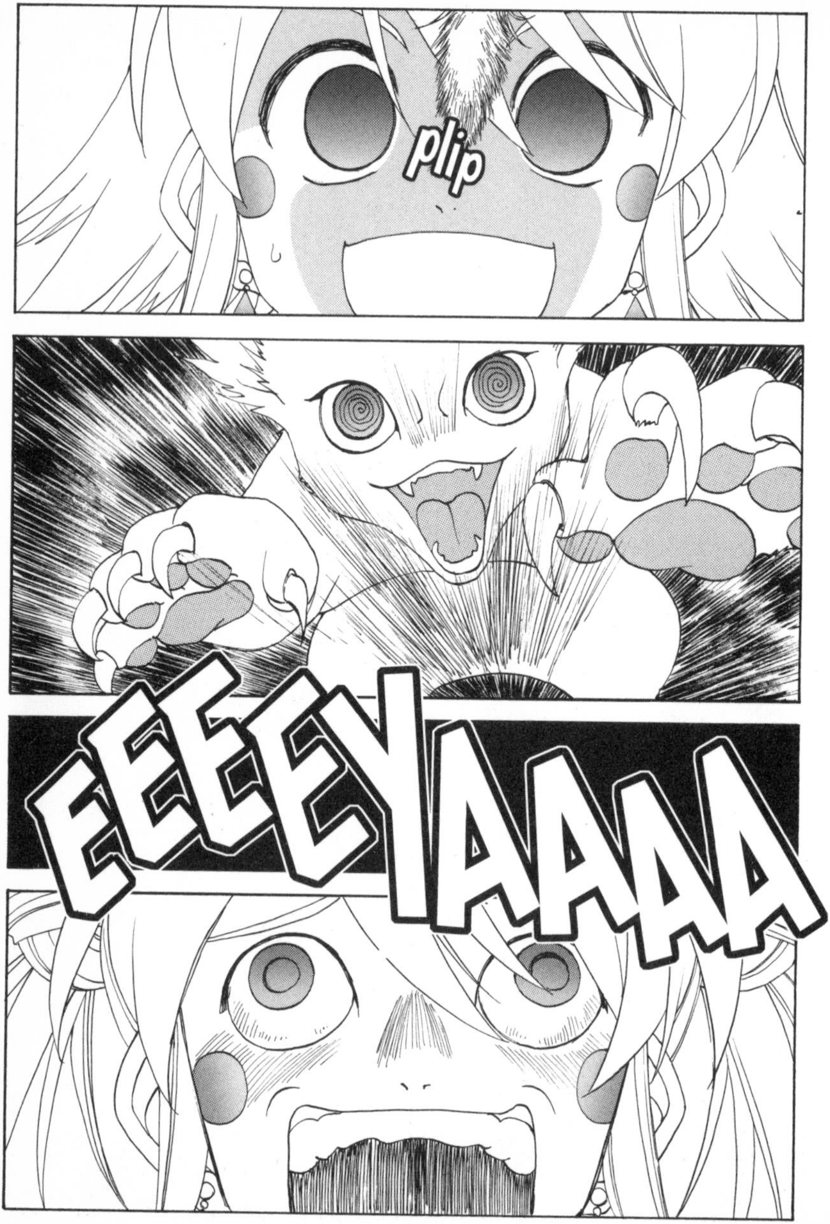
plip
EEEEYAAAA

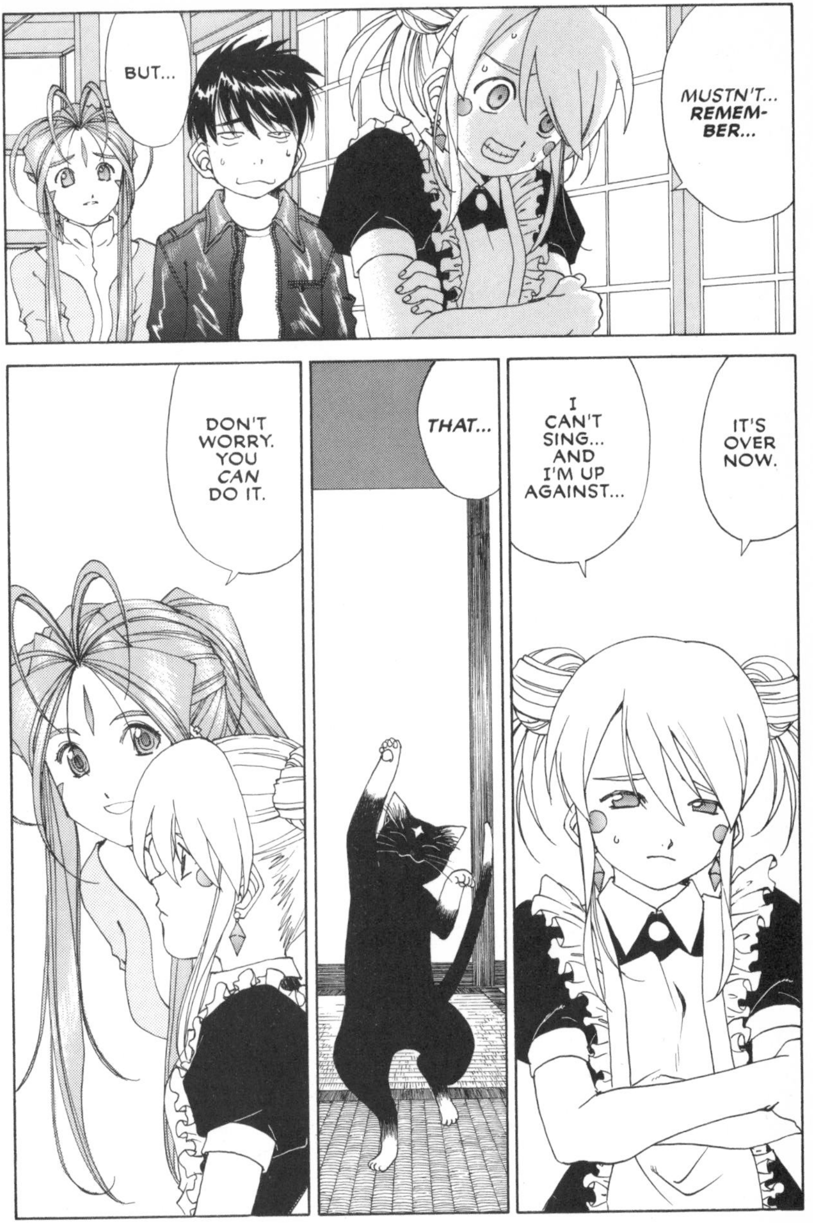
MUSTN'T... REMEMBER...
BUT...
IT'S OVER NOW.
I CAN'T SING... AND I'M UP AGAINST...
THAT...
DON'T WORRY. YOU *CAN* DO IT.

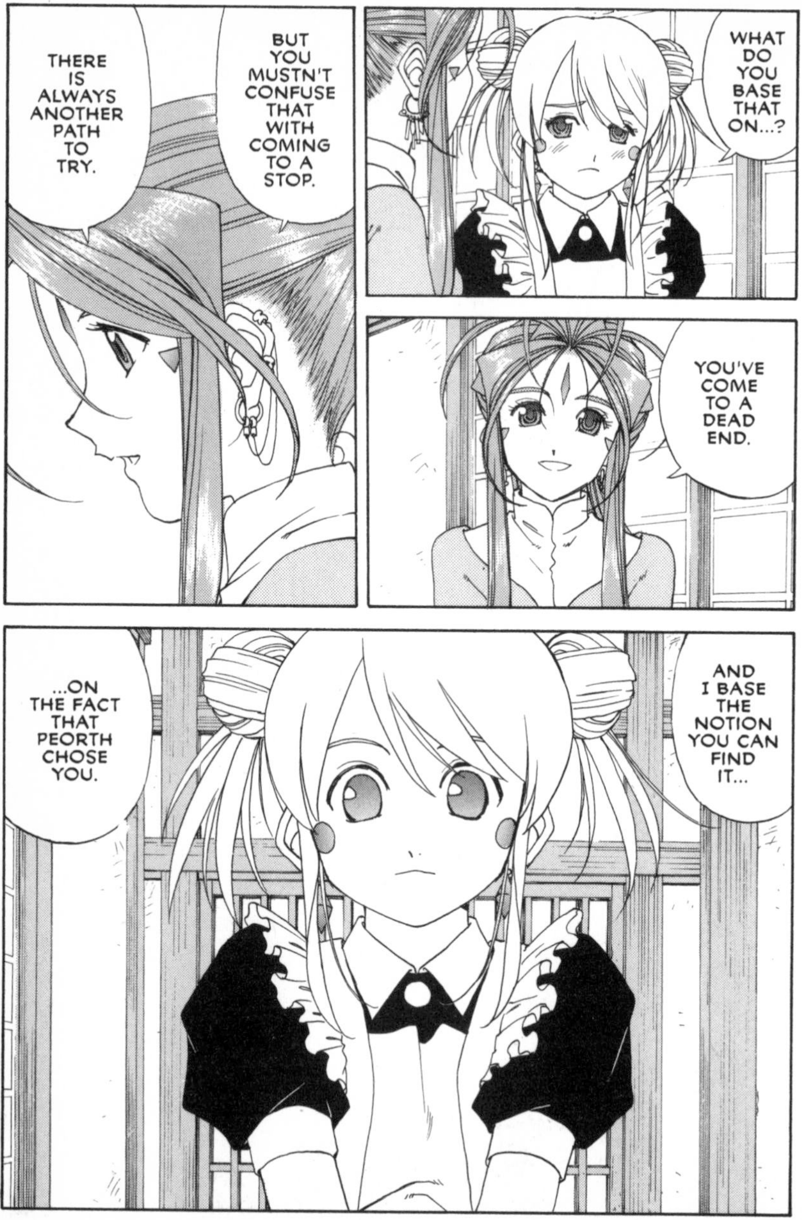
WHAT DO YOU BASE THAT ON...?
YOU'VE COME TO A DEAD END.
BUT YOU MUSTN'T CONFUSE THAT WITH COMING TO A STOP.
THERE IS ALWAYS ANOTHER PATH TO TRY.
AND I BASE THE NOTION YOU CAN FIND IT...
...ON THE FACT THAT PEORTH CHOSE YOU.

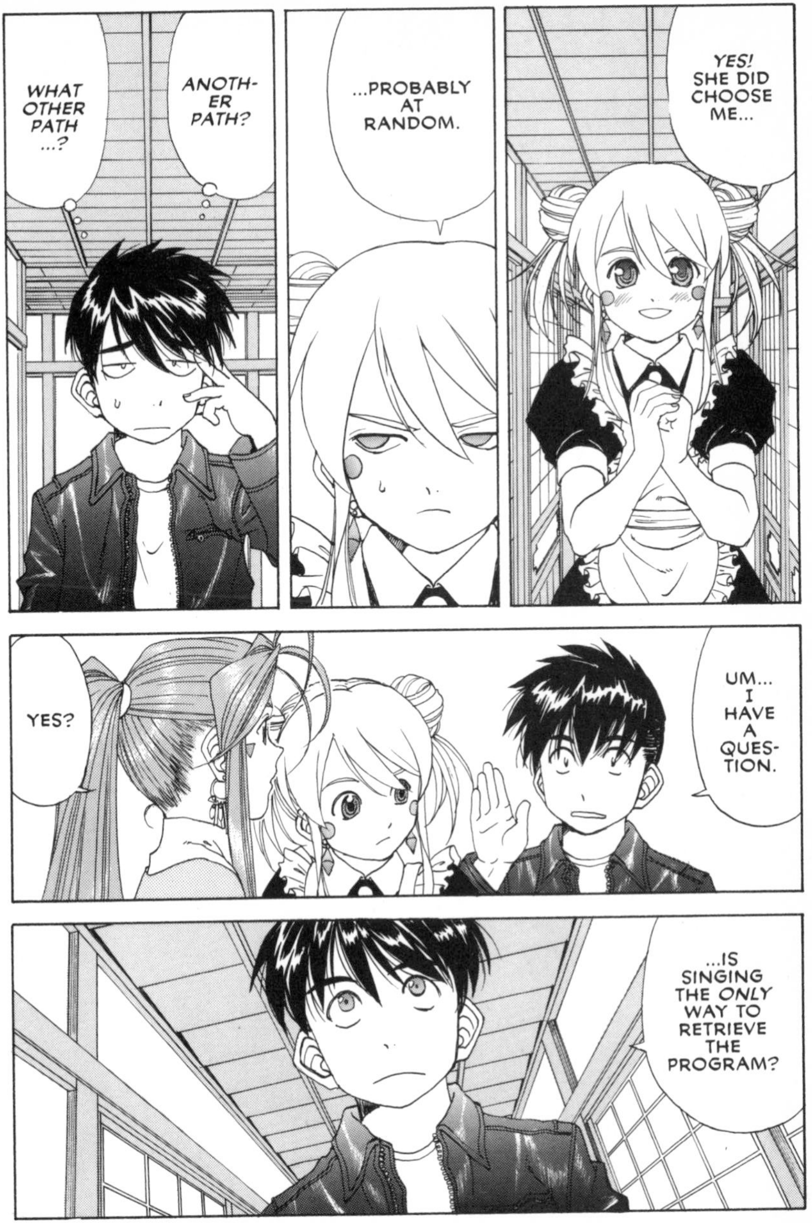
YES! SHE DID CHOOSE ME...
...PROBABLY AT RANDOM.
ANOTH-ER PATH?
WHAT OTHER PATH ...?
UM... I HAVE A QUES-TION.
YES?
...IS SINGING THE *ONLY* WAY TO RETRIEVE THE PROGRAM?

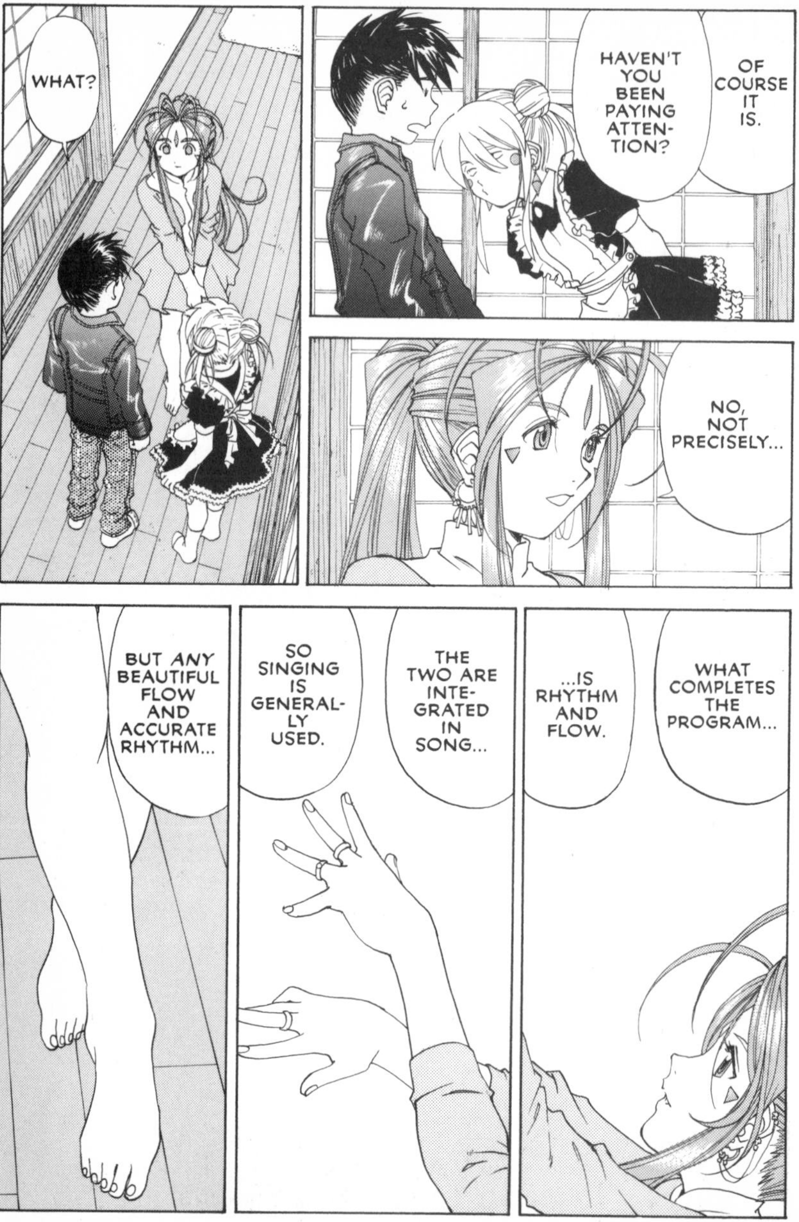
OF COURSE IT IS.
HAVEN'T YOU BEEN PAYING ATTENTION?
NO, NOT PRECISELY...
WHAT?
WHAT COMPLETES THE PROGRAM...
...IS RHYTHM AND FLOW.
THE TWO ARE INTEGRATED IN SONG...
SO SINGING IS GENERALLY USED.
BUT *ANY* BEAUTIFUL FLOW AND ACCURATE RHYTHM...

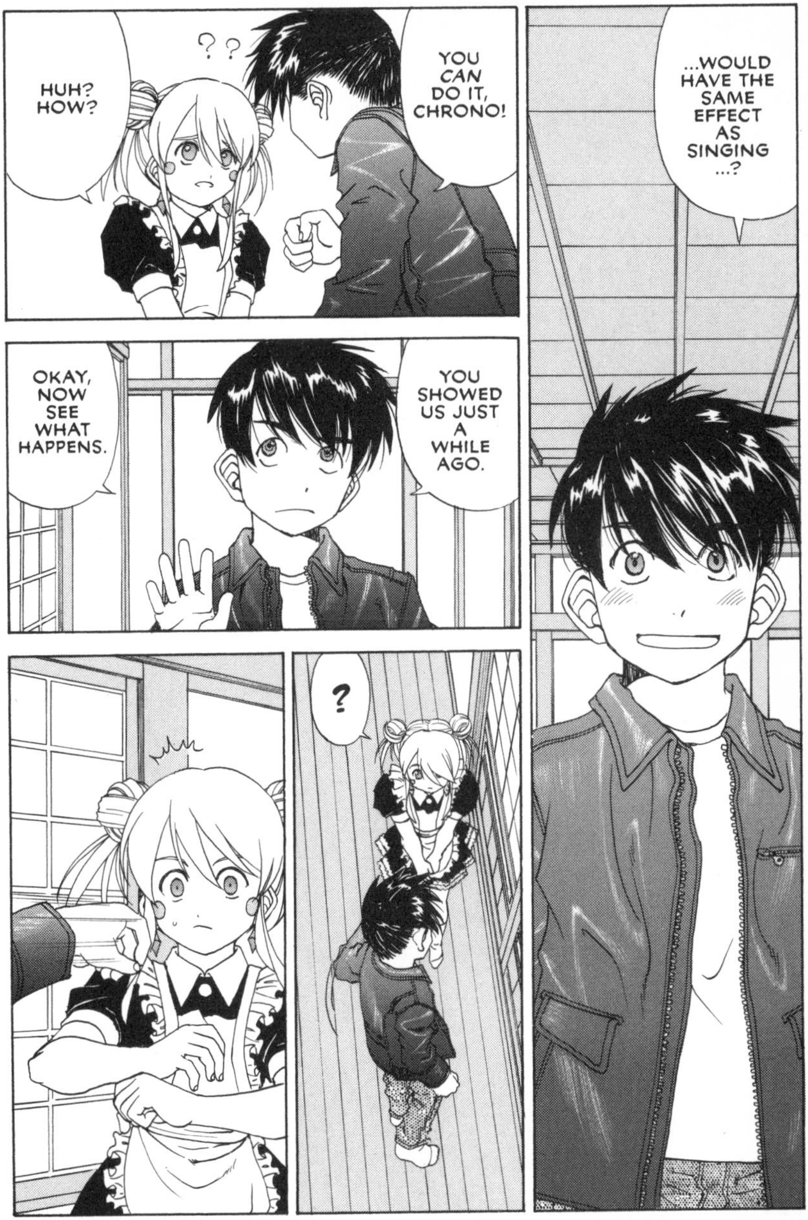
...WOULD HAVE THE SAME EFFECT AS SINGING ...?
YOU CAN DO IT, CHRONO!
HUH? HOW?
??
YOU SHOWED US JUST A WHILE AGO.
OKAY, NOW SEE WHAT HAPPENS.
?

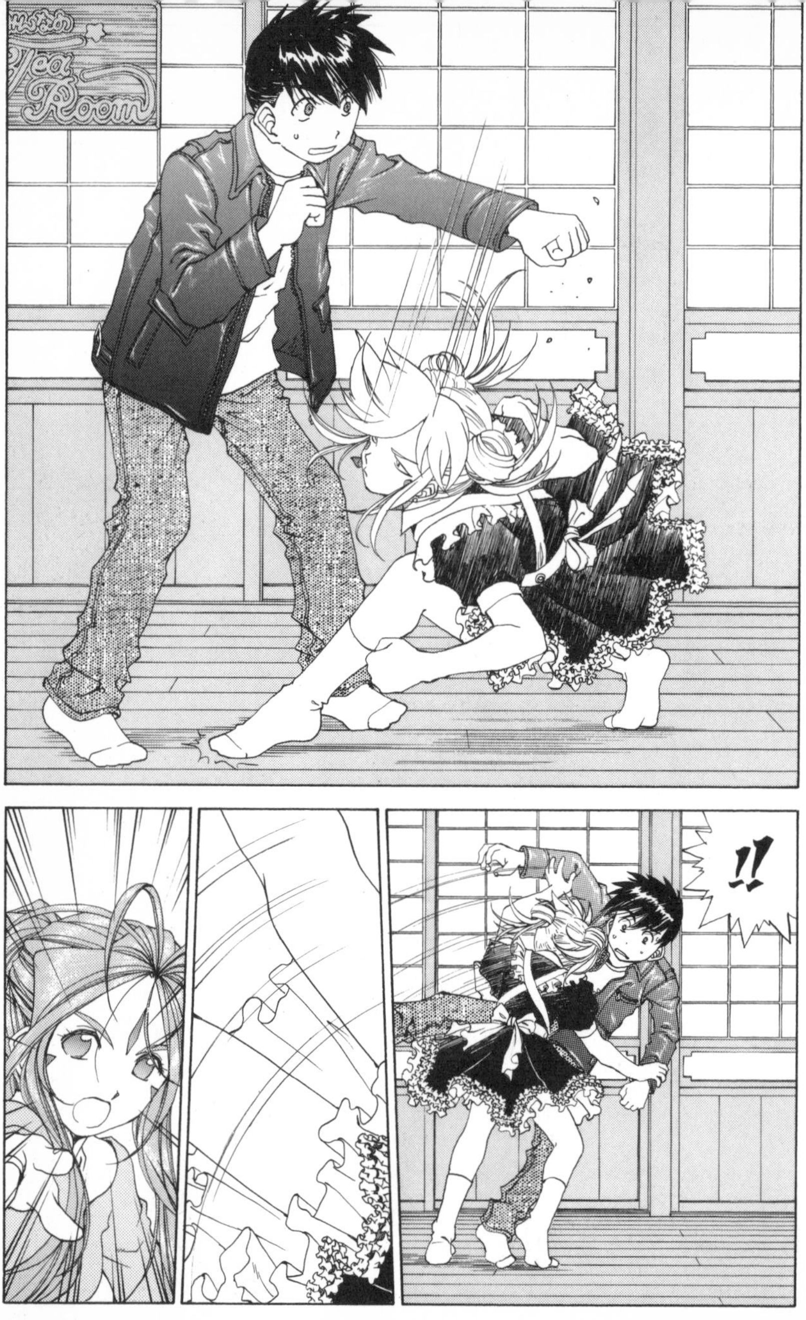
Tea Room
!!

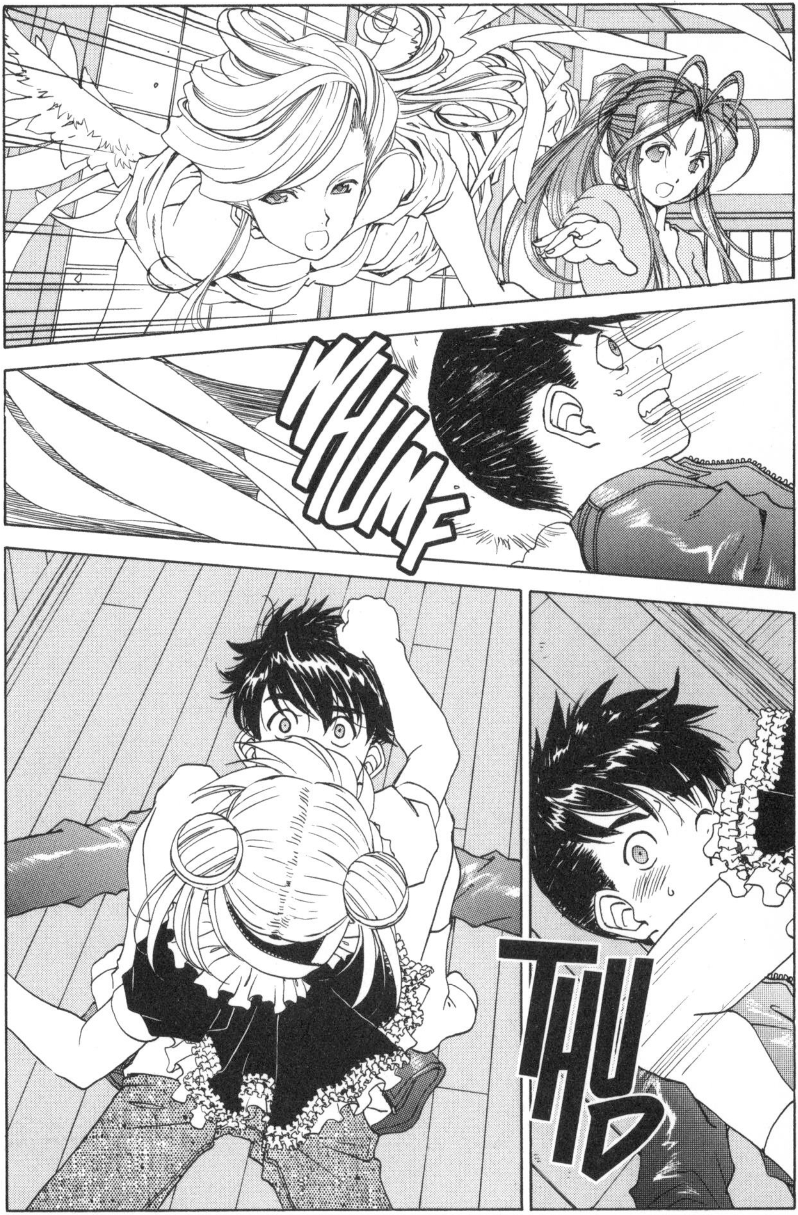
WHUMF
THUD

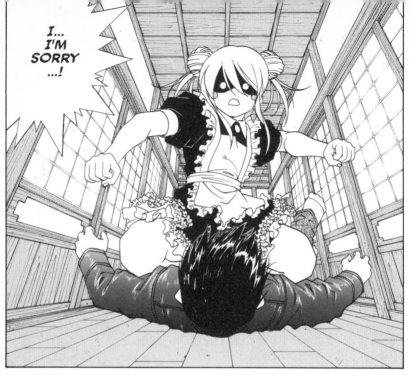

I... I'M SORRY ...!

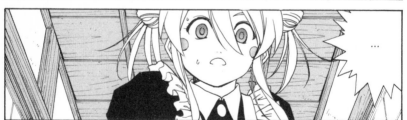

...

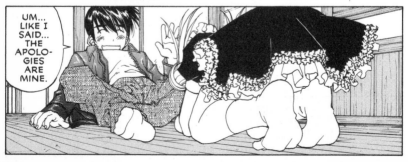

UM... LIKE I SAID... THE APOLO- GIES ARE MINE.

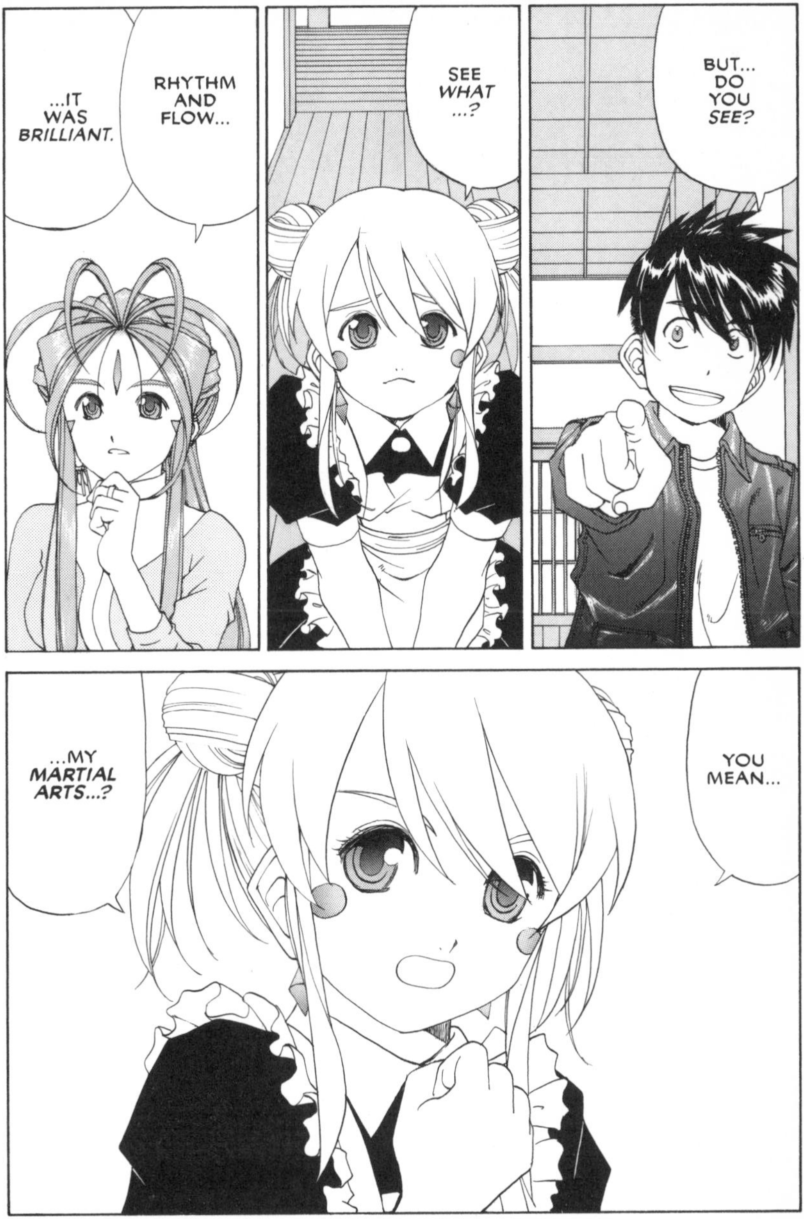
BUT... DO YOU *SEE?*
SEE *WHAT* ...?
RHYTHM AND FLOW...
...IT WAS *BRILLIANT.*
YOU MEAN...
...MY *MARTIAL ARTS...?*

CHAPTER 238

Chrono's Dance Performance

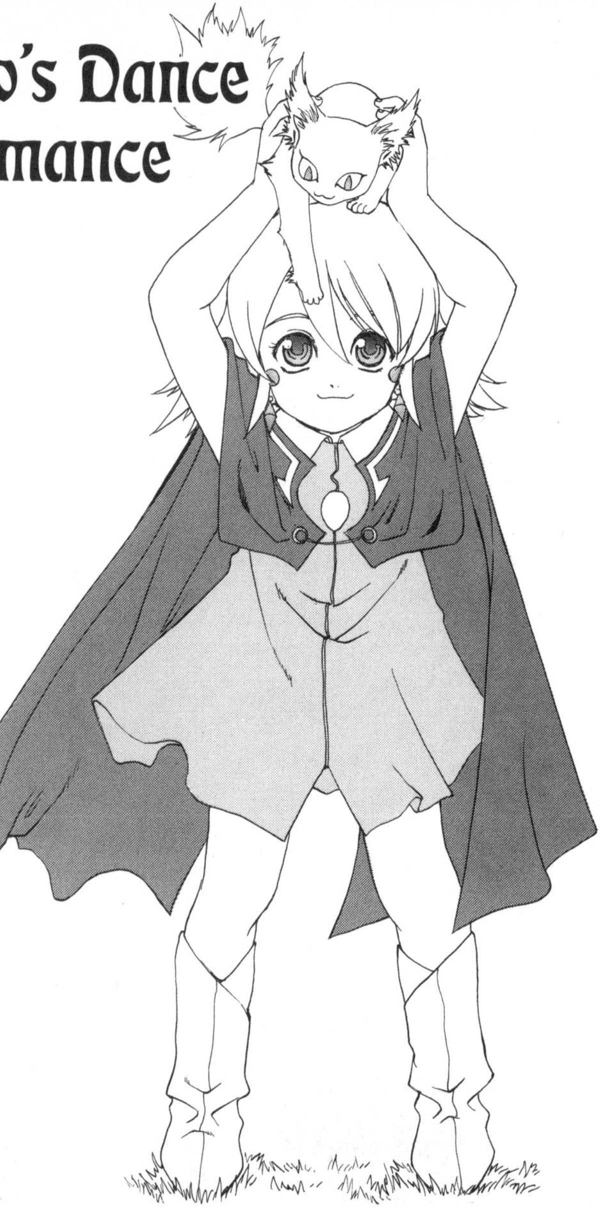

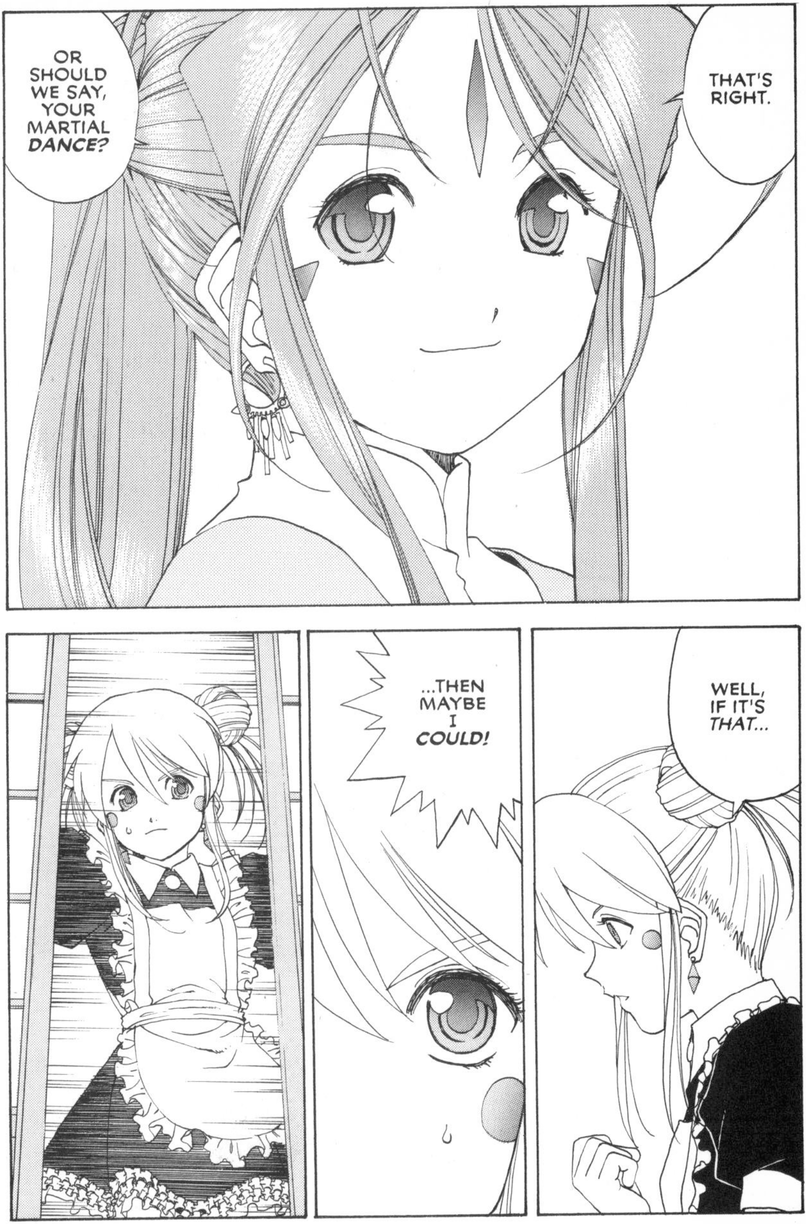

OR SHOULD WE SAY, YOUR MARTIAL *DANCE?*
THAT'S RIGHT.
WELL, IF IT'S *THAT*...
...THEN MAYBE I *COULD!*

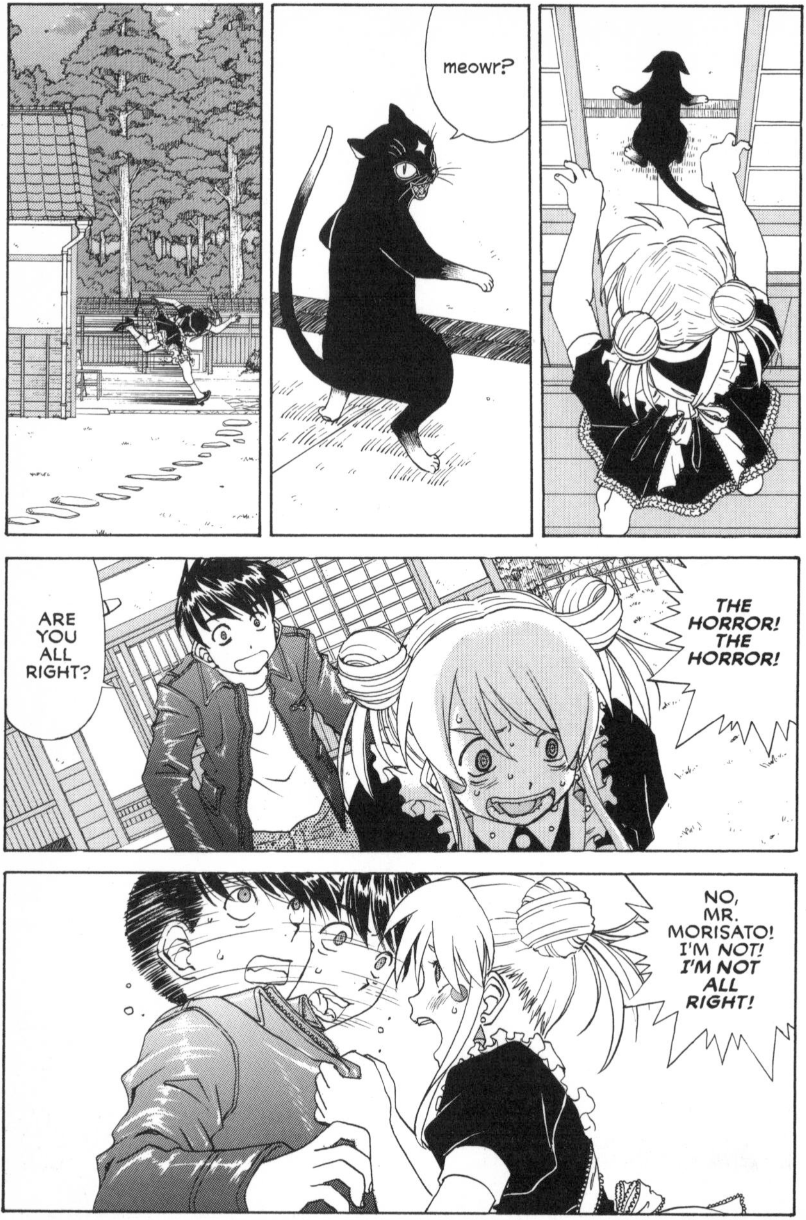
meowr?
THE HORROR! THE HORROR!
ARE YOU ALL RIGHT?
NO, MR. MORISATO! I'M NOT! *I'M NOT ALL RIGHT!*

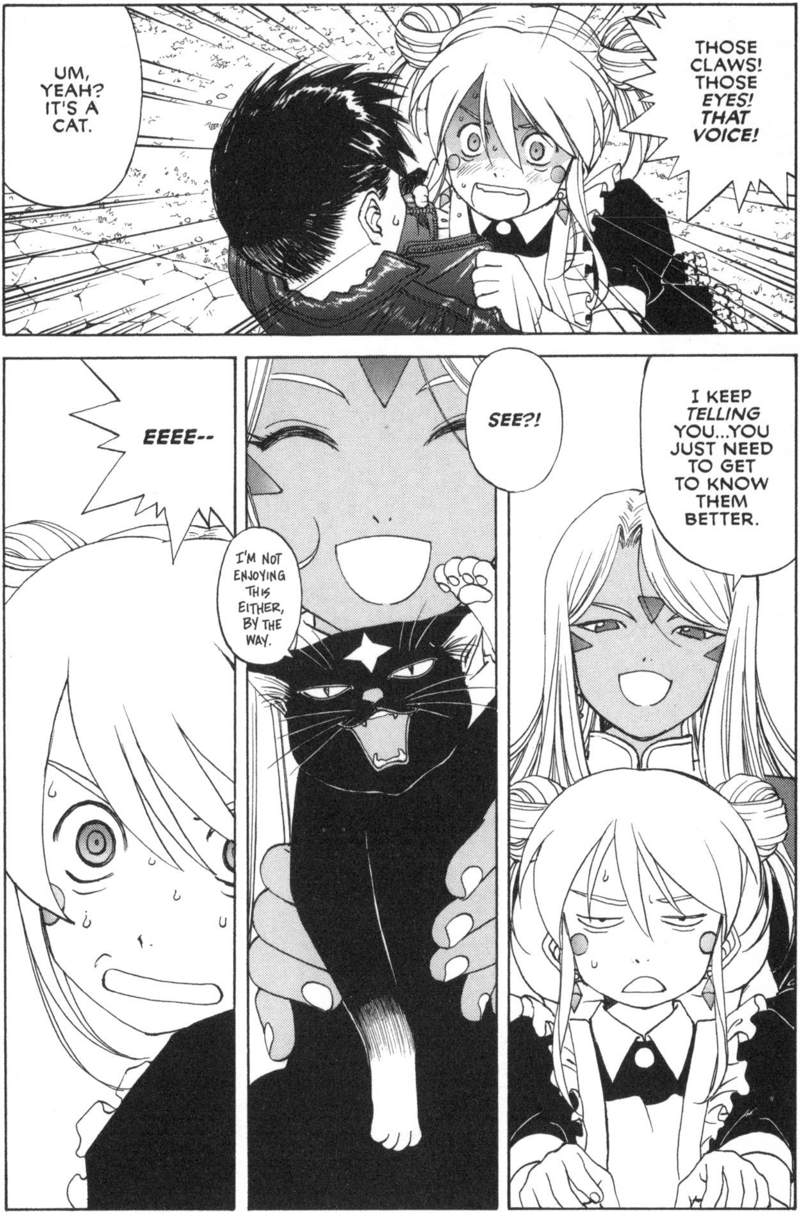
THOSE CLAWS! THOSE EYES! THAT VOICE!
UM, YEAH? IT'S A CAT.
I KEEP TELLING YOU...YOU JUST NEED TO GET TO KNOW THEM BETTER.
SEE?!
I'M NOT ENJOYING THIS EITHER, BY THE WAY.
EEEE--

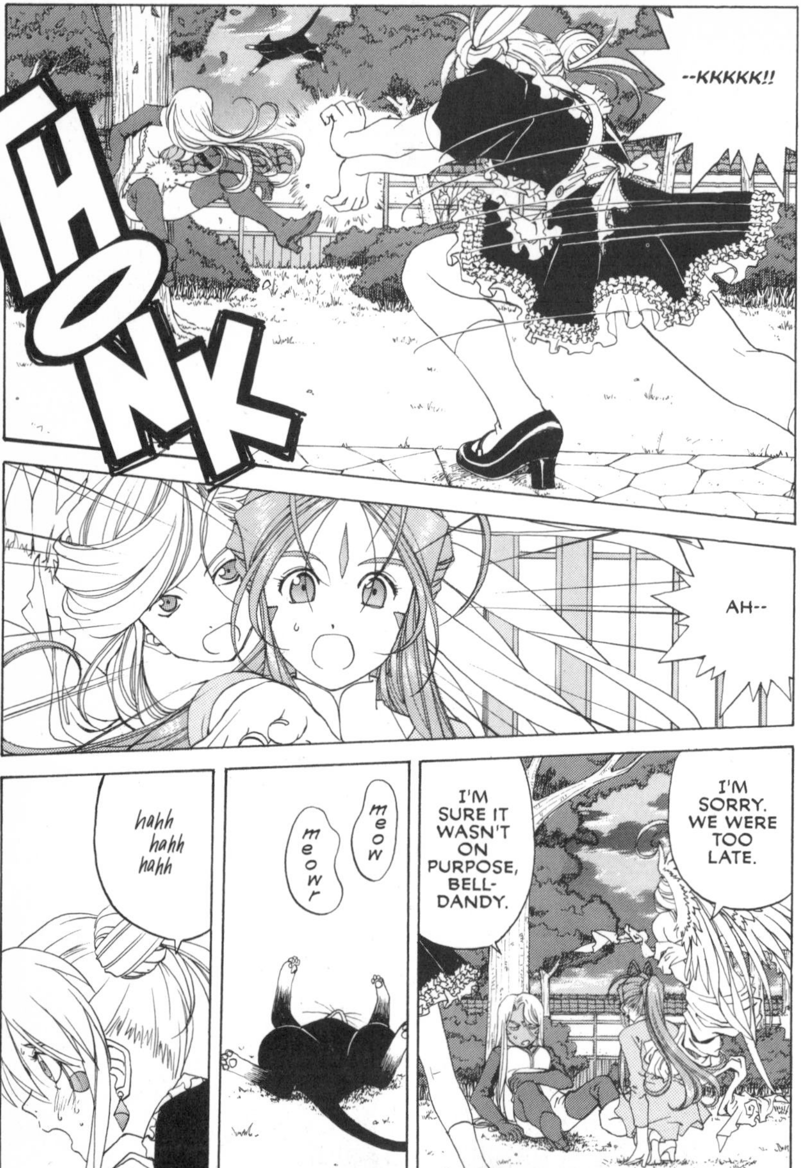
--KKKKK!!
THONK
AH--
I'M SORRY. WE WERE TOO LATE.
I'M SURE IT WASN'T ON PURPOSE, BELL-DANDY.
meow
meowr
hahh hahh hahh

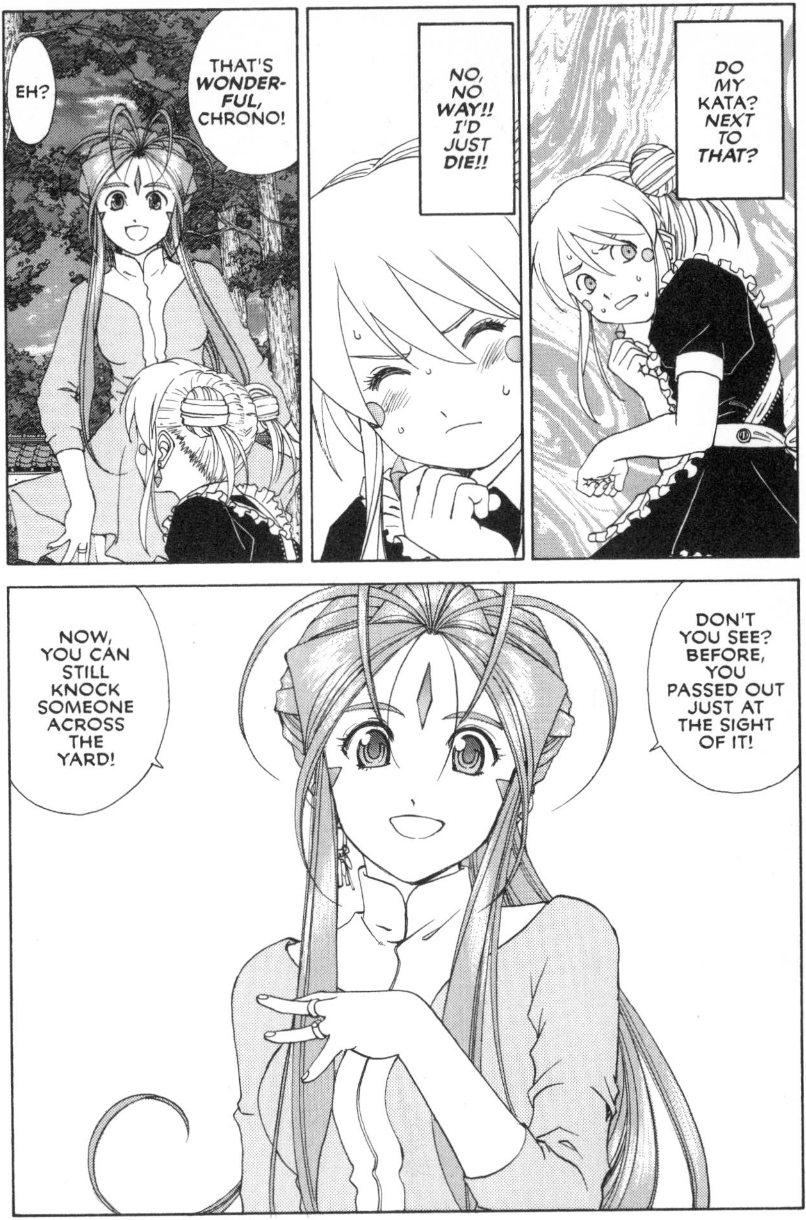
DO MY KATA? NEXT TO THAT?
NO, NO WAY!! I'D JUST DIE!!
THAT'S WONDER-FUL, CHRONO!
EH?
DON'T YOU SEE? BEFORE, YOU PASSED OUT JUST AT THE SIGHT OF IT!
NOW, YOU CAN STILL KNOCK SOMEONE ACROSS THE YARD!

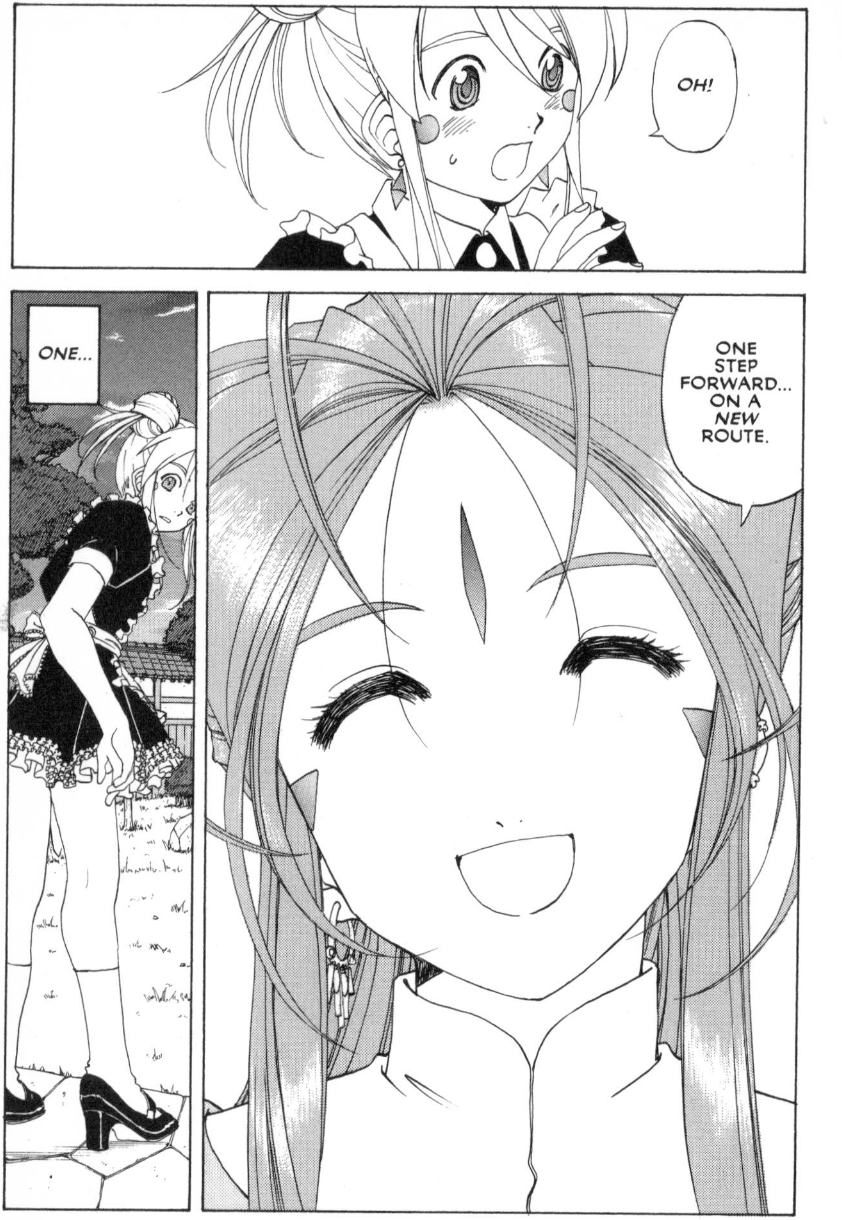
OH!
ONE STEP FORWARD... ON A *NEW* ROUTE.
ONE...

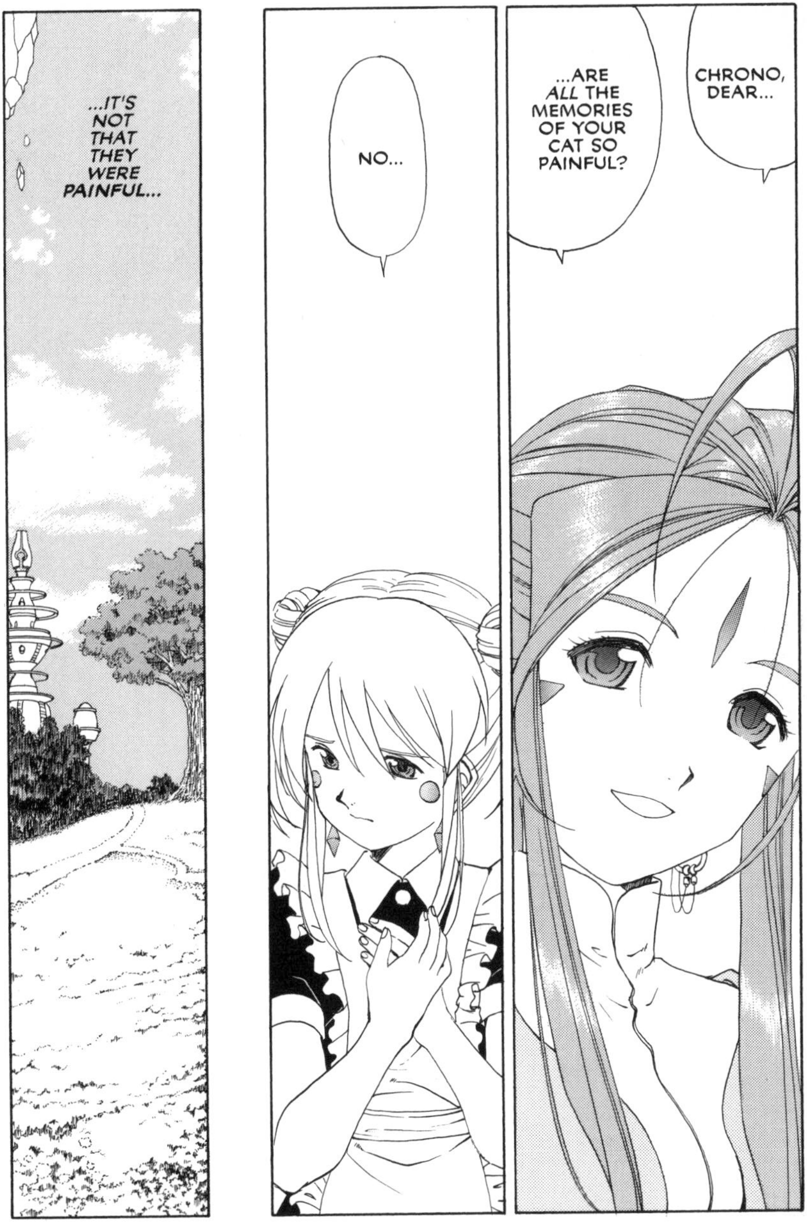
CHRONO, DEAR...
...ARE *ALL* THE MEMORIES OF YOUR CAT SO PAINFUL?
NO...
...IT'S NOT THAT THEY WERE PAINFUL...

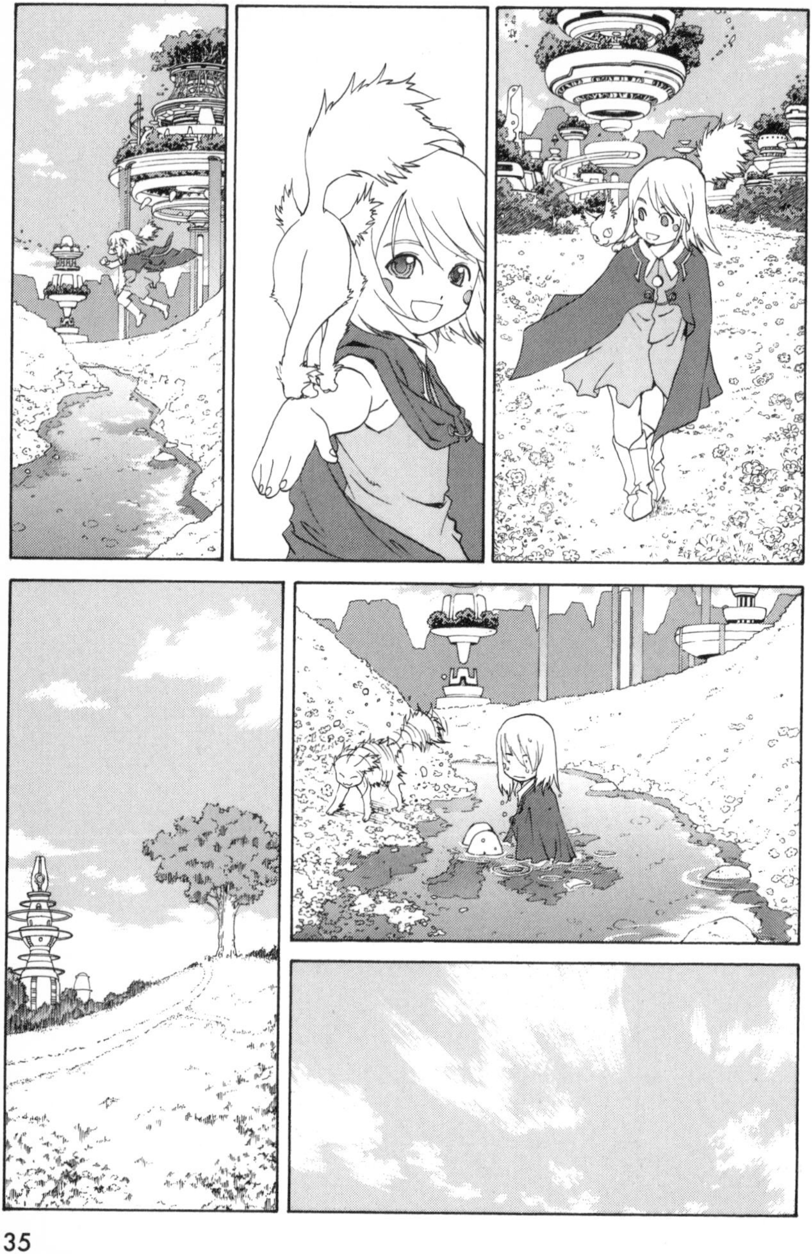

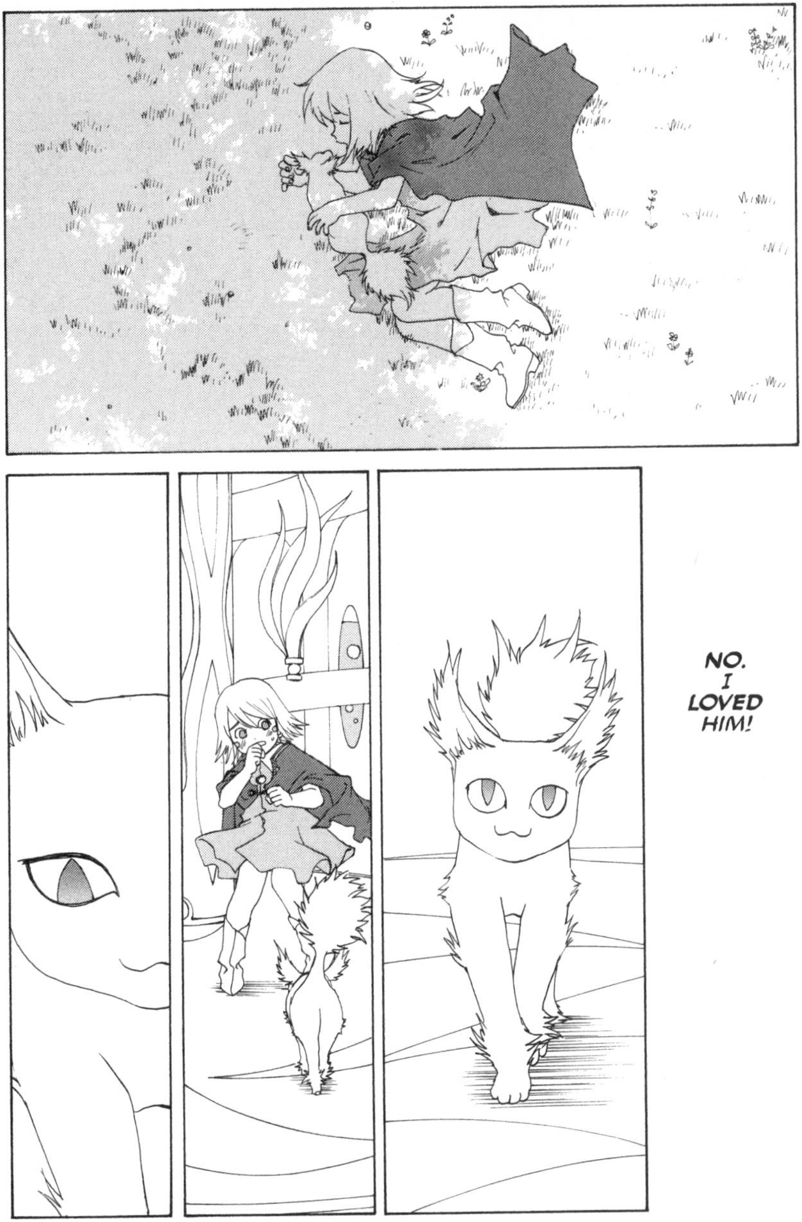
NO. I LOVED HIM!

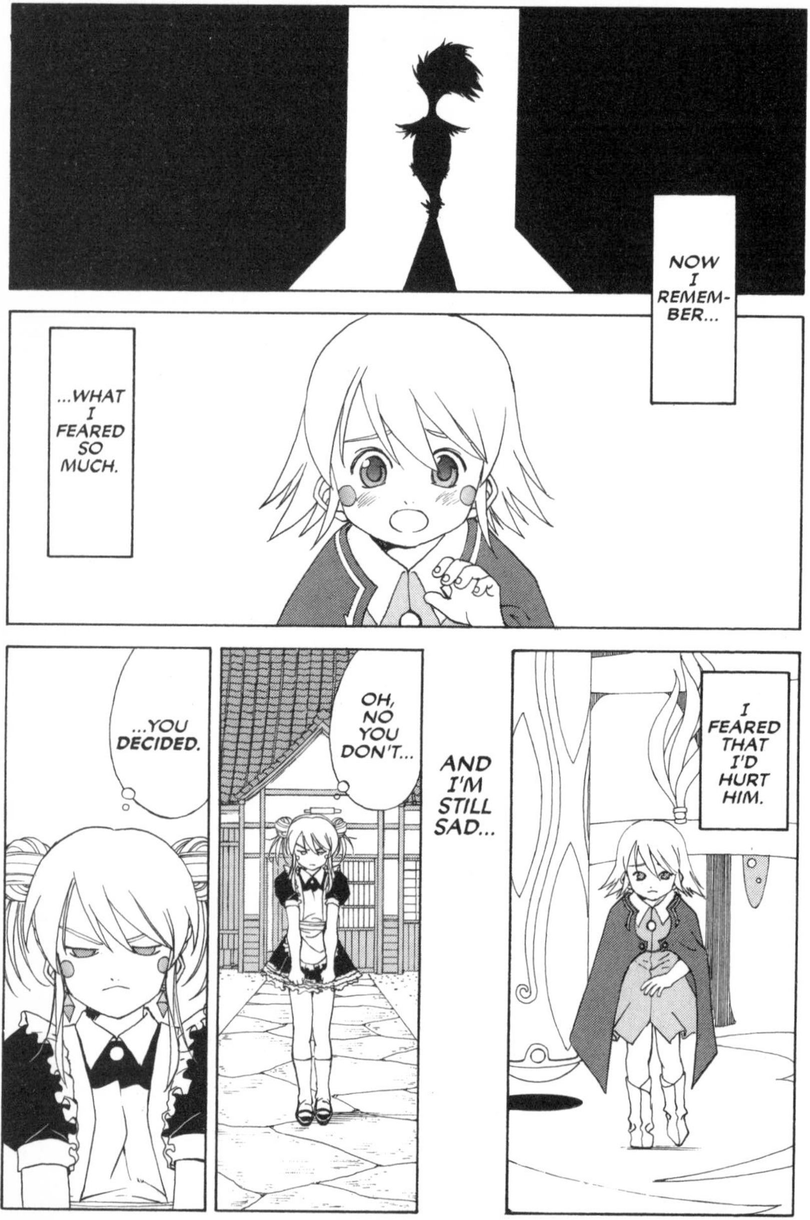
NOW I REMEMBER...
...WHAT I FEARED SO MUCH.
I FEARED THAT I'D HURT HIM.
AND I'M STILL SAD...
OH, NO YOU DON'T...
...YOU DECIDED.

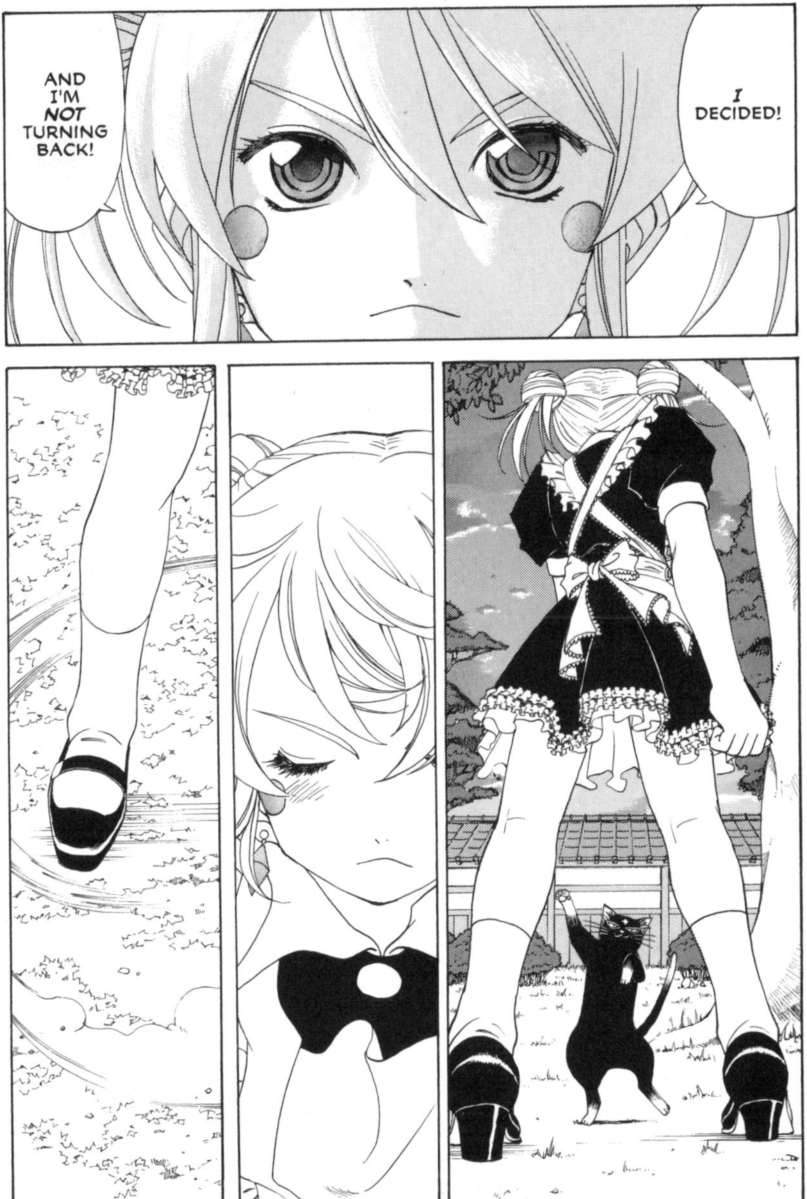
I DECIDED!
AND I'M ***NOT*** TURNING BACK!

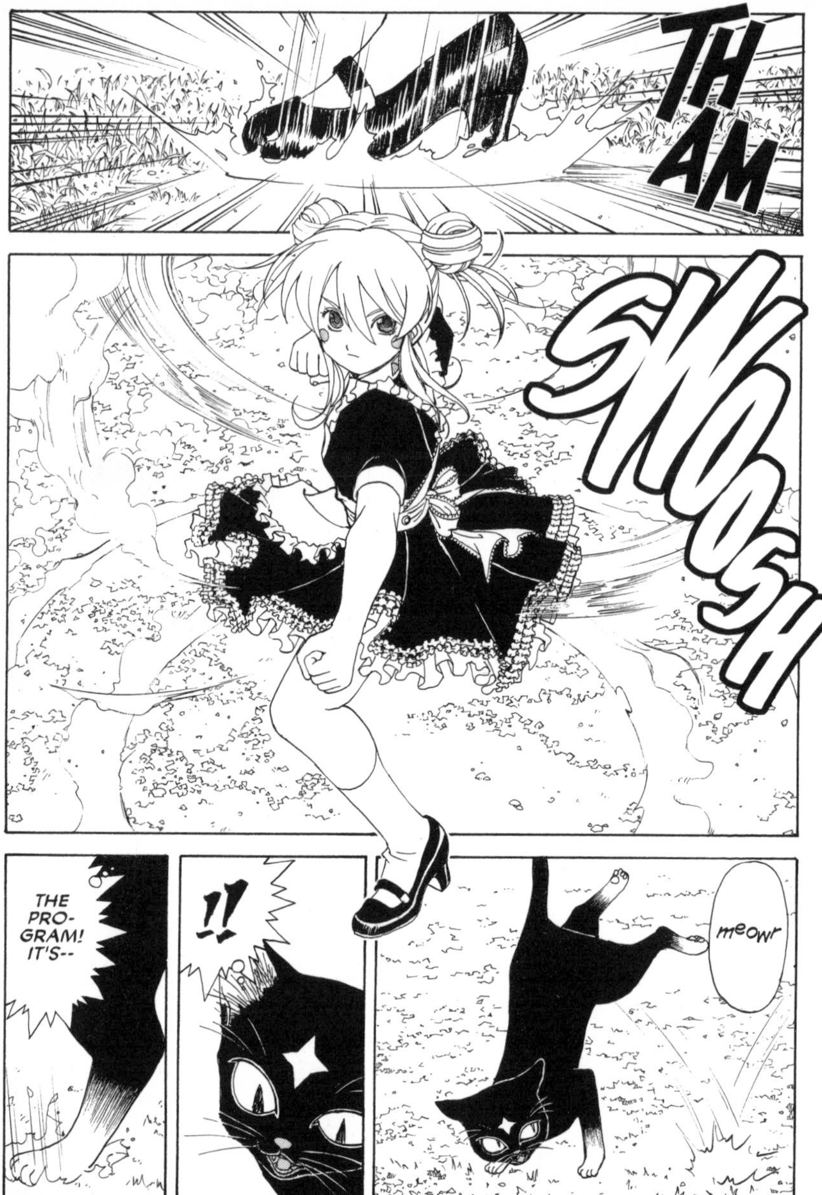
THAM
SWOOSH
meowr
!!
THE PRO-GRAM! IT'S--

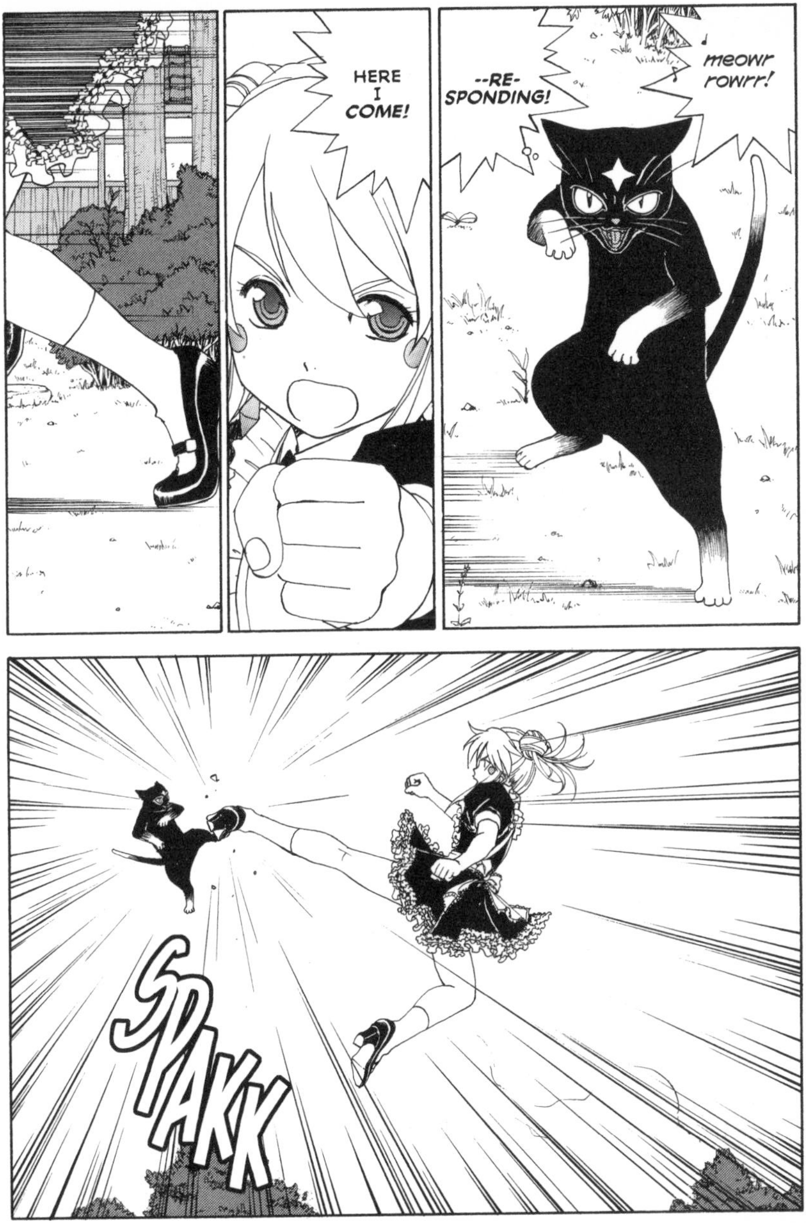
meowr rowrr!
--RE-SPONDING!
HERE I COME!
SPAKK

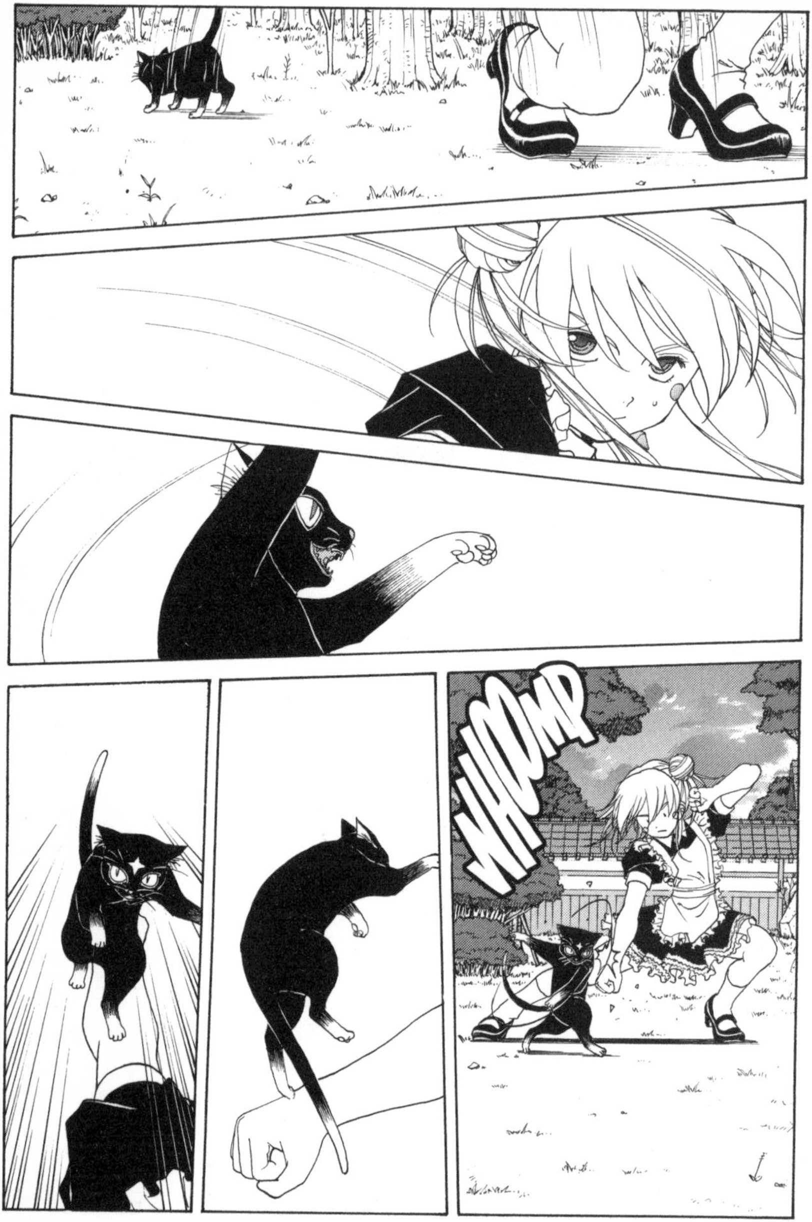
WHOMP

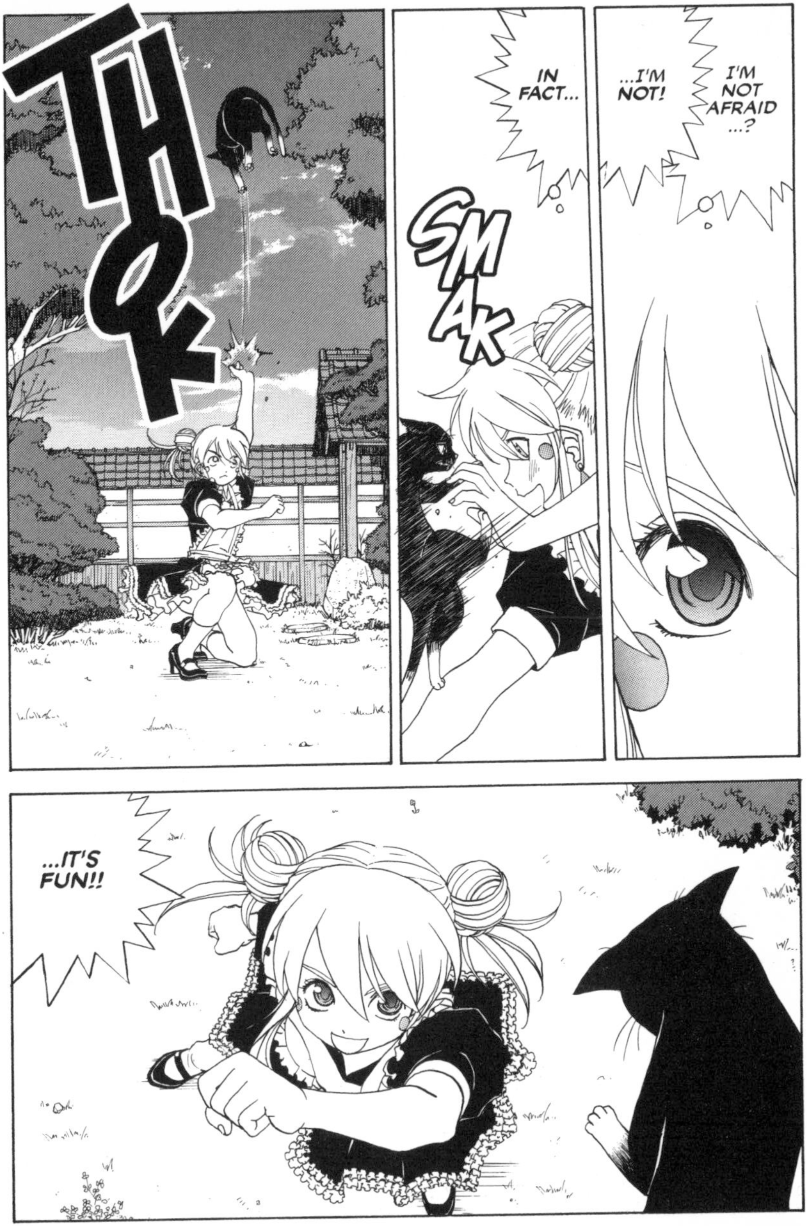
I'M NOT AFRAID ...?
...I'M NOT!
IN FACT...
SMAK
THOK
...IT'S FUN!!

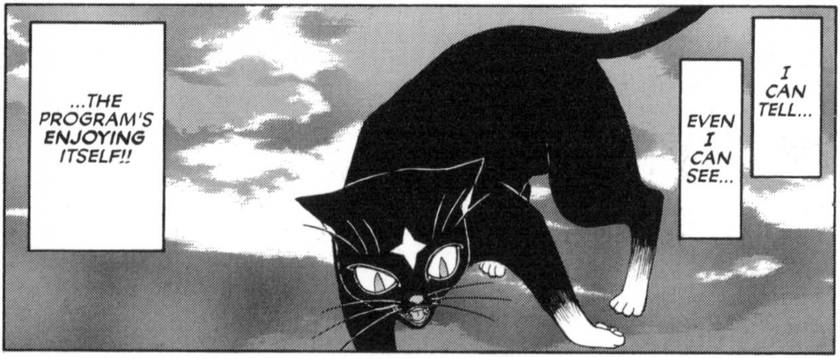
I CAN TELL...
EVEN I CAN SEE...
...THE PROGRAM'S ENJOYING ITSELF!!
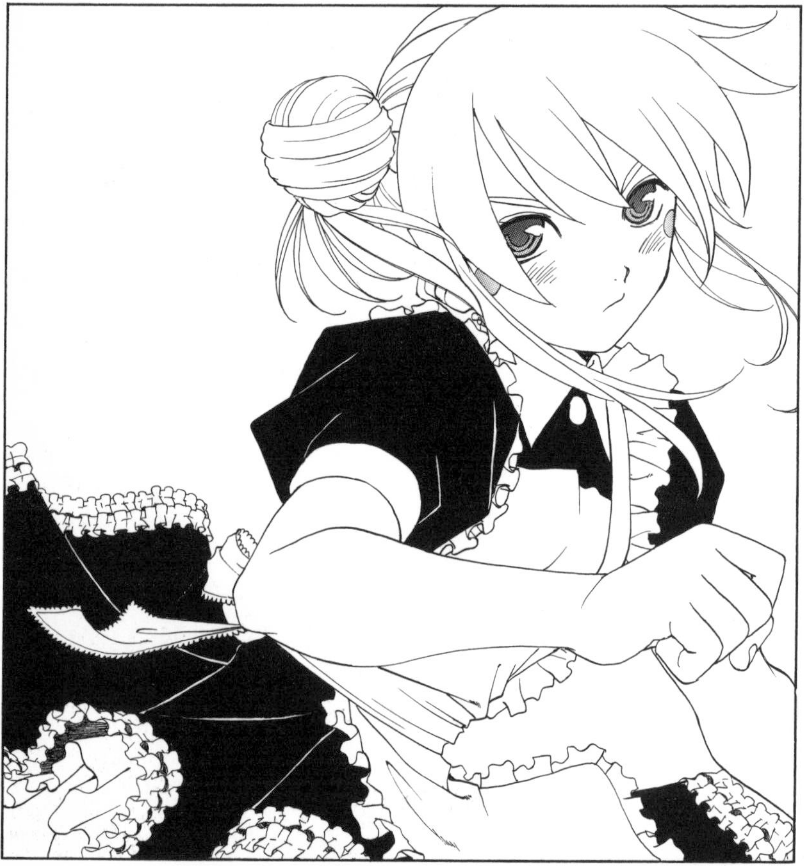

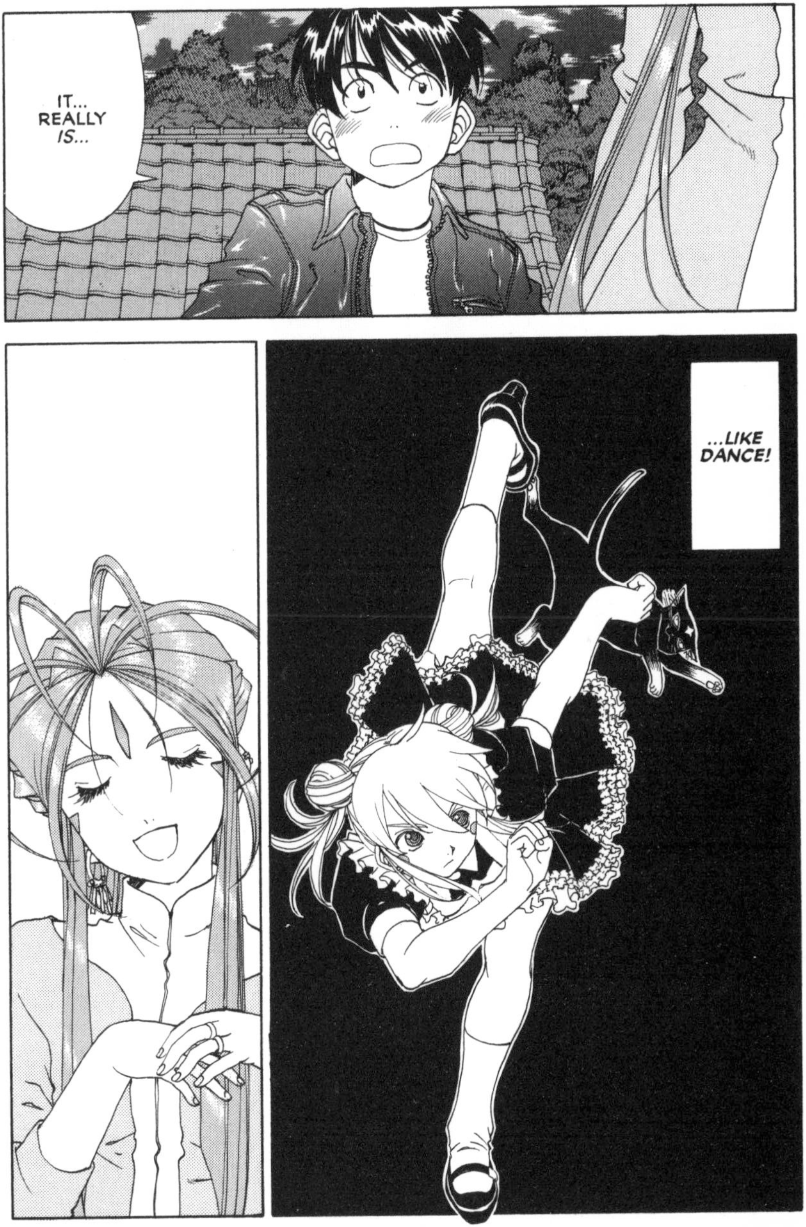
IT... REALLY IS...
...LIKE DANCE!

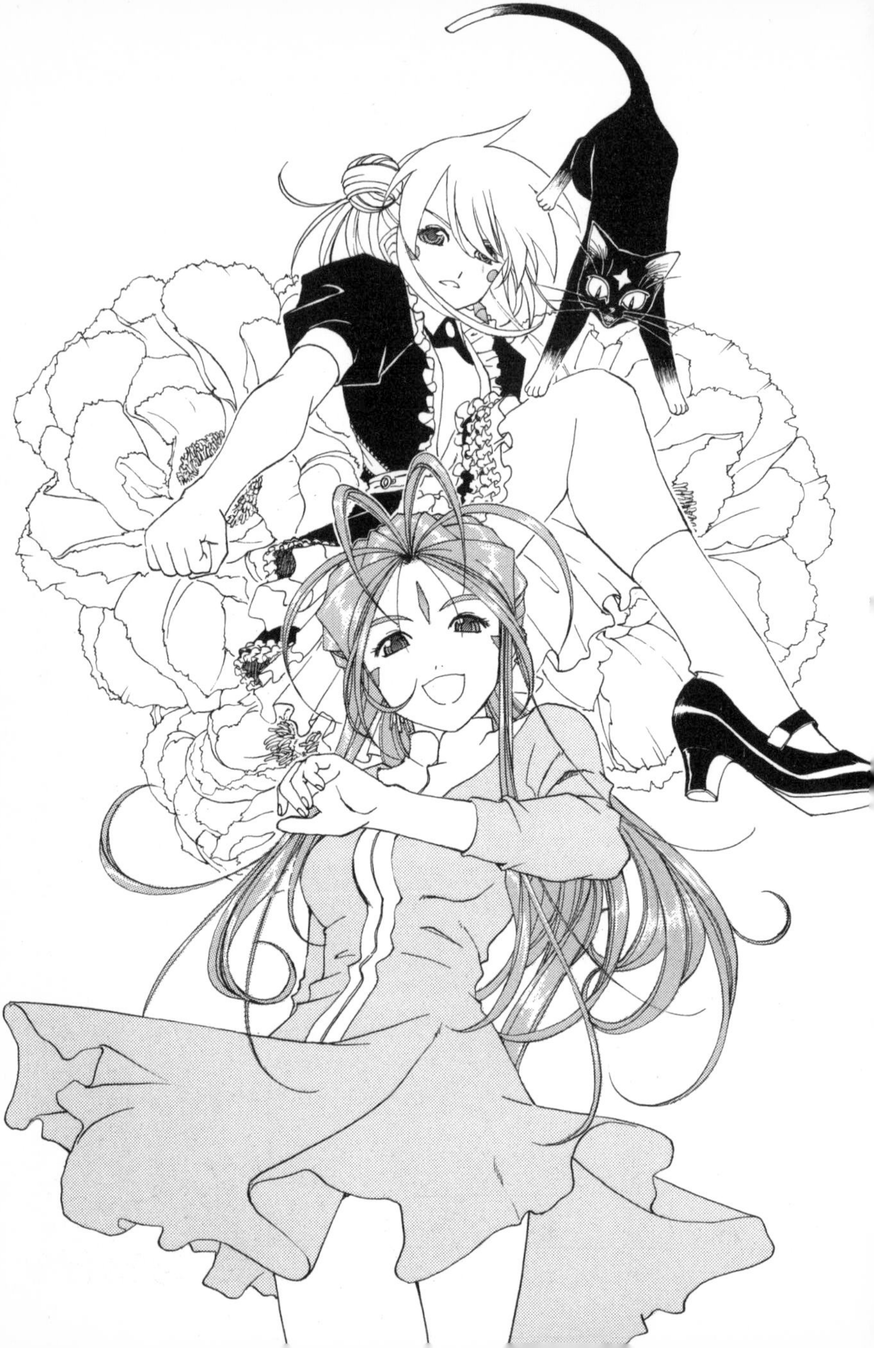

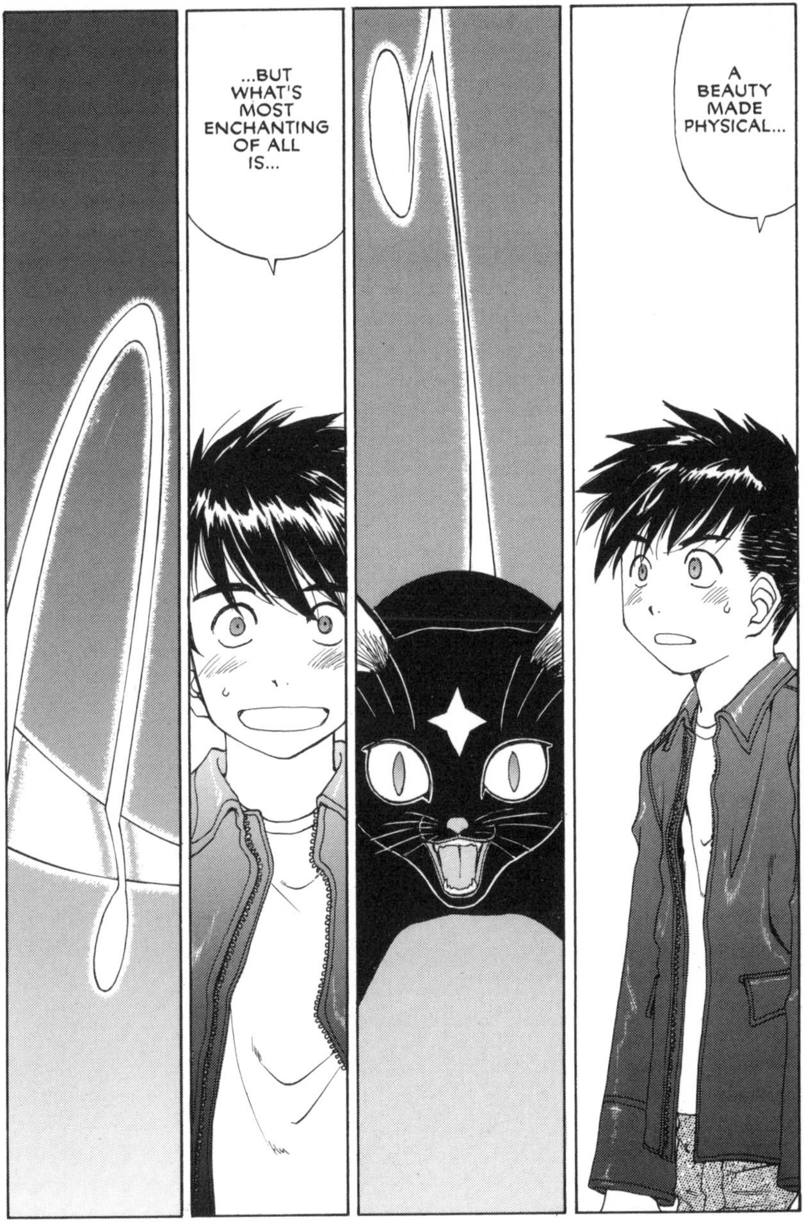
A BEAUTY MADE PHYSICAL...
...BUT WHAT'S MOST ENCHANTING OF ALL IS...

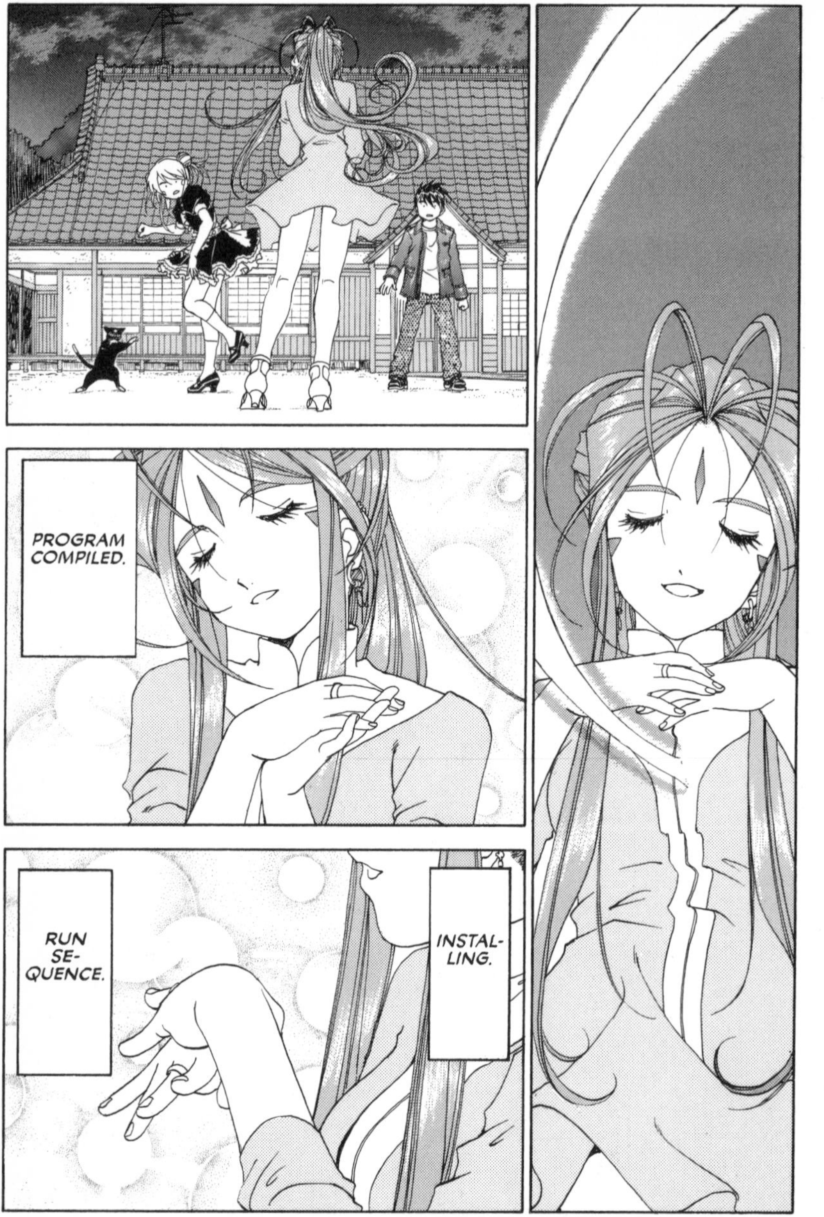
PROGRAM COMPILED.
INSTALLING.
RUN SEQUENCE.

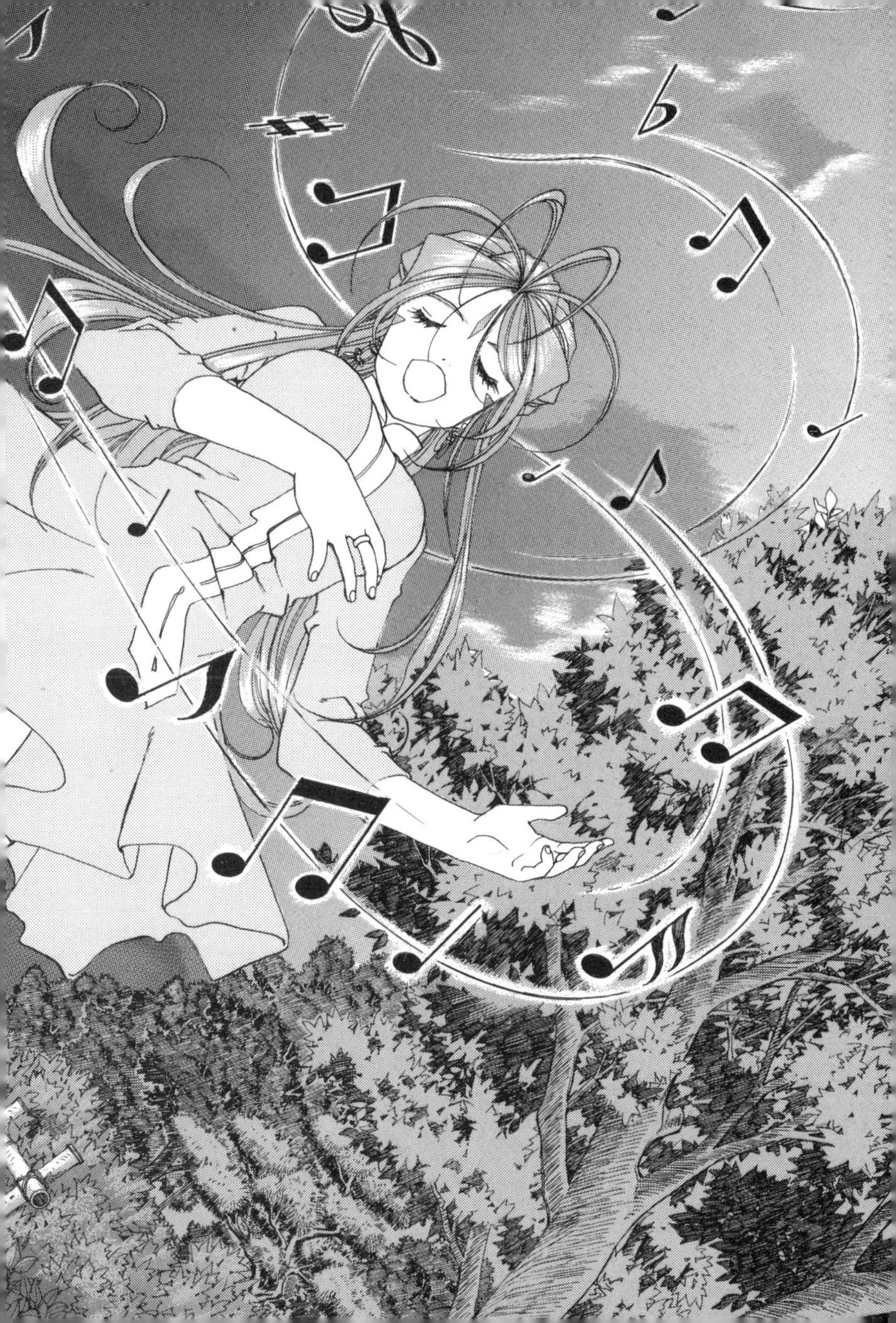

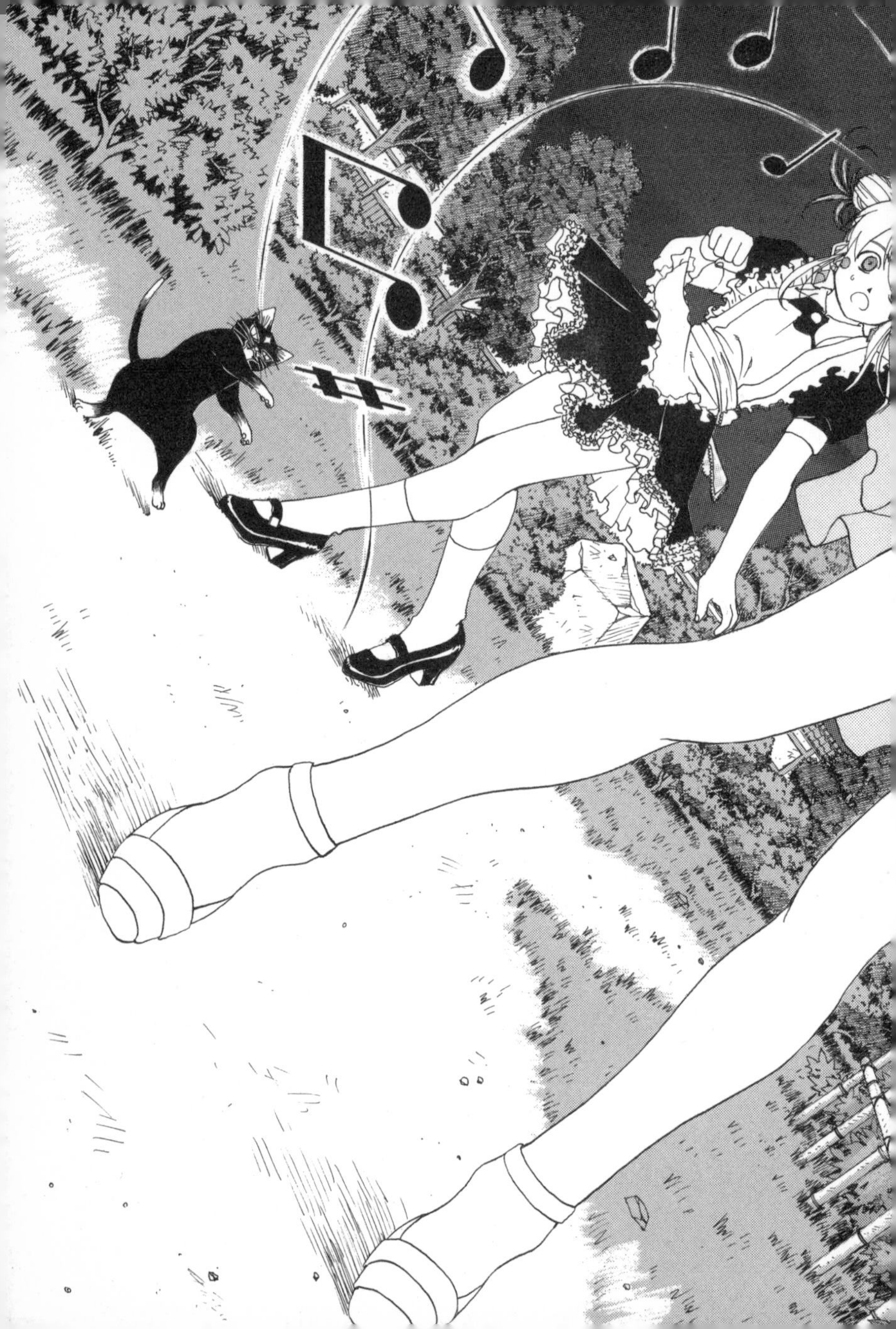

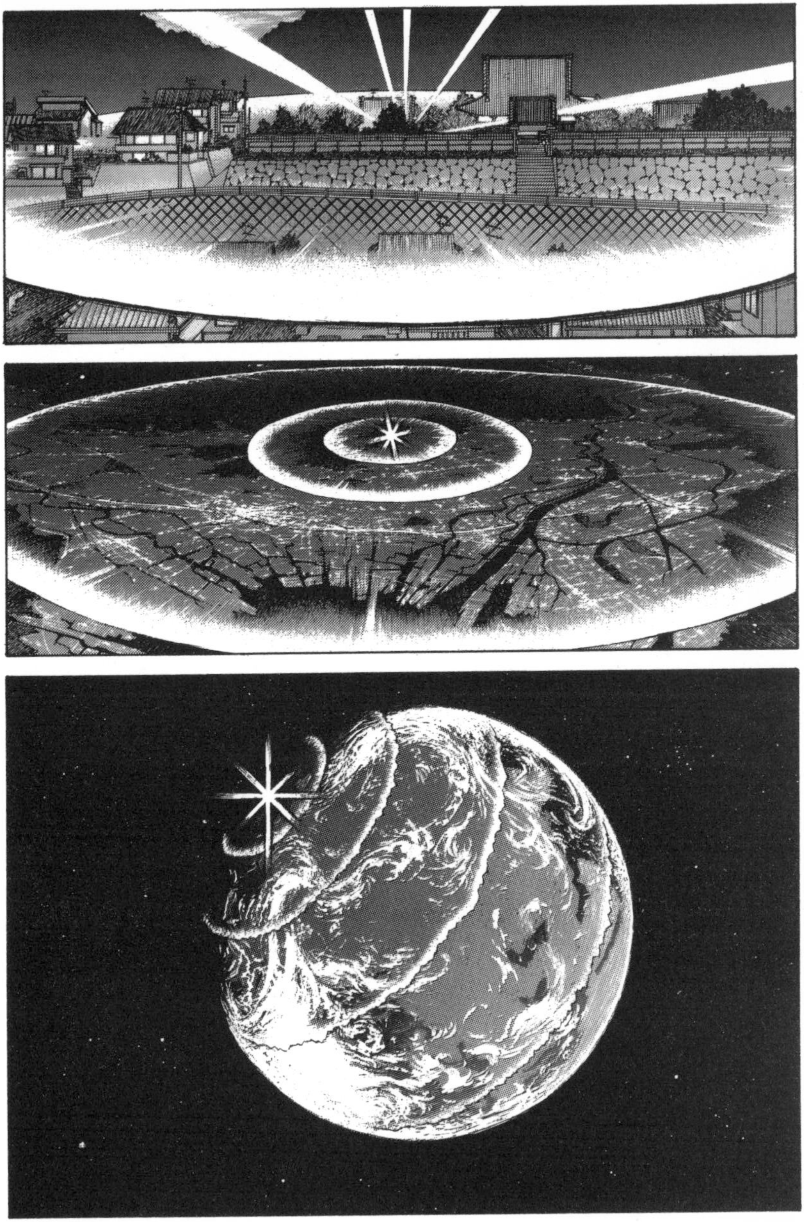

CHAPTER 239

Goddesses First Class Don't Lie

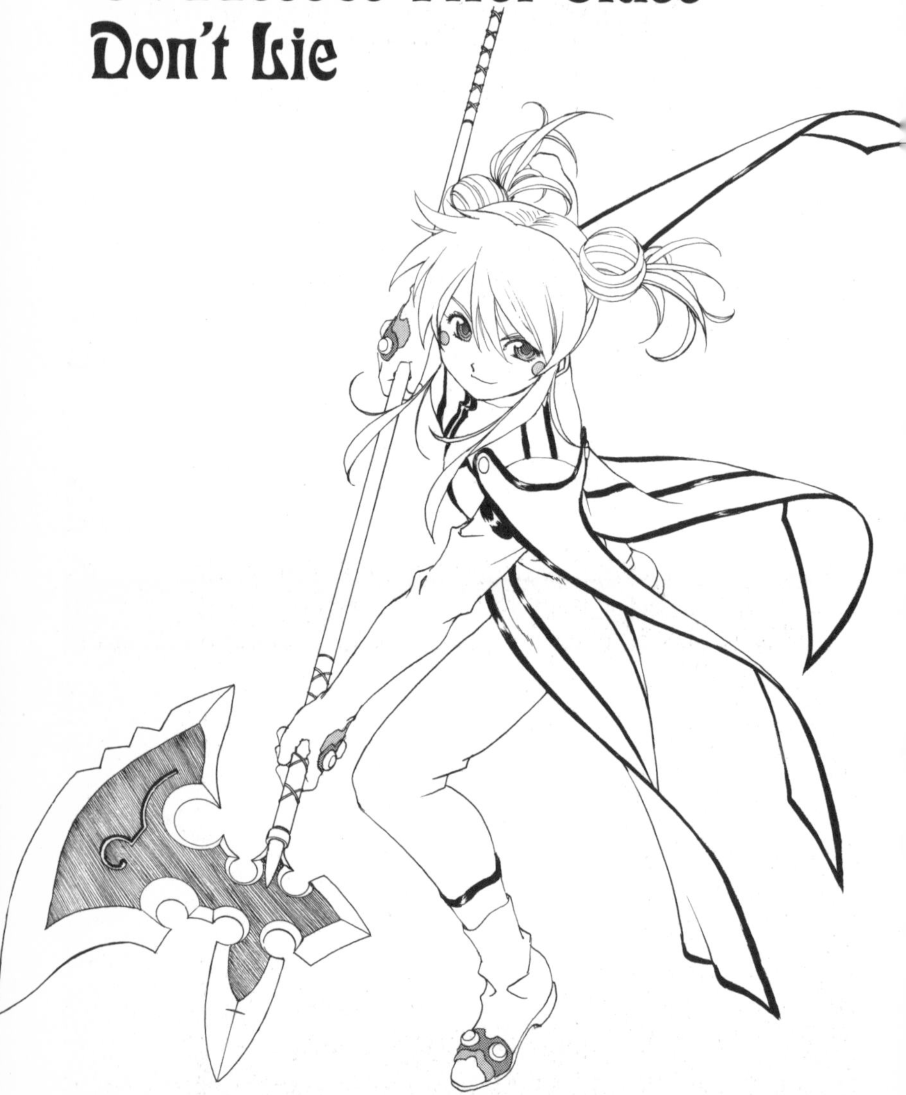

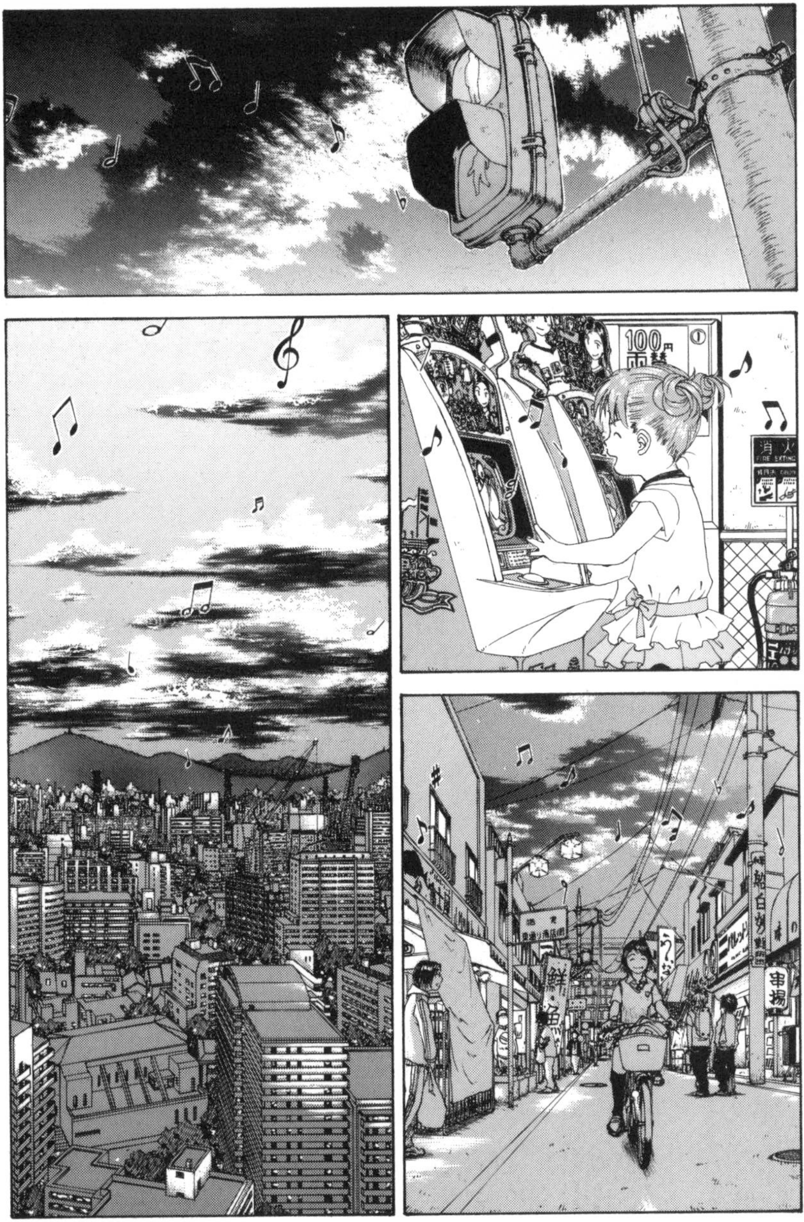
100円
FIRE EXTING
串揚

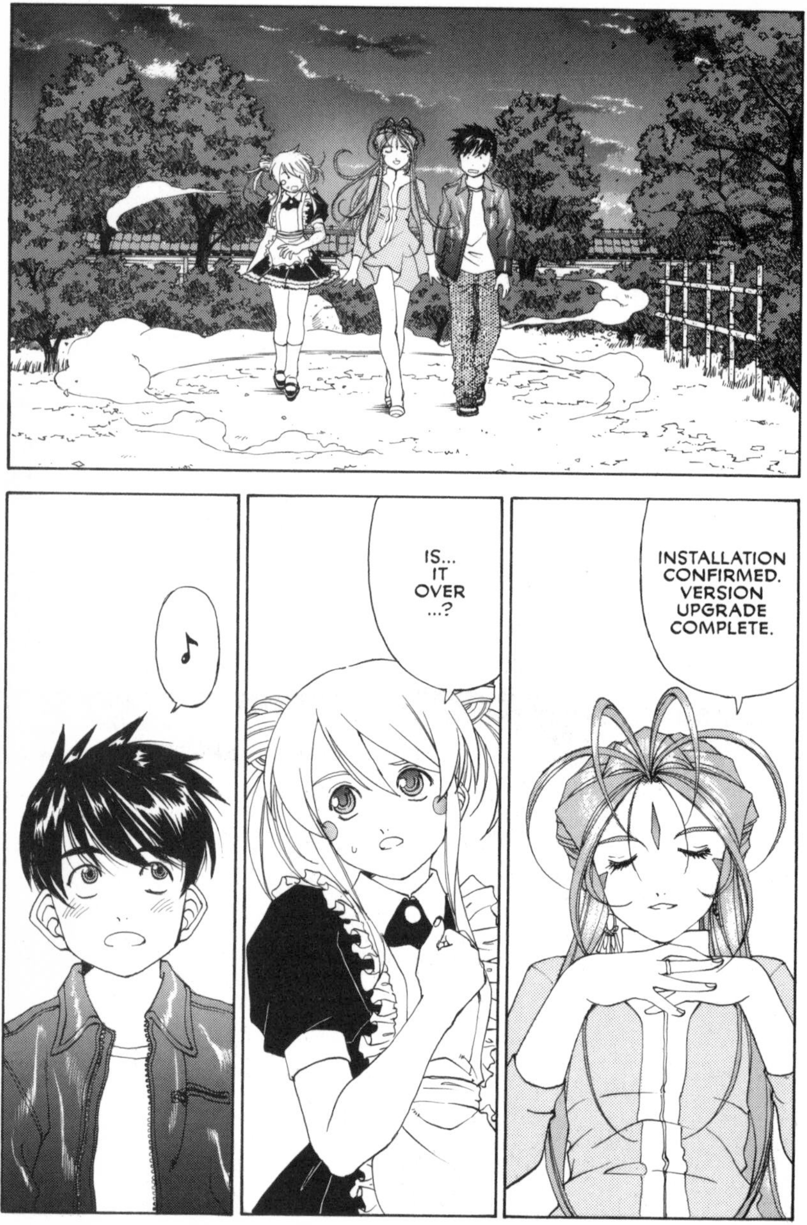

INSTALLATION CONFIRMED. VERSION UPGRADE COMPLETE.
IS... IT OVER ...?
♪

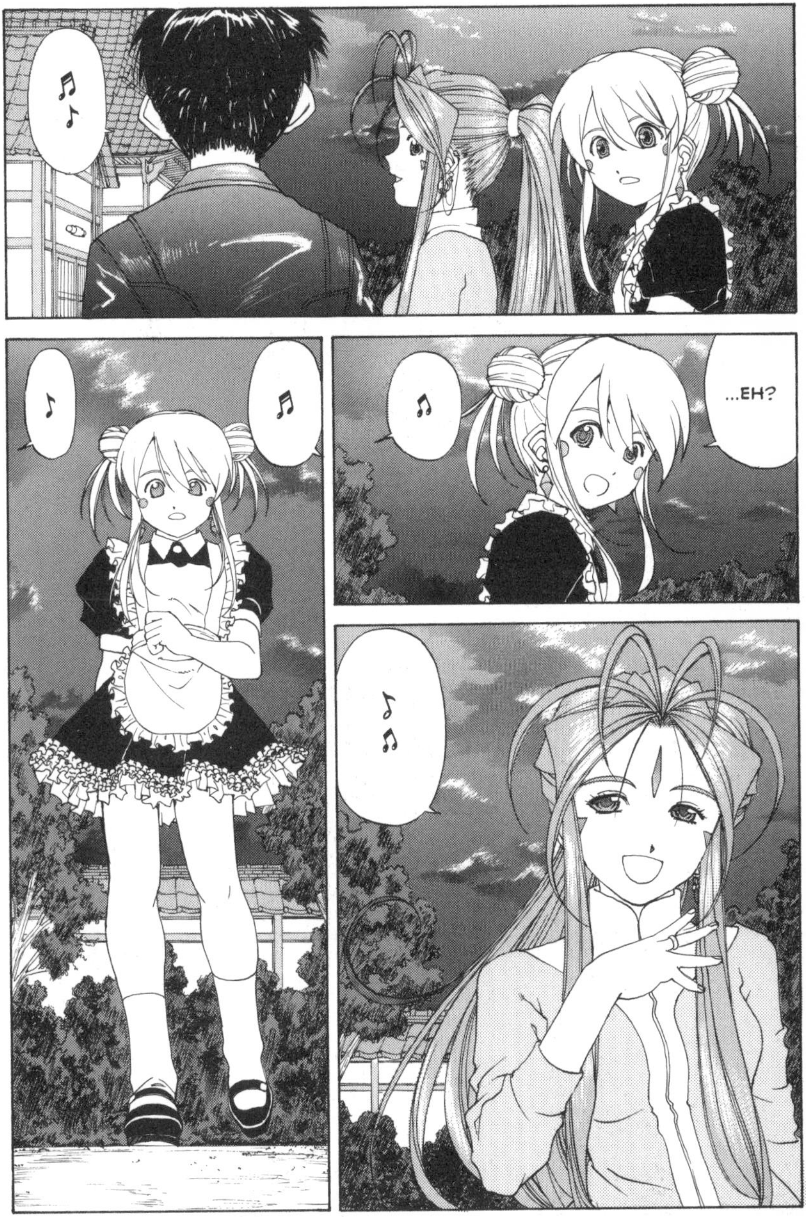
♫ ♪
...EH?
♫
♪ ♫
♫
♪

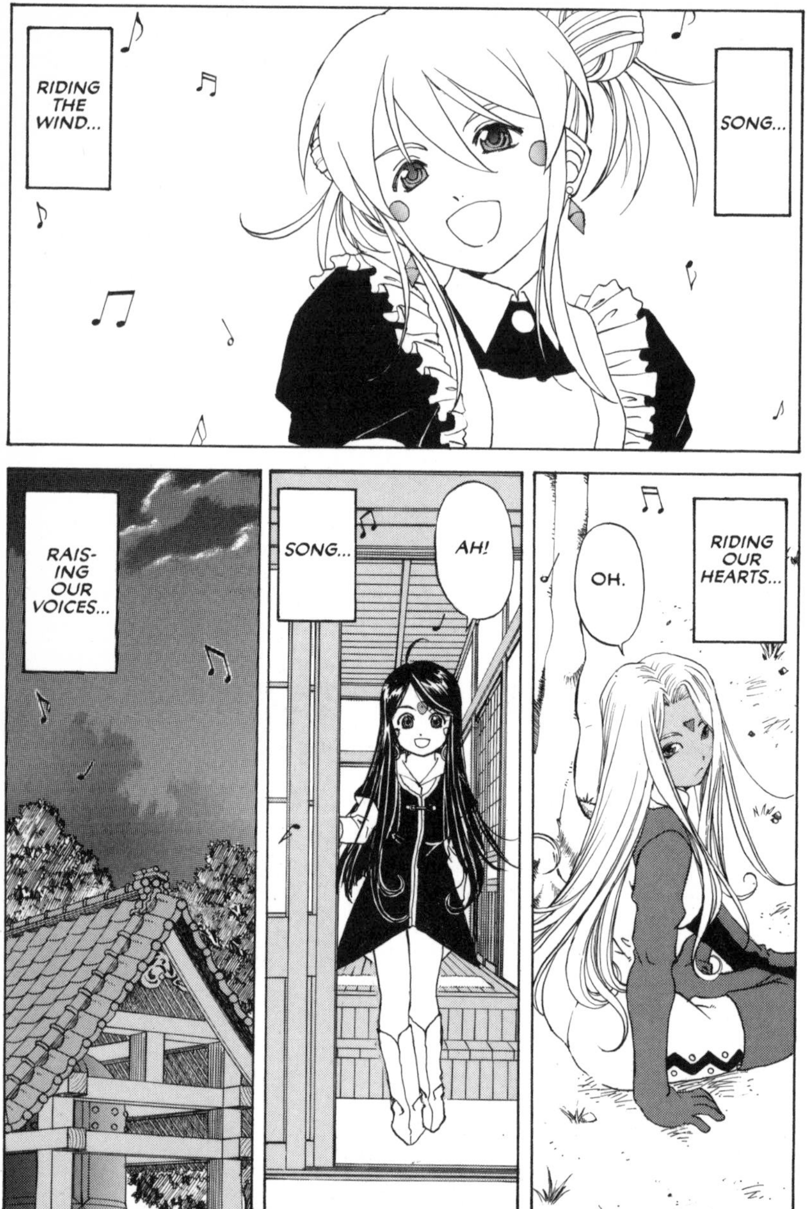
SONG...
RIDING THE WIND...
RIDING OUR HEARTS...
OH.
AH!
SONG...
RAIS-ING OUR VOICES...

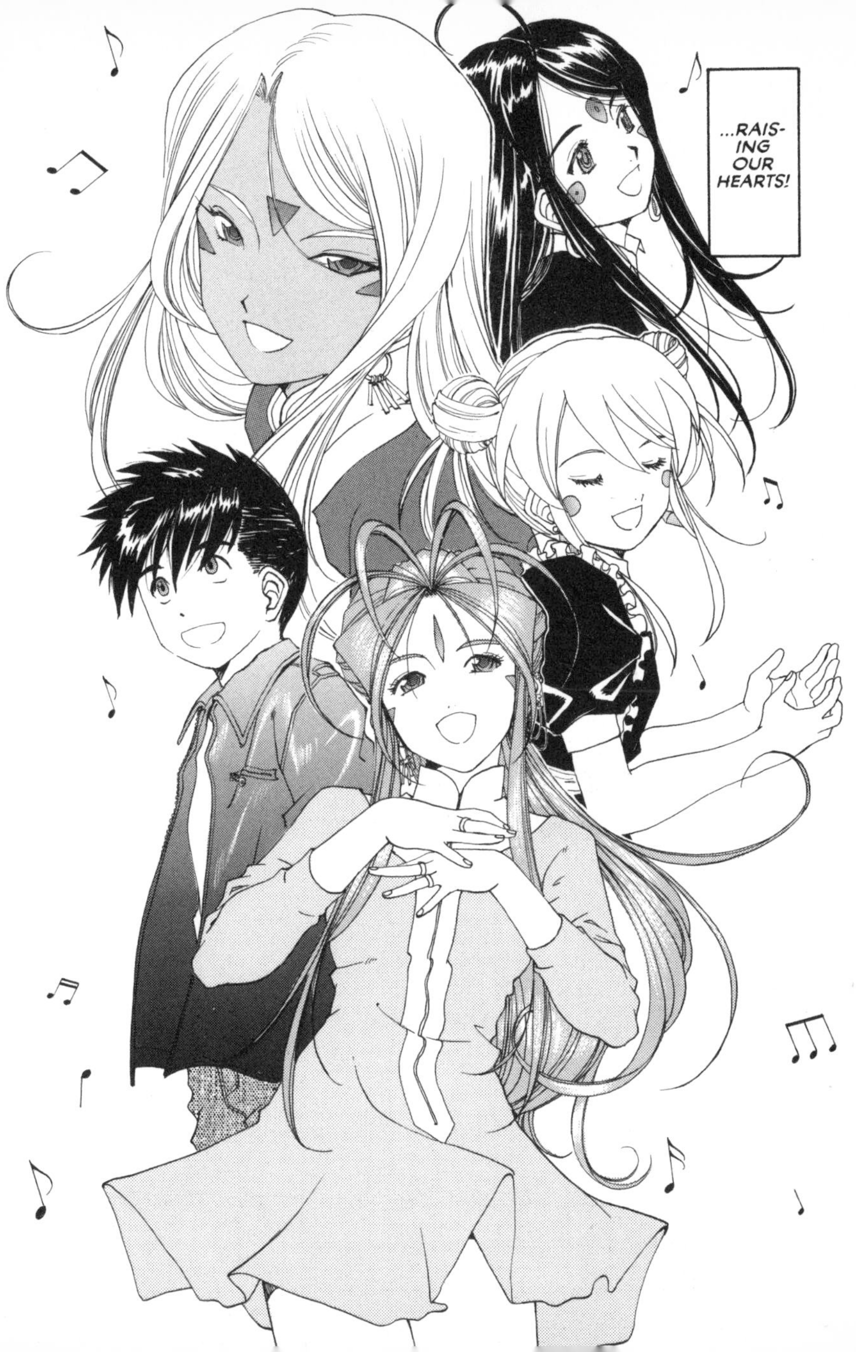
...RAIS-ING OUR HEARTS!

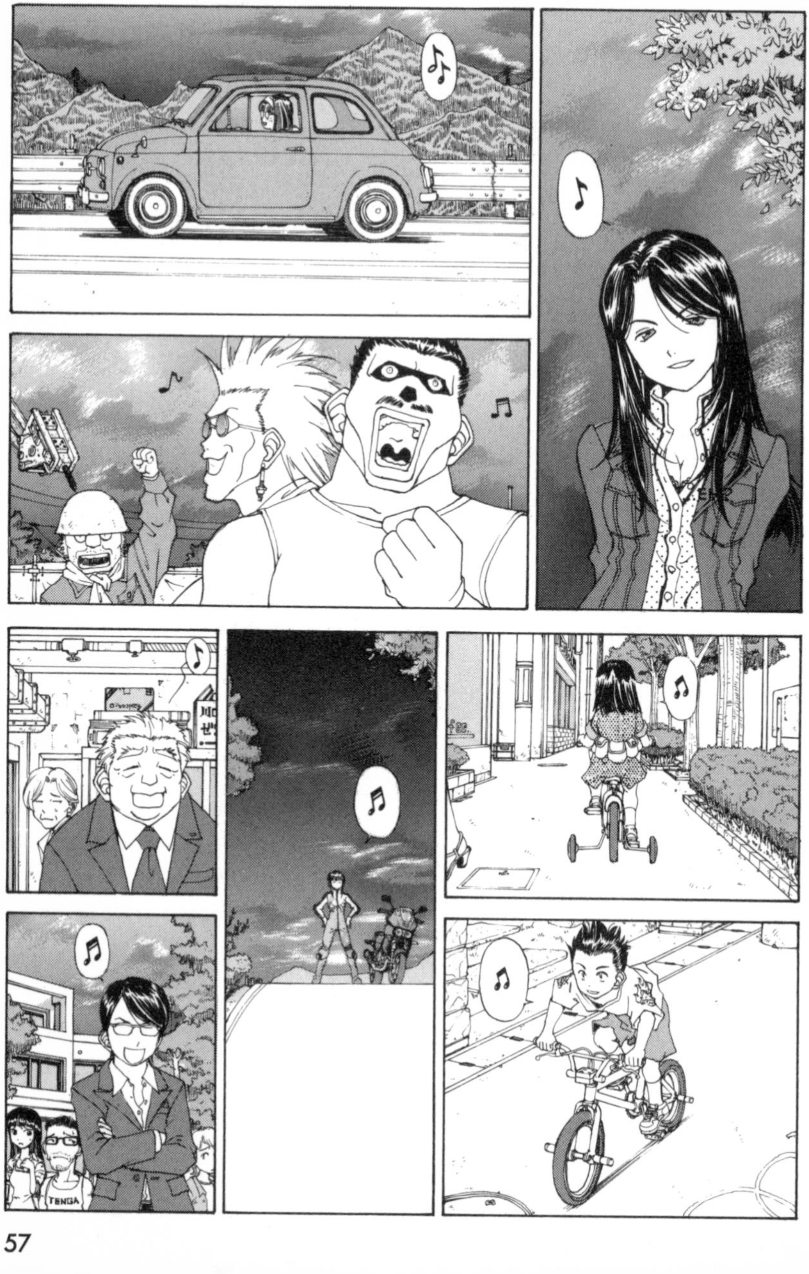
TENGA

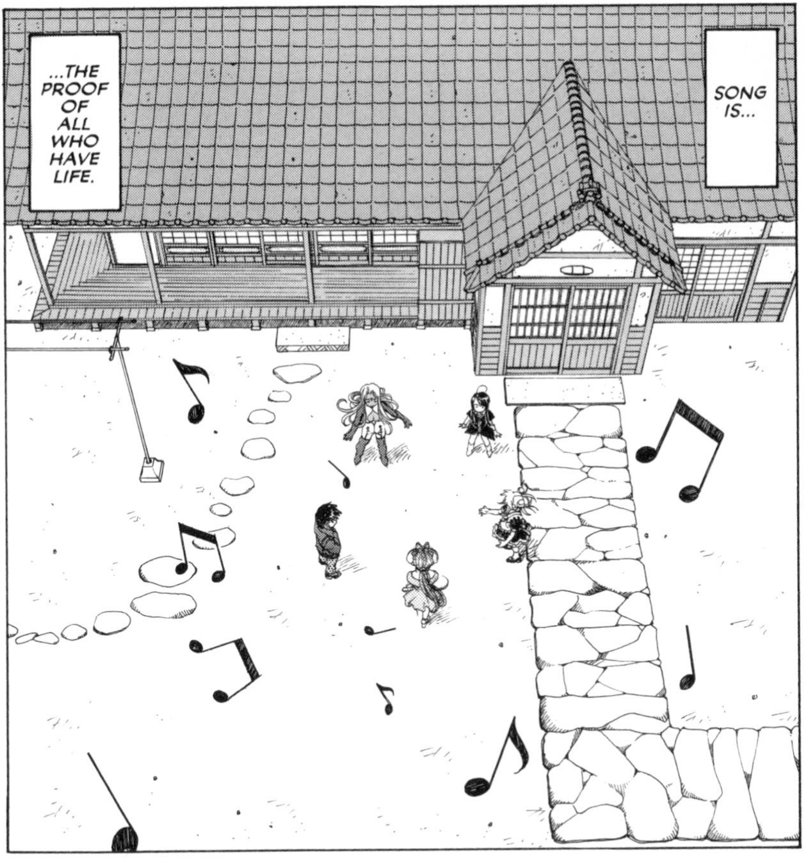
SONG IS...
...THE PROOF OF ALL WHO HAVE LIFE.

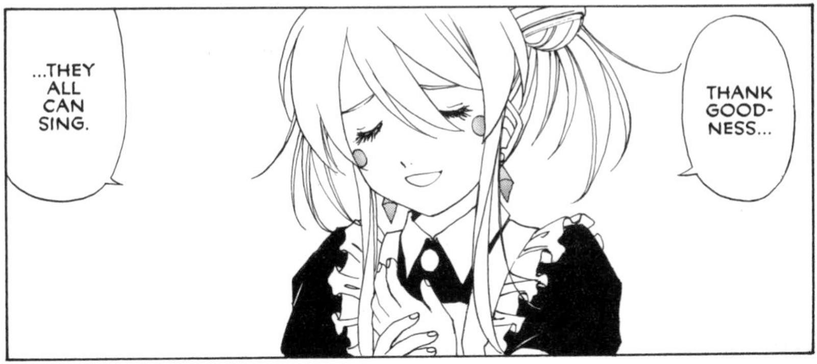
THANK GOOD-NESS...
...THEY ALL CAN SING.

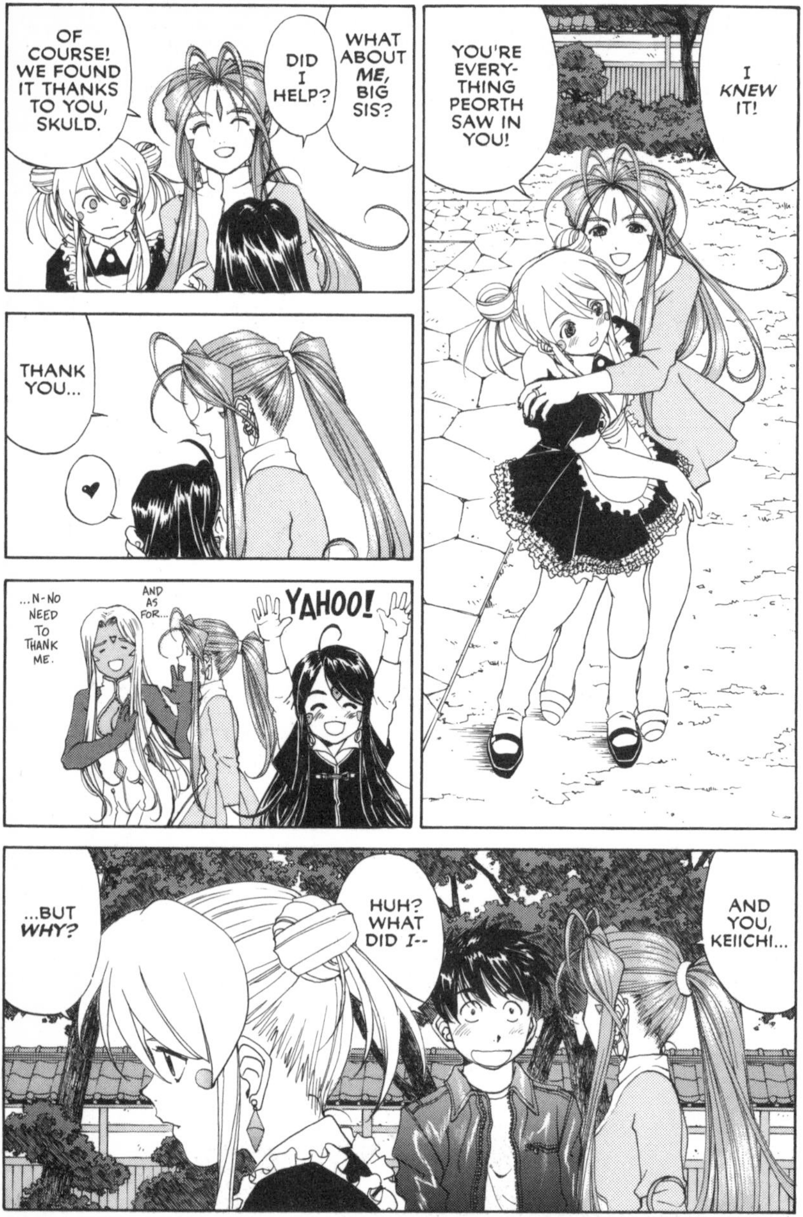
I KNEW IT!
YOU'RE EVERYTHING PEORTH SAW IN YOU!
WHAT ABOUT ME, BIG SIS?
DID I HELP?
OF COURSE! WE FOUND IT THANKS TO YOU, SKULD.
THANK YOU...
♥
YAHOO!
AND AS FOR...
...N-NO NEED TO THANK ME.
AND YOU, KEIICHI...
HUH? WHAT DID I--
...BUT WHY?

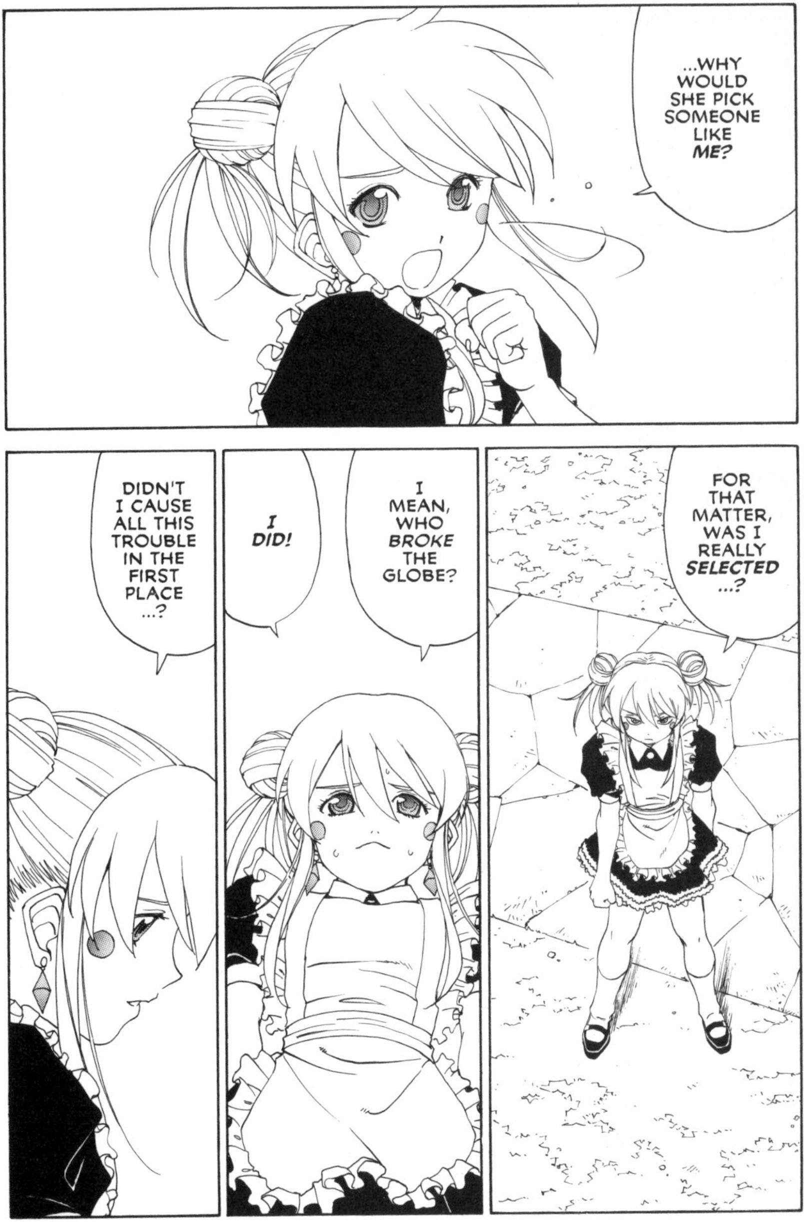
...WHY WOULD SHE PICK SOMEONE LIKE *ME?*
FOR THAT MATTER, WAS I REALLY *SELECTED* ...?
I MEAN, WHO *BROKE* THE GLOBE?
I DID!
DIDN'T I CAUSE ALL THIS TROUBLE IN THE FIRST PLACE ...?

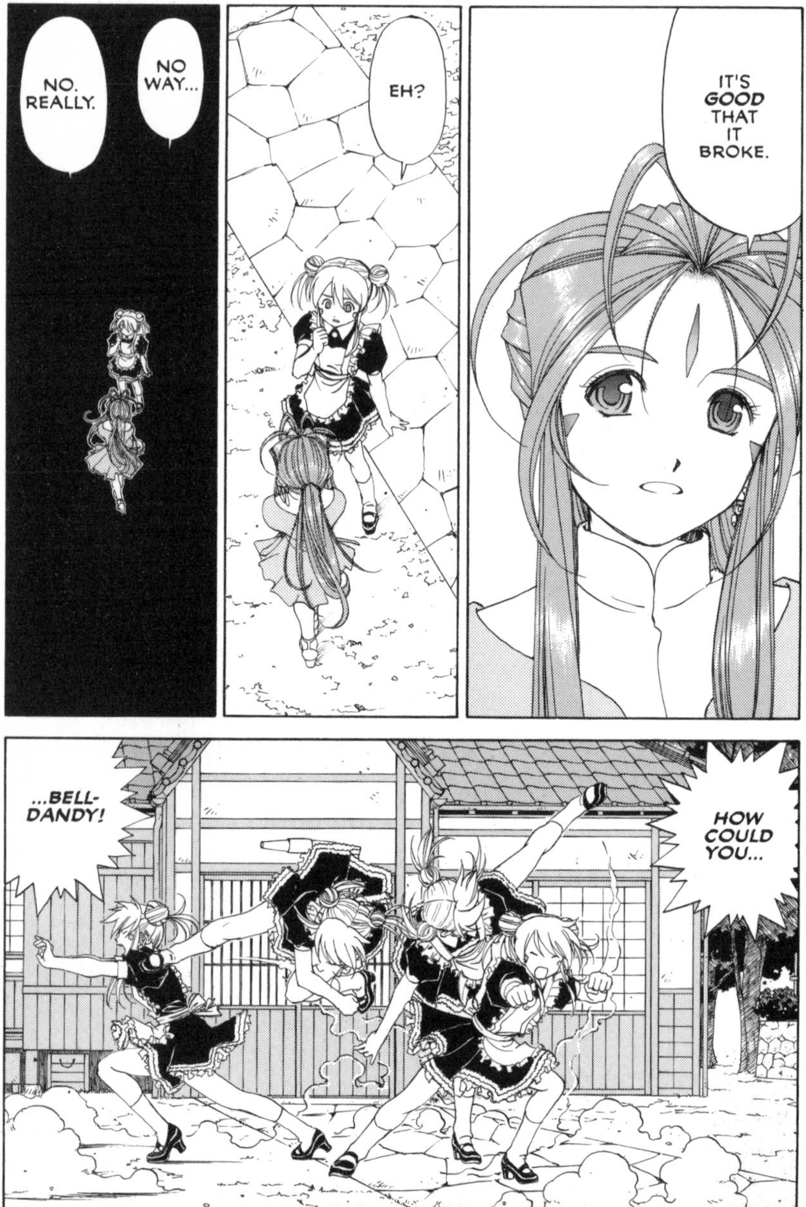
IT'S GOOD THAT IT BROKE.
EH?
NO WAY...
NO. REALLY.
HOW COULD YOU...
...BELL-DANDY!

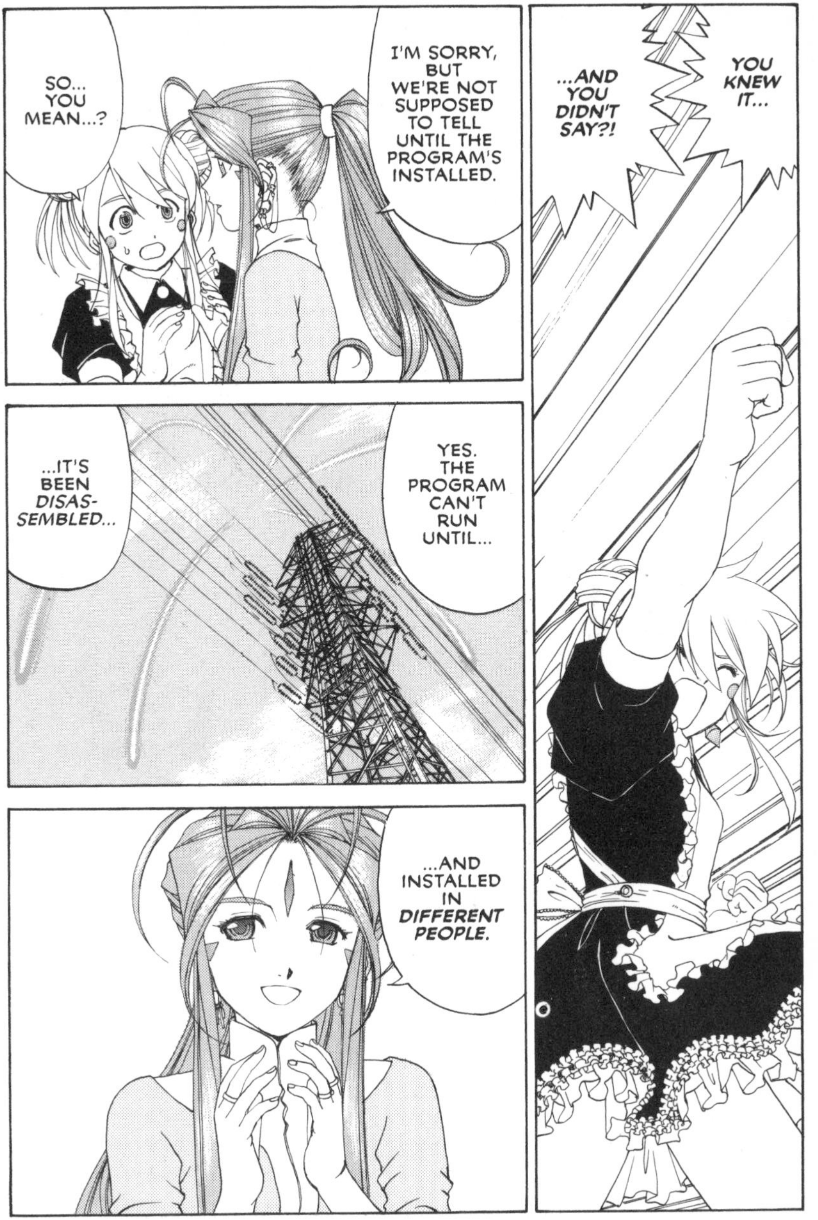
YOU KNEW IT...
...*AND* YOU *DIDN'T SAY?!*
I'M SORRY, BUT WE'RE NOT SUPPOSED TO TELL UNTIL THE PROGRAM'S INSTALLED.
SO... YOU MEAN...?
YES. THE PROGRAM CAN'T RUN UNTIL...
...IT'S BEEN *DISAS-SEMBLED...*
...AND INSTALLED IN *DIFFERENT PEOPLE.*

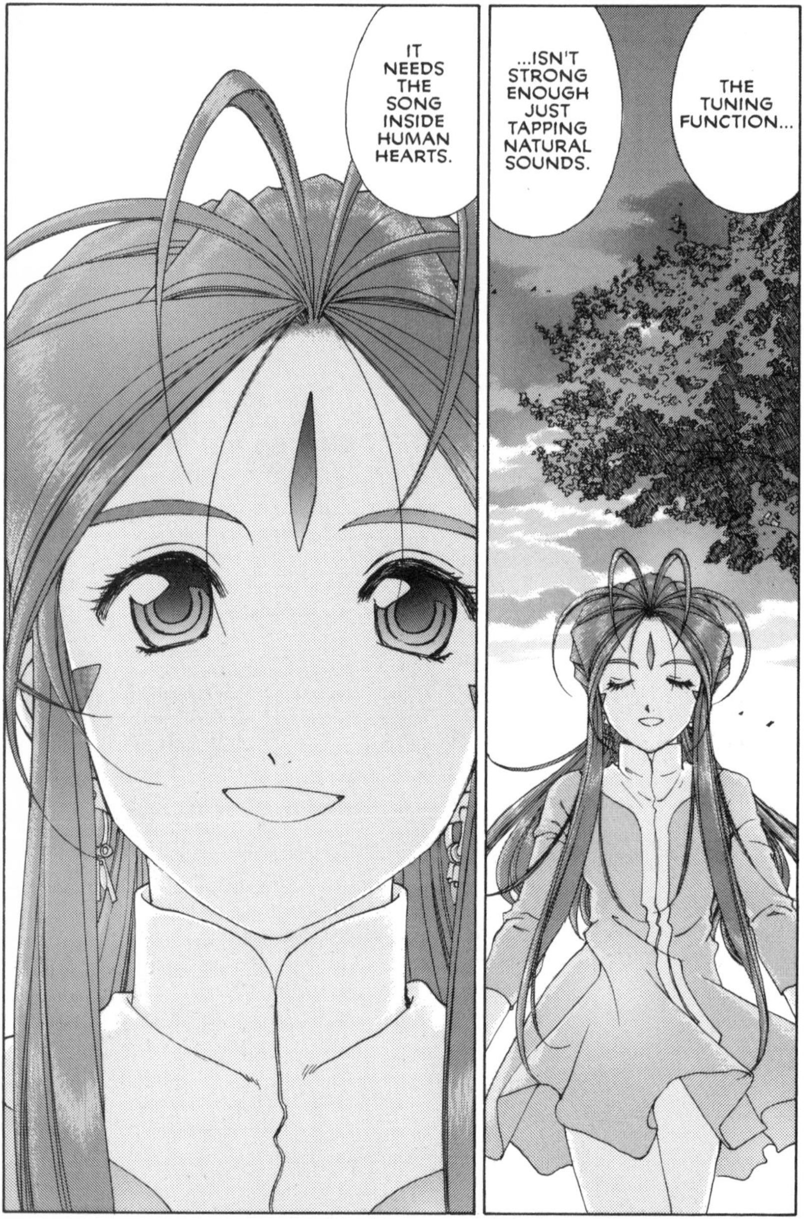
THE TUNING FUNCTION...
...ISN'T STRONG ENOUGH JUST TAPPING NATURAL SOUNDS.
IT NEEDS THE SONG INSIDE HUMAN HEARTS.

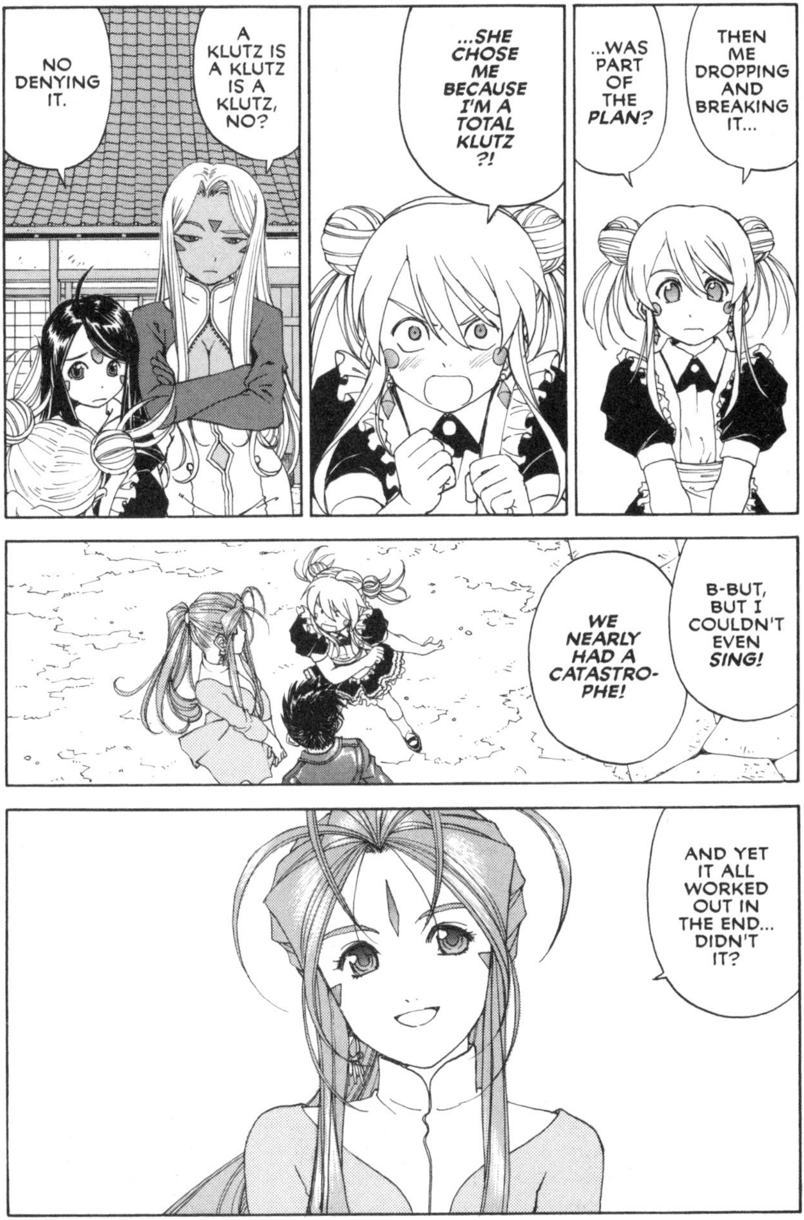
THEN ME DROPPING AND BREAKING IT...
...WAS PART OF THE PLAN?
...SHE CHOSE ME BECAUSE I'M A TOTAL KLUTZ ?!
A KLUTZ IS A KLUTZ IS A KLUTZ, NO?
NO DENYING IT.
B-BUT, BUT I COULDN'T EVEN SING!
WE NEARLY HAD A CATASTROPHE!
AND YET IT ALL WORKED OUT IN THE END... DIDN'T IT?

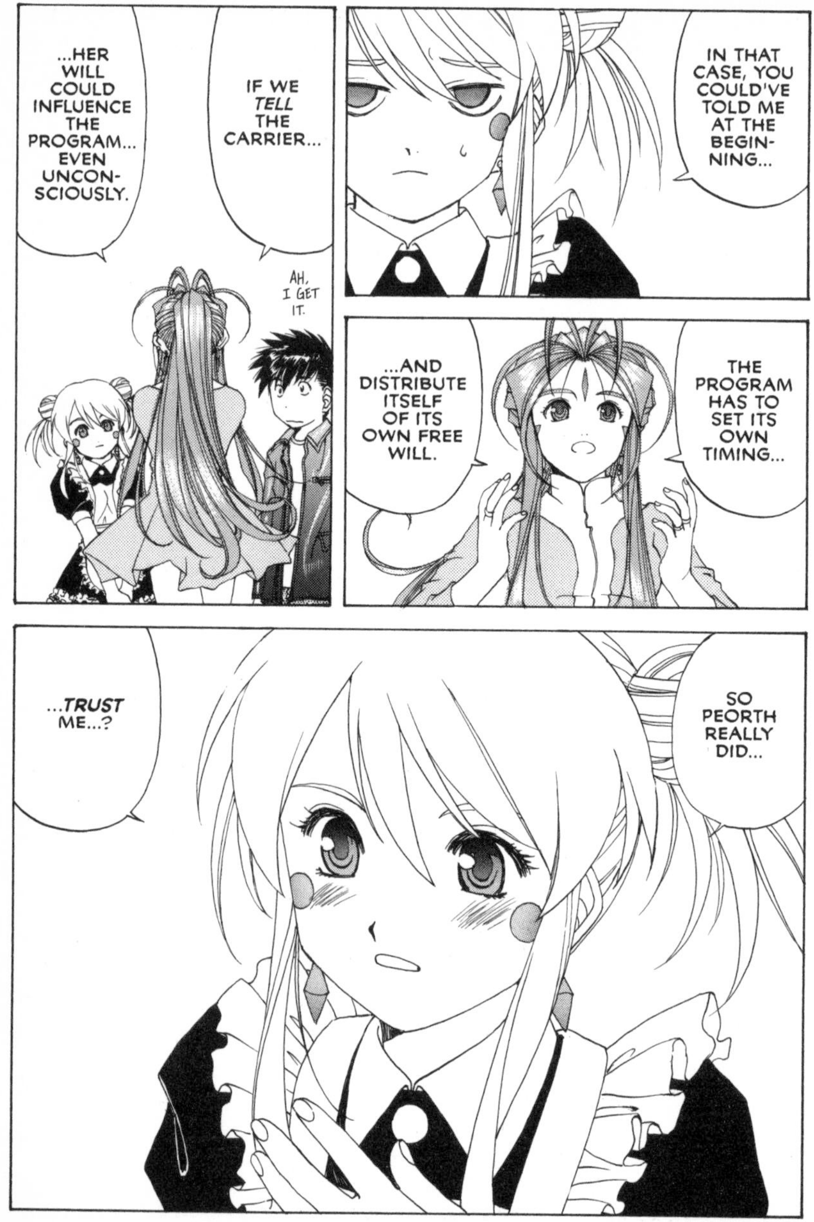
IN THAT CASE, YOU COULD'VE TOLD ME AT THE BEGIN-NING...
THE PROGRAM HAS TO SET ITS OWN TIMING...
...AND DISTRIBUTE ITSELF OF ITS OWN FREE WILL.
IF WE *TELL* THE CARRIER...
...HER WILL COULD INFLUENCE THE PROGRAM... EVEN UNCON-SCIOUSLY.
AH, I GET IT.
SO PEORTH REALLY DID...
...*TRUST* ME...?

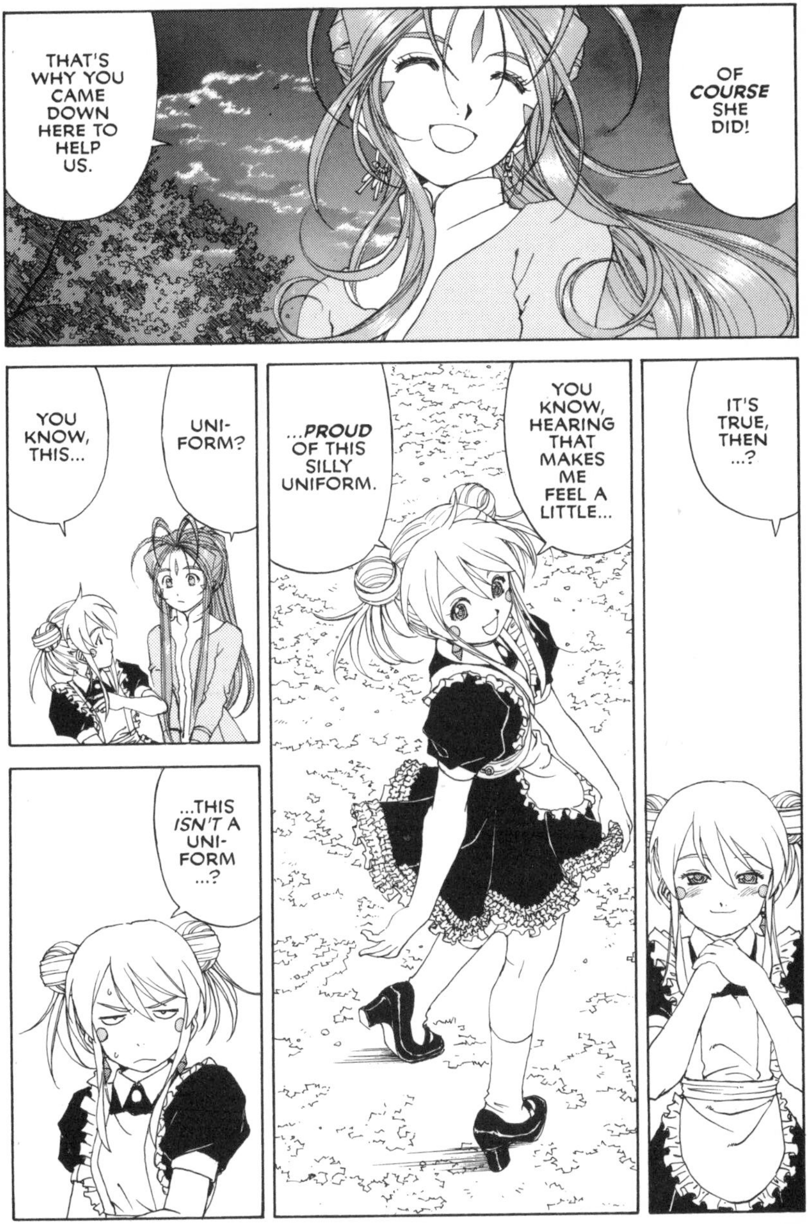
THAT'S WHY YOU CAME DOWN HERE TO HELP US.
OF *COURSE* SHE DID!
YOU KNOW, THIS...
UNI-FORM?
...THIS *ISN'T* A UNI-FORM ...?
YOU KNOW, HEARING THAT MAKES ME FEEL A LITTLE...
...*PROUD* OF THIS SILLY UNIFORM.
IT'S TRUE, THEN ...?

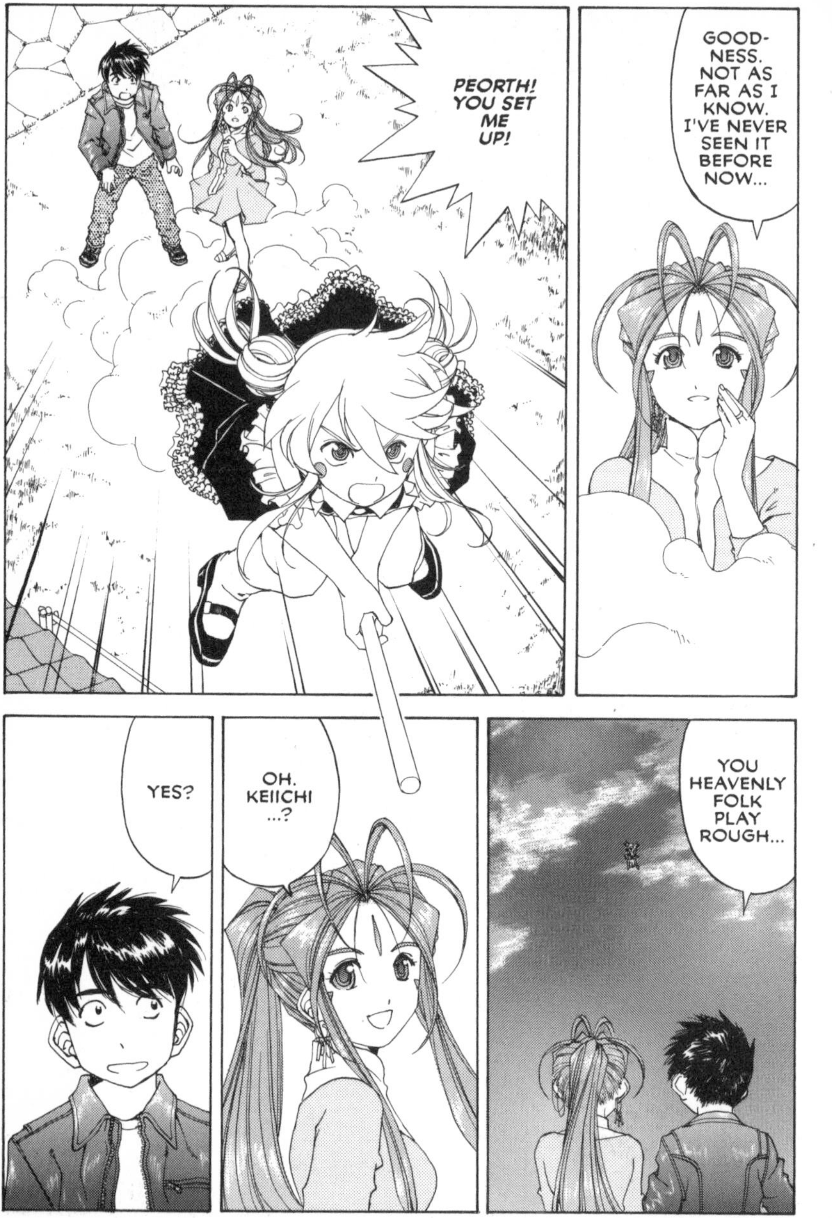
GOOD-NESS. NOT AS FAR AS I KNOW. I'VE NEVER SEEN IT BEFORE NOW...
PEORTH! YOU SET ME UP!
YOU HEAVENLY FOLK PLAY ROUGH...
OH. KEIICHI ...?
YES?

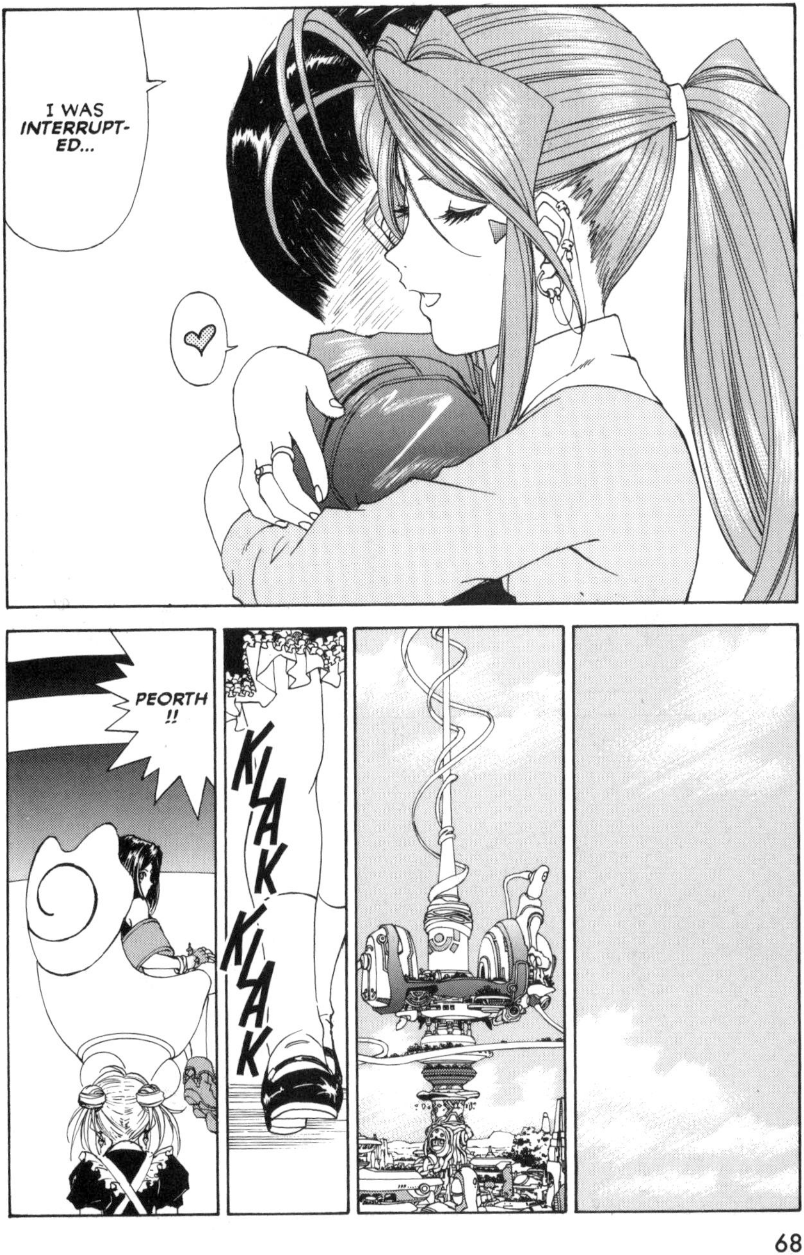
I WAS INTERRUPT-ED...
KLAK KLAK
PEORTH !!

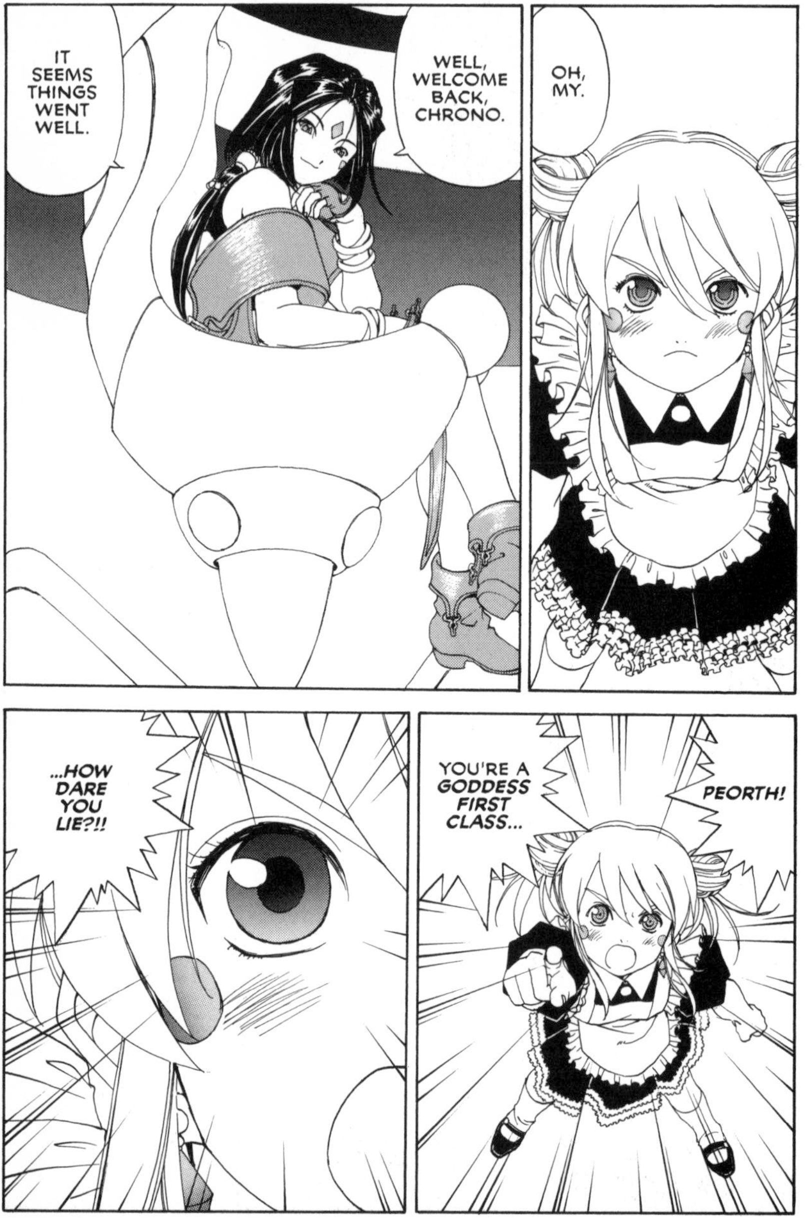
OH, MY.
WELL, WELCOME BACK, CHRONO.
IT SEEMS THINGS WENT WELL.
PEORTH!
YOU'RE A *GODDESS FIRST CLASS*...
...HOW DARE YOU LIE?!!

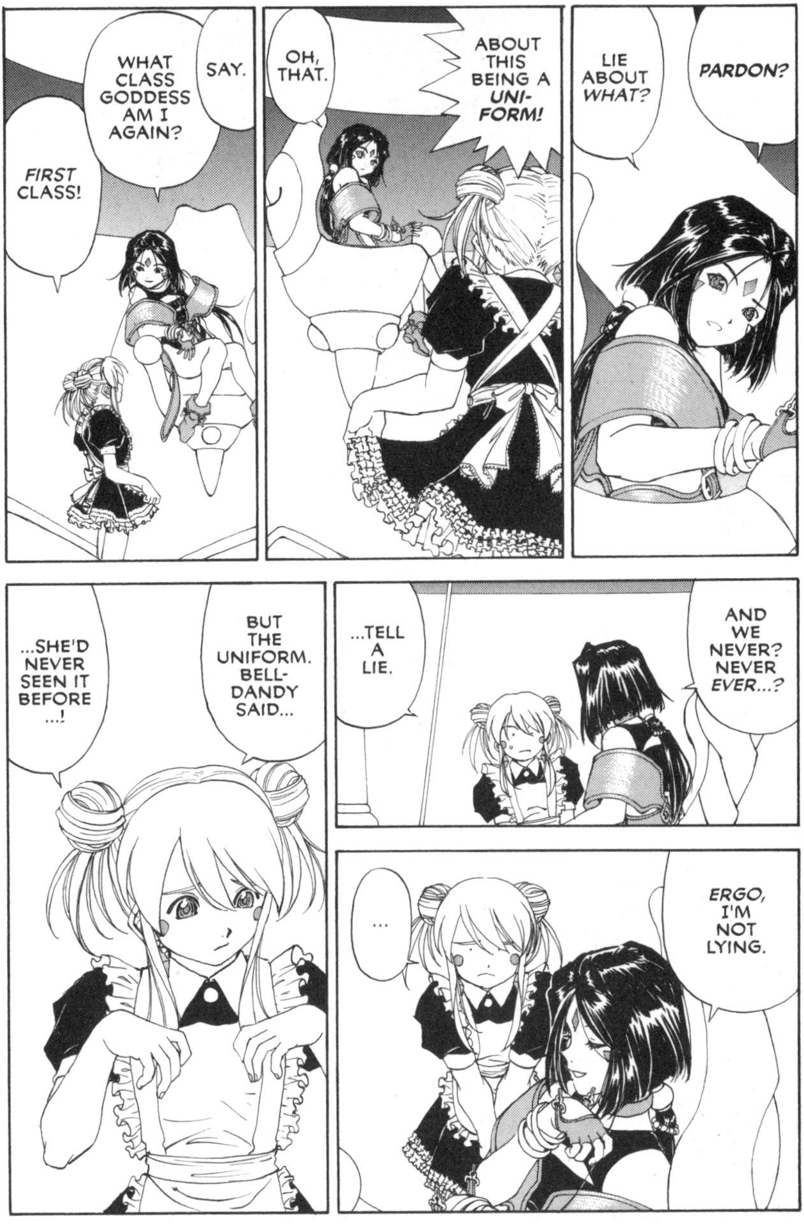
PARDON?
LIE ABOUT WHAT?
ABOUT THIS BEING A UNI-FORM!
OH, THAT.
SAY.
WHAT CLASS GODDESS AM I AGAIN?
FIRST CLASS!
AND WE NEVER? NEVER EVER...?
...TELL A LIE.
ERGO, I'M NOT LYING.
...
BUT THE UNIFORM. BELL-DANDY SAID...
...SHE'D NEVER SEEN IT BEFORE ...!

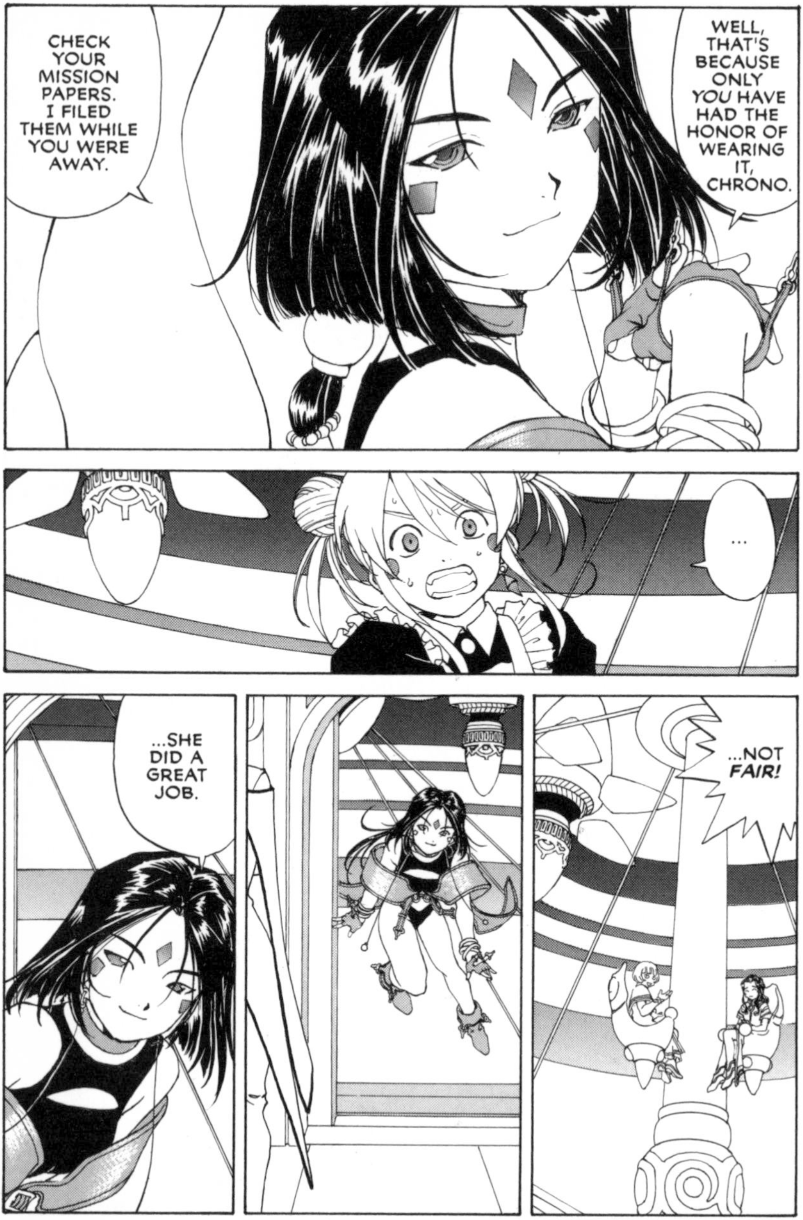
WELL, THAT'S BECAUSE ONLY *YOU* HAVE HAD THE HONOR OF WEARING IT, CHRONO.
CHECK YOUR MISSION PAPERS. I FILED THEM WHILE YOU WERE AWAY.
...
...NOT ***FAIR!***
...SHE DID A GREAT JOB.

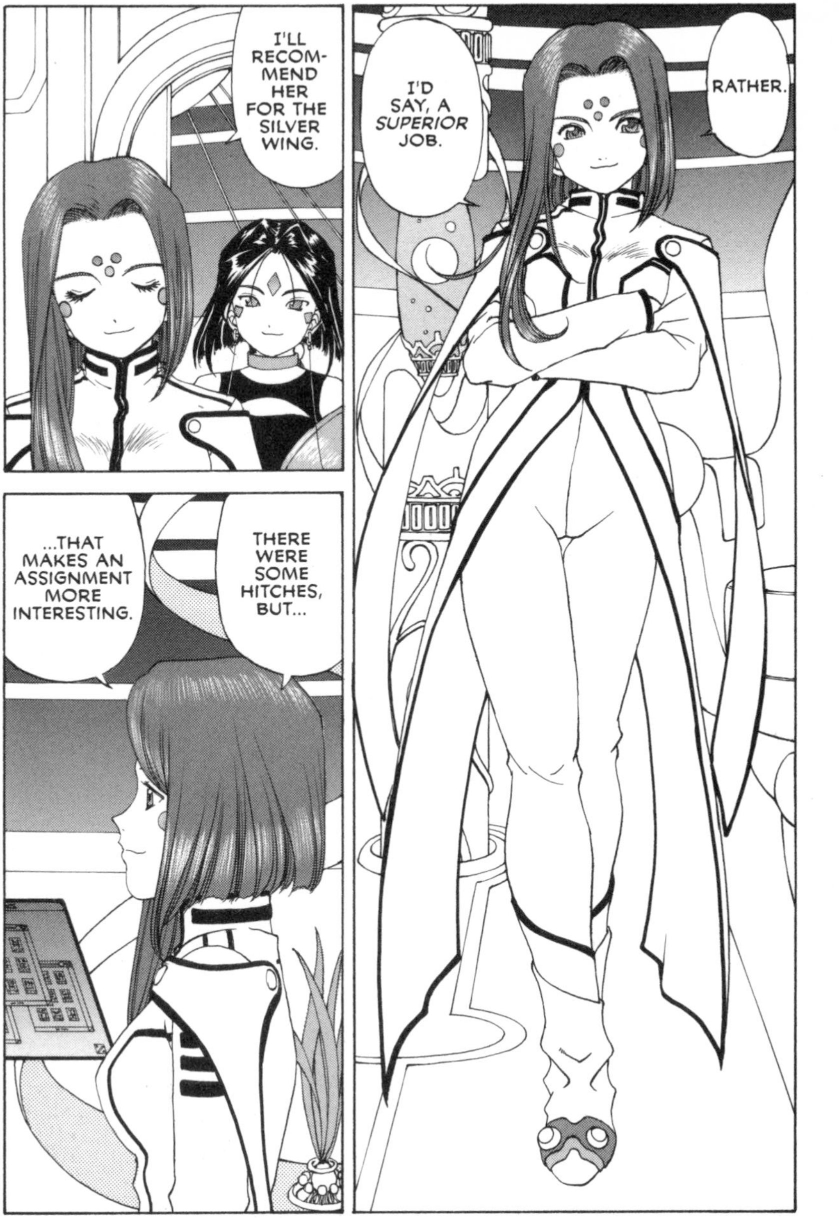
RATHER.
I'D SAY, A *SUPERIOR* JOB.
I'LL RECOMMEND HER FOR THE SILVER WING.
THERE WERE SOME HITCHES, BUT...
...THAT MAKES AN ASSIGNMENT MORE INTERESTING.

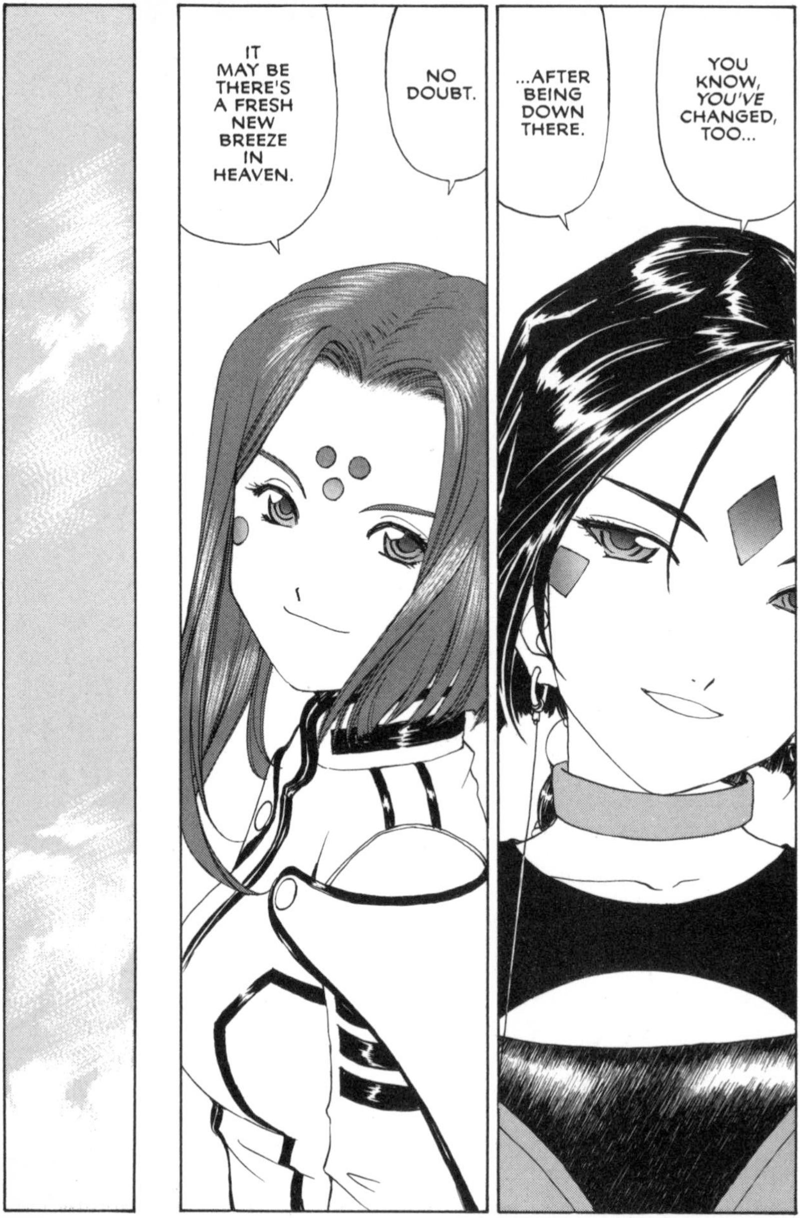
YOU KNOW, *YOU'VE* CHANGED, TOO...
...AFTER BEING DOWN THERE.
NO DOUBT.
IT MAY BE THERE'S A FRESH NEW BREEZE IN HEAVEN.

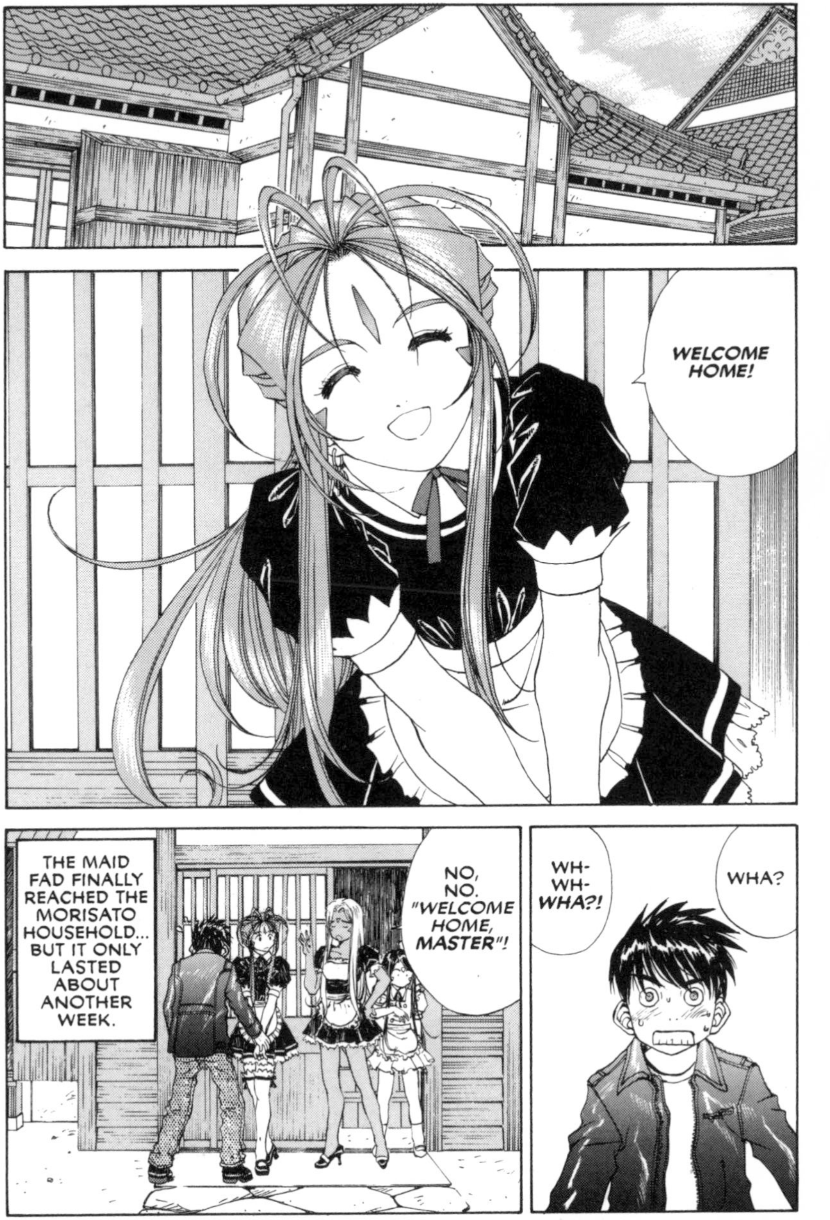
WELCOME HOME!
WHA?
WH- WH- WHA?!
NO, NO. "WELCOME HOME, MASTER"!
THE MAID FAD FINALLY REACHED THE MORISATO HOUSEHOLD... BUT IT ONLY LASTED ABOUT ANOTHER WEEK.

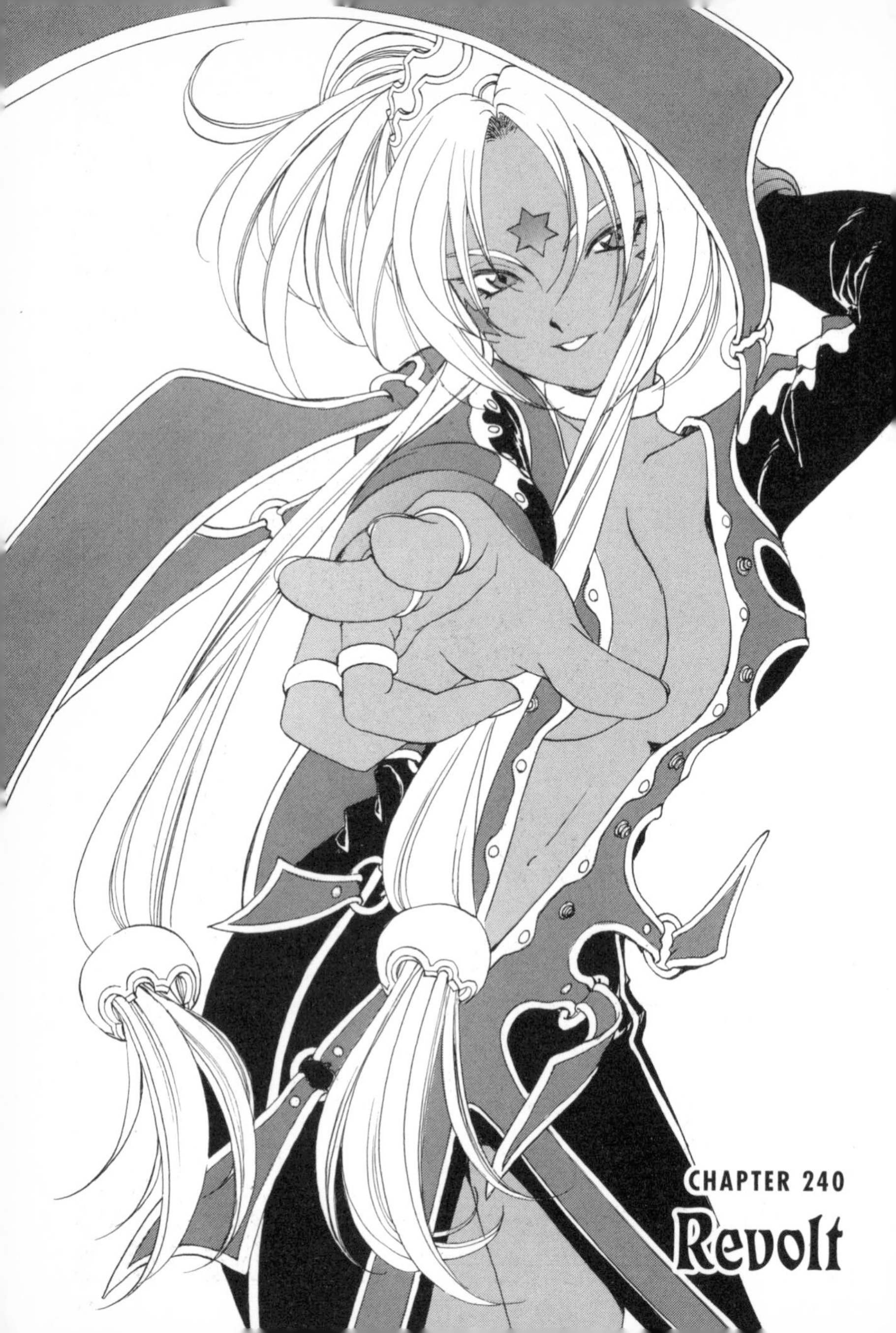

CHAPTER 240

Revolt

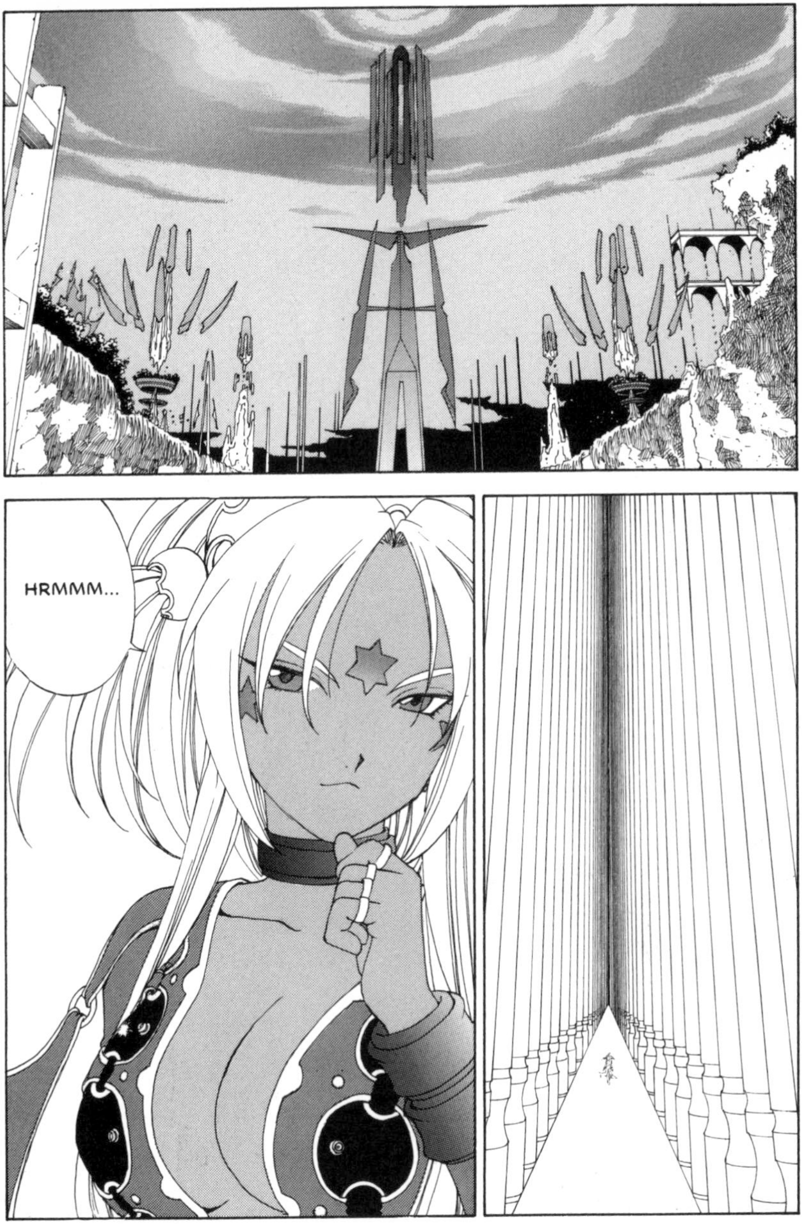
HRMMM...

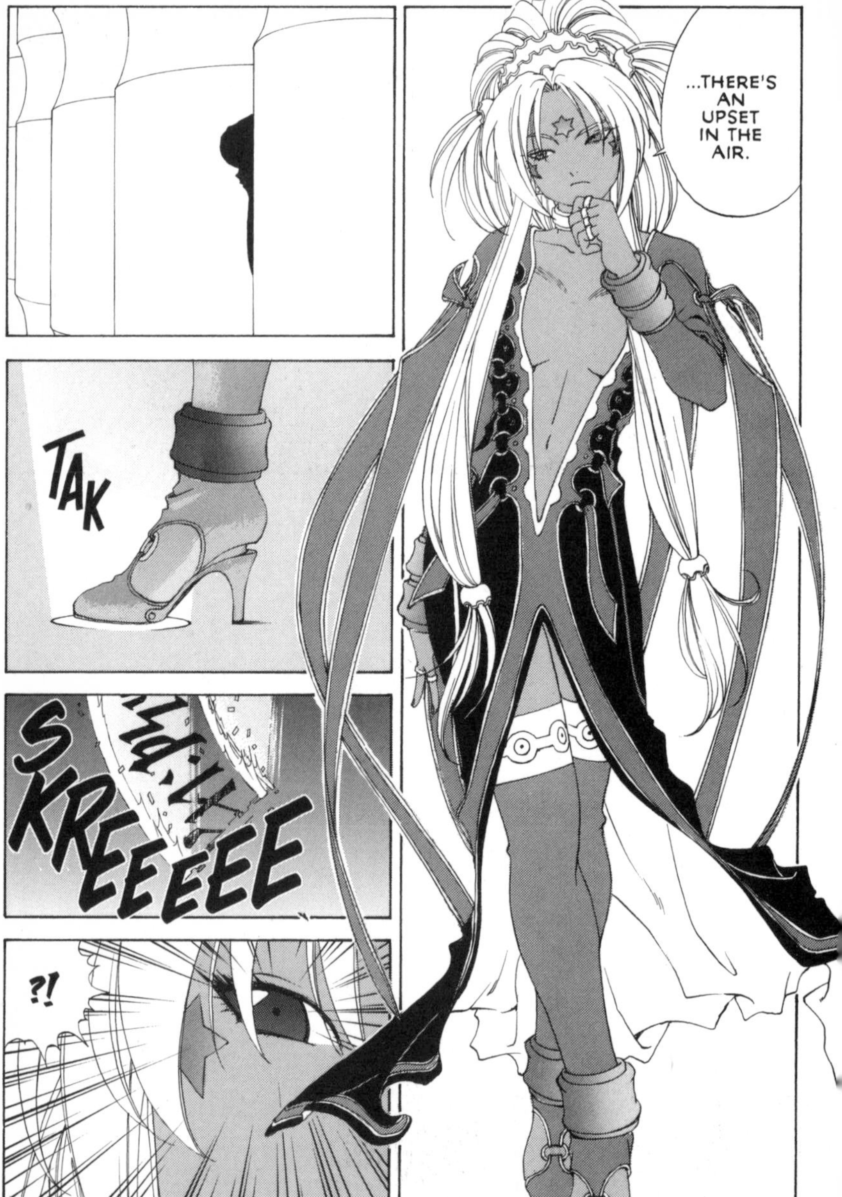
...THERE'S AN UPSET IN THE AIR.
TAK
SKREEEEEE
?!

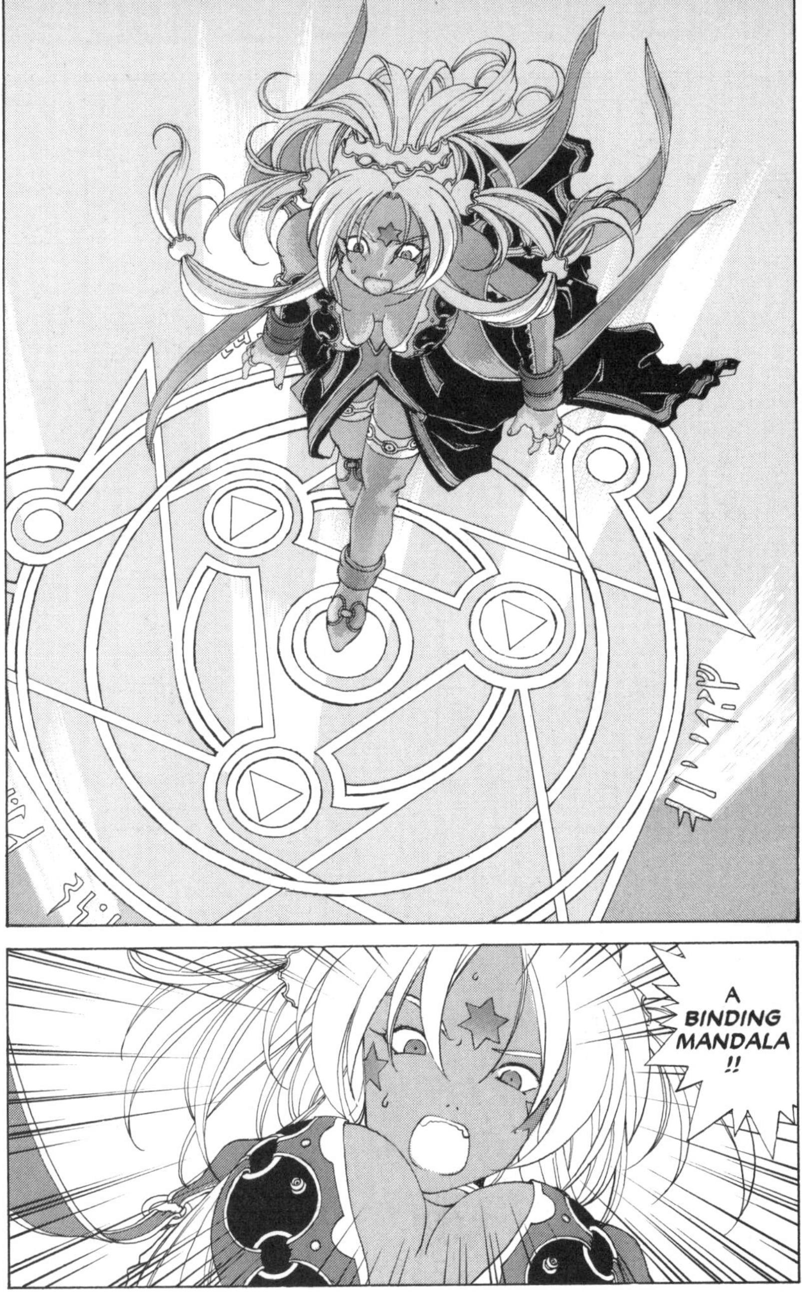
A BINDING MANDALA !!

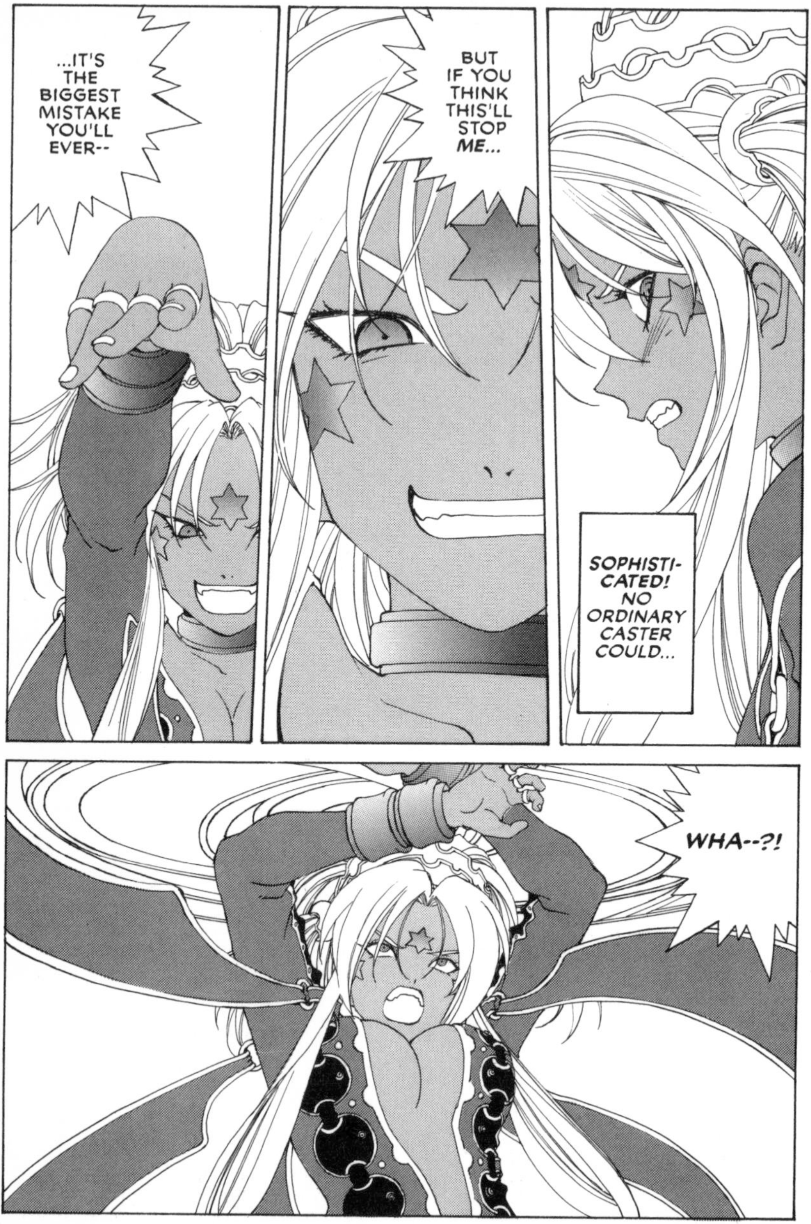
SOPHISTI-CATED! NO ORDINARY CASTER COULD...
BUT IF YOU THINK THIS'LL STOP *ME*...
...IT'S THE BIGGEST MISTAKE YOU'LL EVER--
WHA--?!

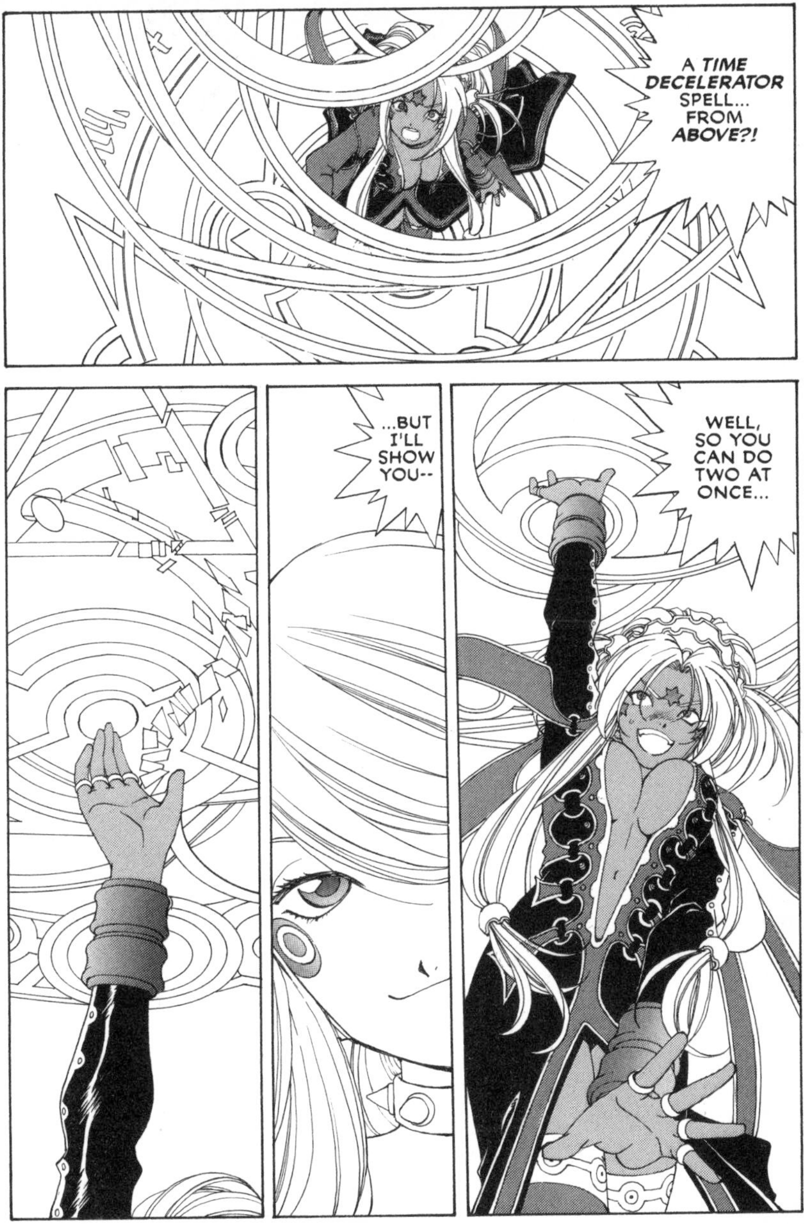
A *TIME DECELERATOR* SPELL... FROM *ABOVE?!*
WELL, SO YOU CAN DO TWO AT ONCE...
...BUT I'LL SHOW YOU--

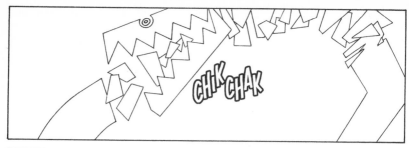

CHIK CHAK

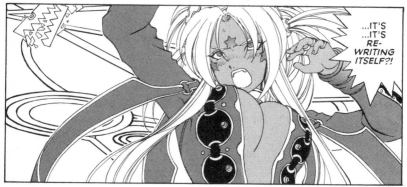

...IT'S ...IT'S RE-WRITING ITSELF?!

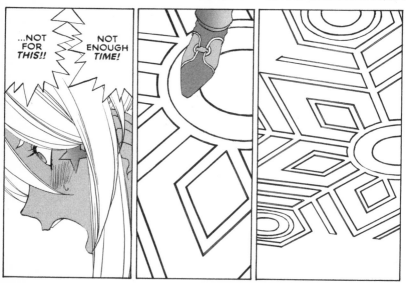

...NOT FOR *THIS*!!

NOT ENOUGH *TIME*!

81

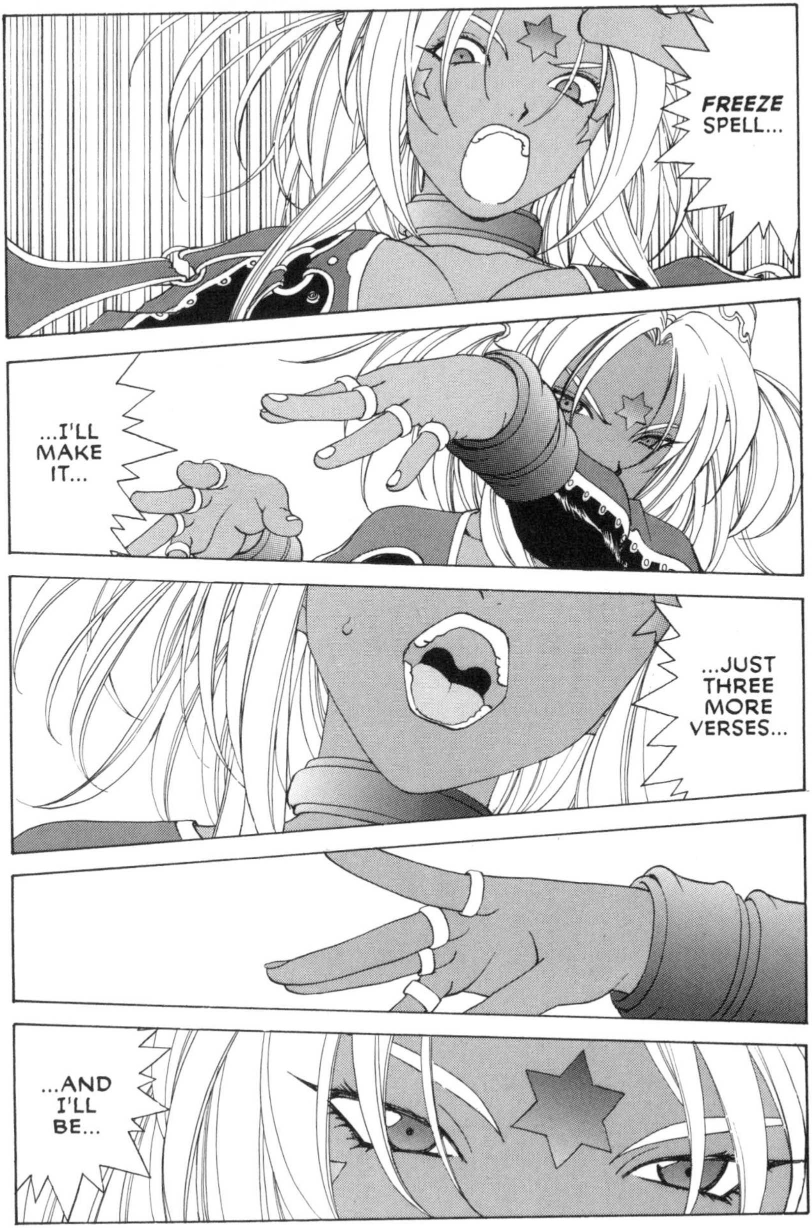
FREEZE SPELL...
...I'LL MAKE IT...
...JUST THREE MORE VERSES...
...AND I'LL BE...

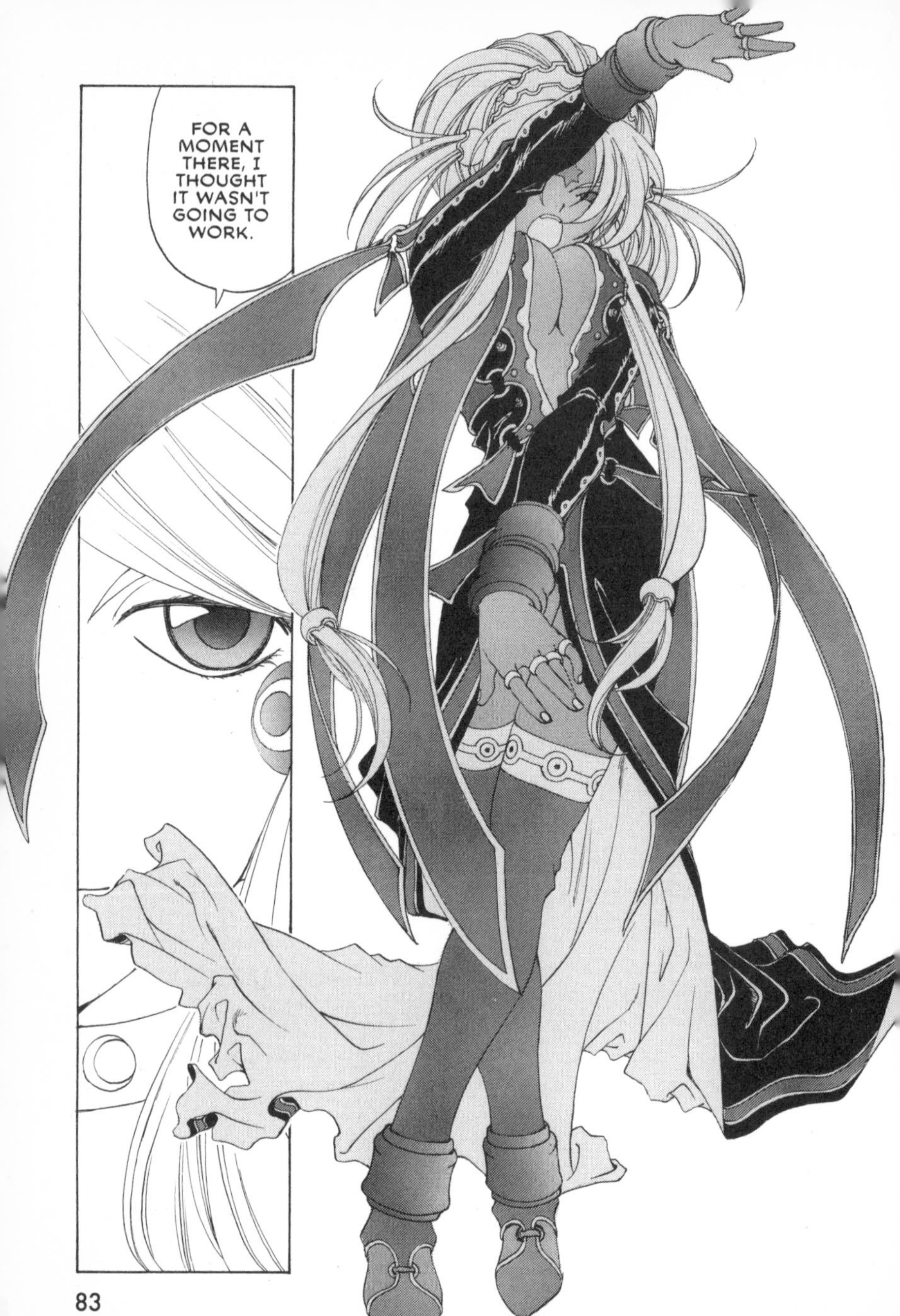
FOR A MOMENT THERE, I THOUGHT IT WASN'T GOING TO WORK.

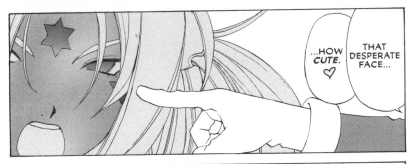

...HOW *CUTE.* ♥

THAT DESPERATE FACE...

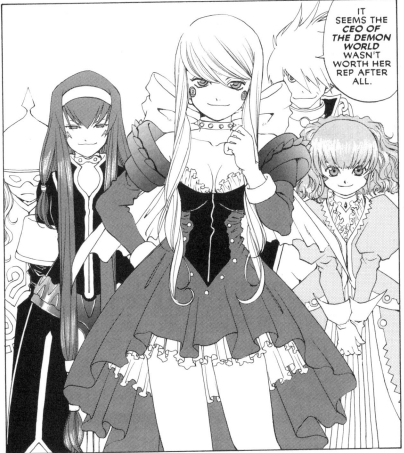

IT SEEMS THE *CEO OF THE DEMON WORLD* WASN'T WORTH HER REP AFTER ALL.

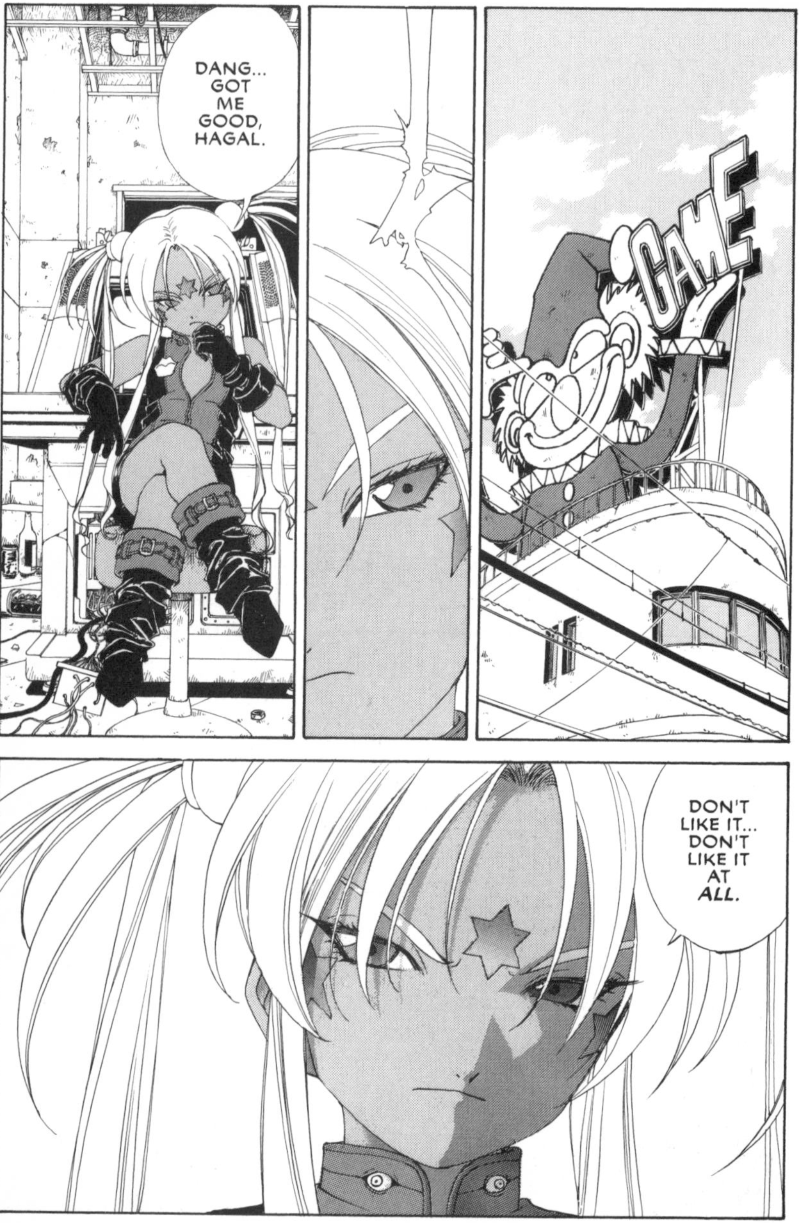
GAME
DANG... GOT ME GOOD, HAGAL.
DON'T LIKE IT... DON'T LIKE IT AT *ALL*.

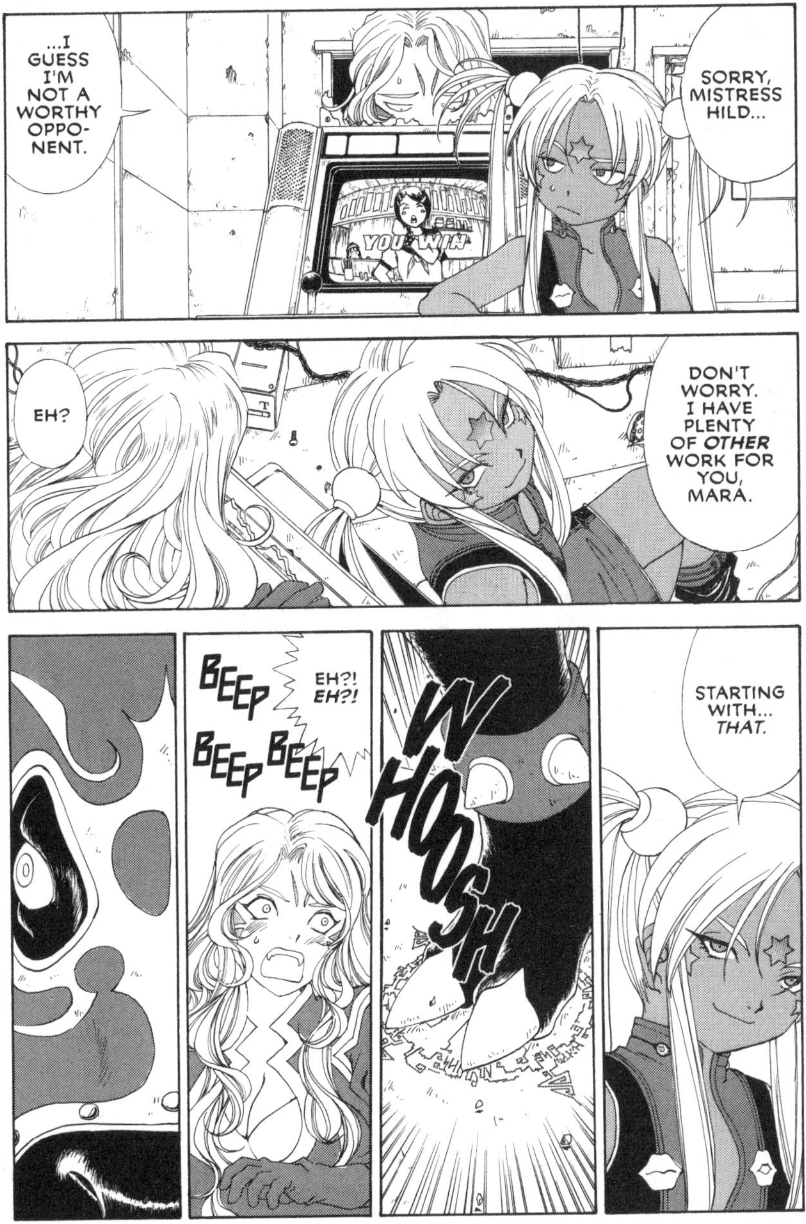
SORRY, MISTRESS HILD...
...I GUESS I'M NOT A WORTHY OPPONENT.
YOU WIN
DON'T WORRY. I HAVE PLENTY OF *OTHER* WORK FOR YOU, MARA.
EH?
STARTING WITH... *THAT.*
WHOOSH
EH?! EH?!
BEEP BEEP BEEP

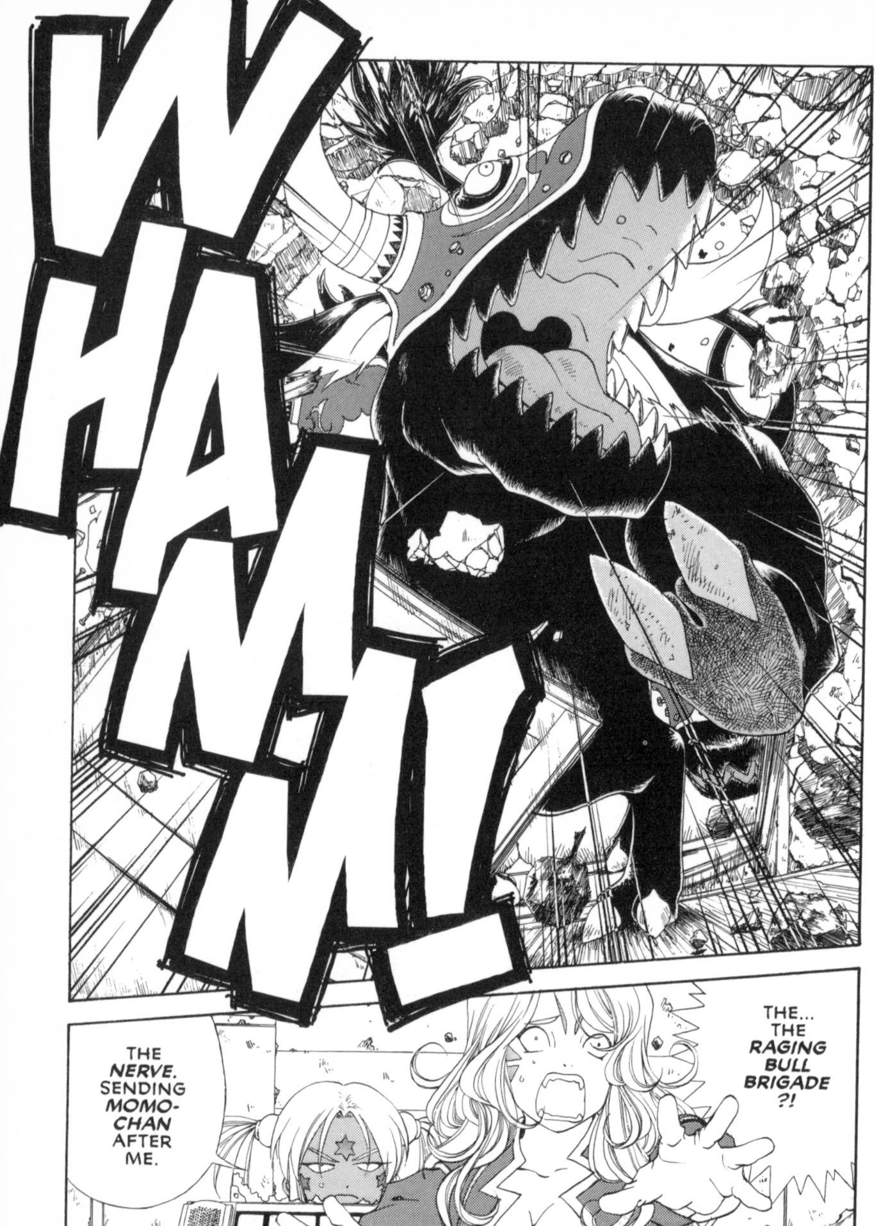
WHAMM!
THE... THE RAGING BULL BRIGADE?!
THE NERVE. SENDING MOMO-CHAN AFTER ME.

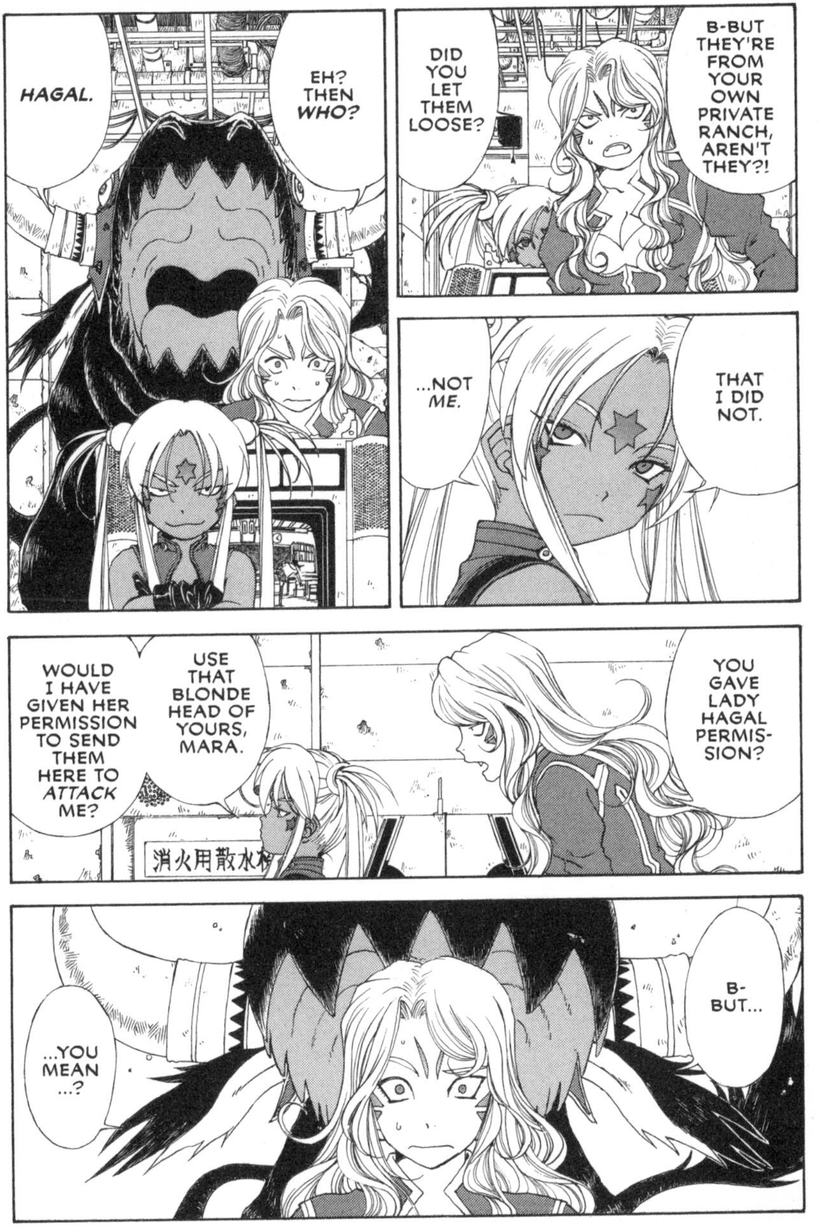
B-BUT THEY'RE FROM YOUR OWN PRIVATE RANCH, AREN'T THEY?!
DID YOU LET THEM LOOSE?
THAT I DID NOT.
...NOT *ME.*
EH? THEN *WHO?*
HAGAL.
YOU GAVE LADY HAGAL PERMISSION?
USE THAT BLONDE HEAD OF YOURS, MARA.
WOULD I HAVE GIVEN HER PERMISSION TO SEND THEM HERE TO *ATTACK* ME?
消火用散水
B-BUT...
...YOU MEAN ...?

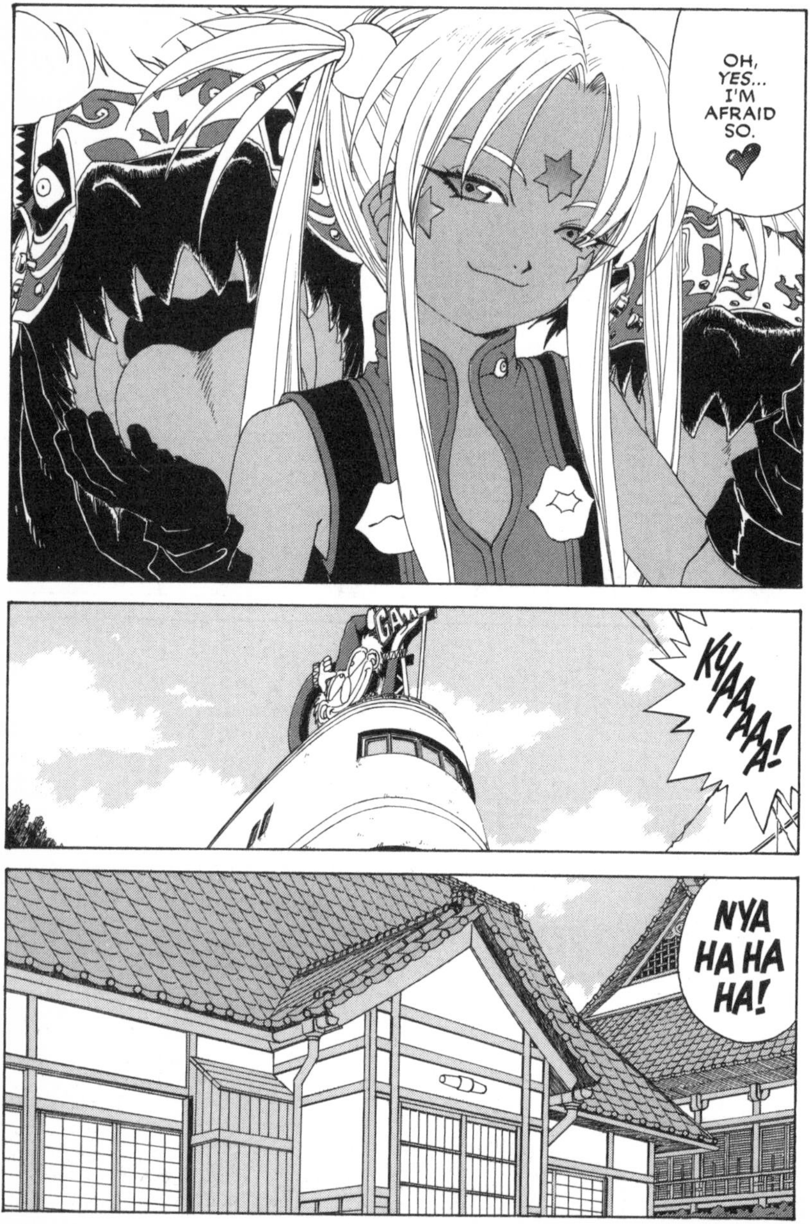
OH, YES... I'M AFRAID SO. ♥
KYAAAAAA!
NYA HA HA HA HA!

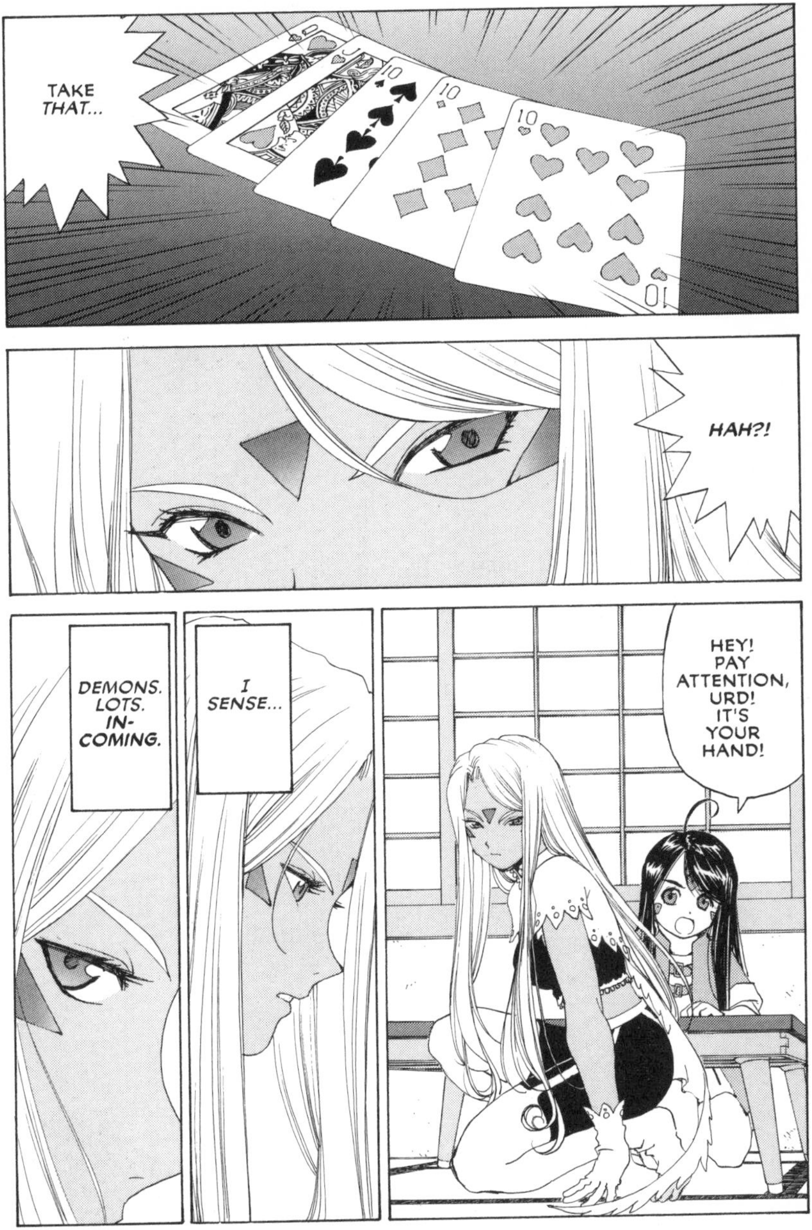
TAKE THAT...
HAH?!
HEY! PAY ATTENTION, URD! IT'S YOUR HAND!
I SENSE...
DEMONS. LOTS. IN-COMING.

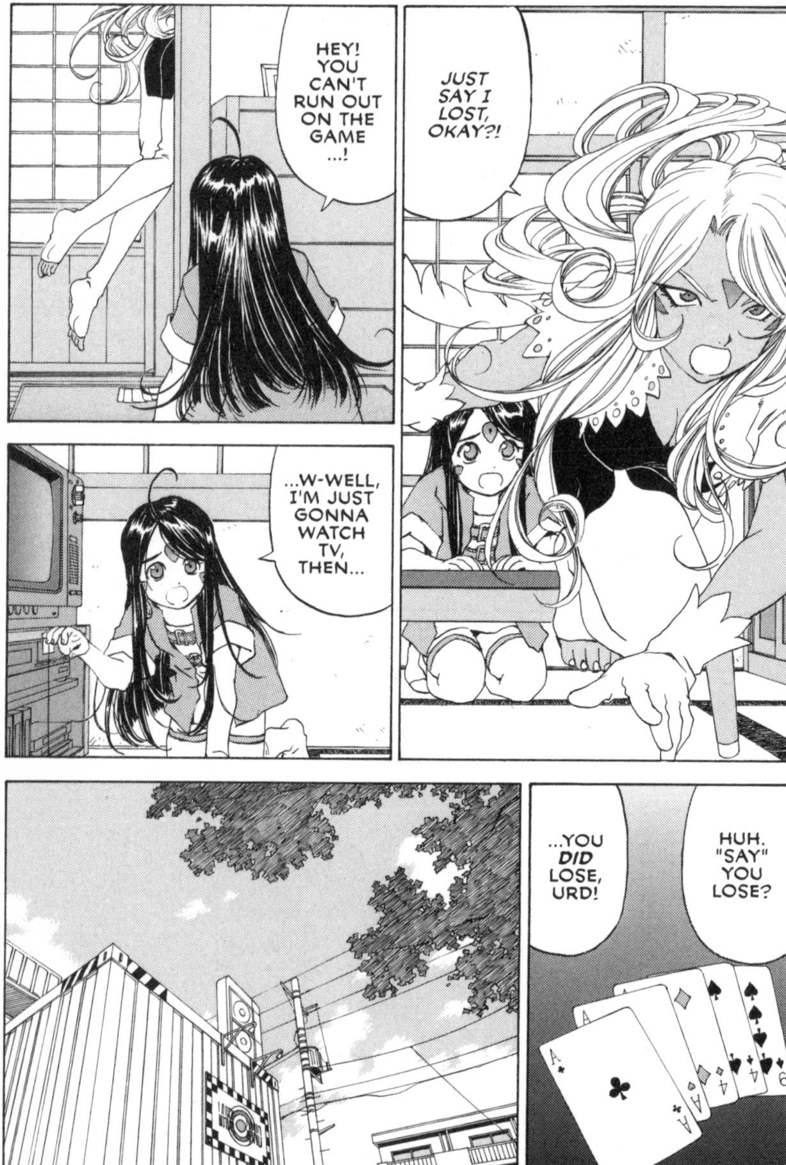
JUST SAY I LOST, OKAY?!
HEY! YOU CAN'T RUN OUT ON THE GAME ...!
...W-WELL, I'M JUST GONNA WATCH TV, THEN...
HUH. "SAY" YOU LOSE?
...YOU *DID* LOSE, URD!

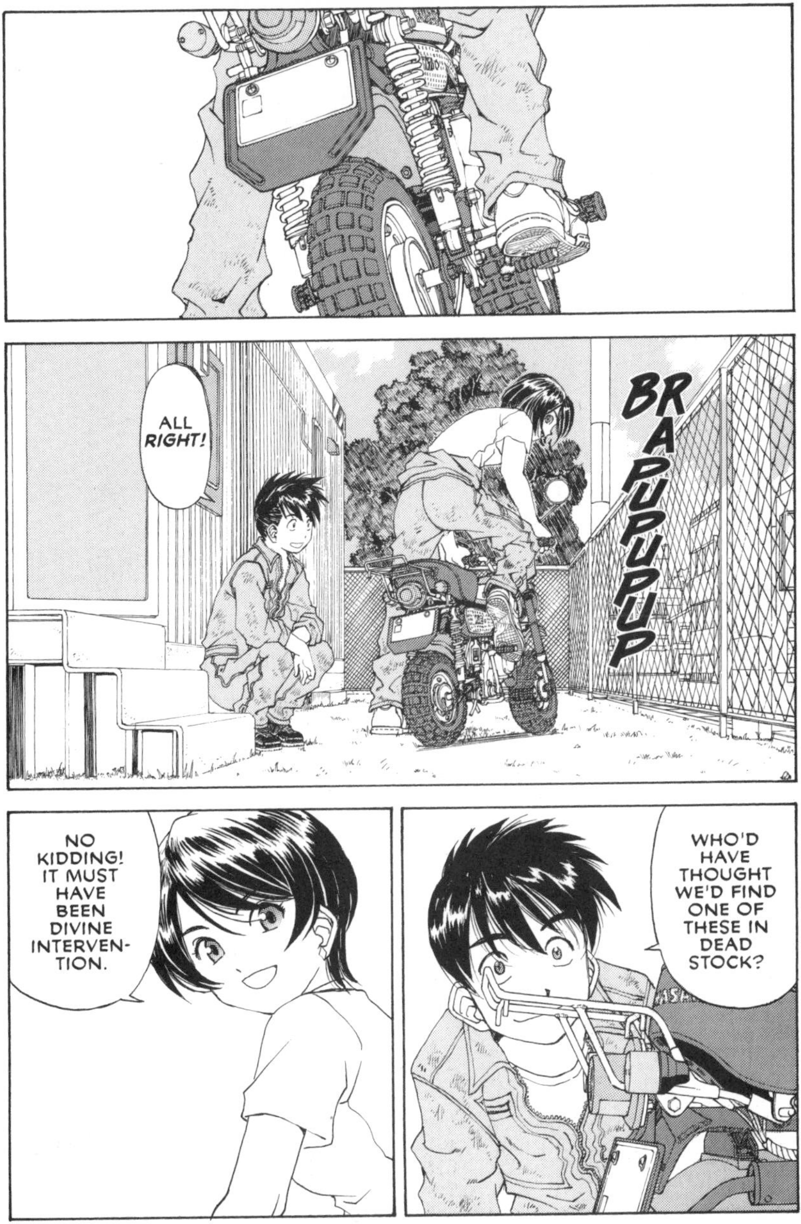
BRAPUPUPUPUP
ALL RIGHT!
WHO'D HAVE THOUGHT WE'D FIND ONE OF THESE IN DEAD STOCK?
NO KIDDING! IT MUST HAVE BEEN DIVINE INTERVENTION.

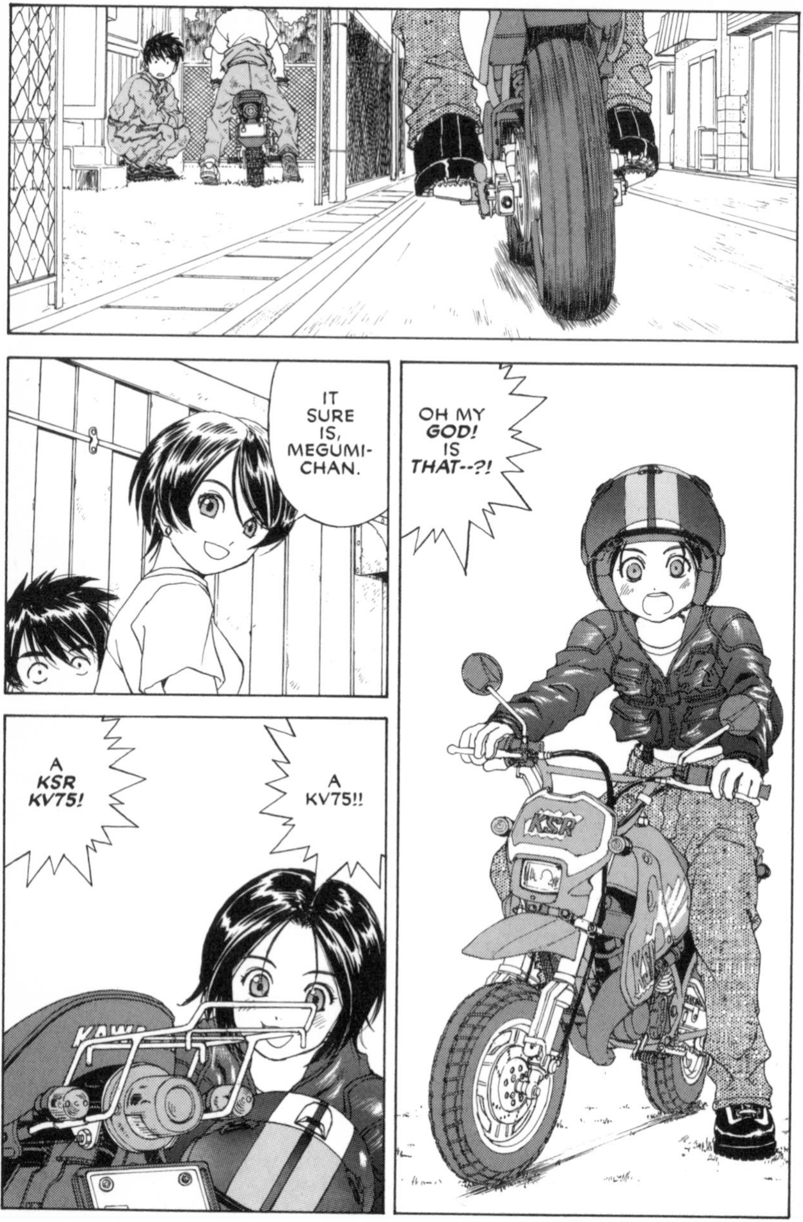
OH MY GOD! IS THAT--?!
IT SURE IS, MEGUMI-CHAN.
A KV75!!
A KSR KV75!

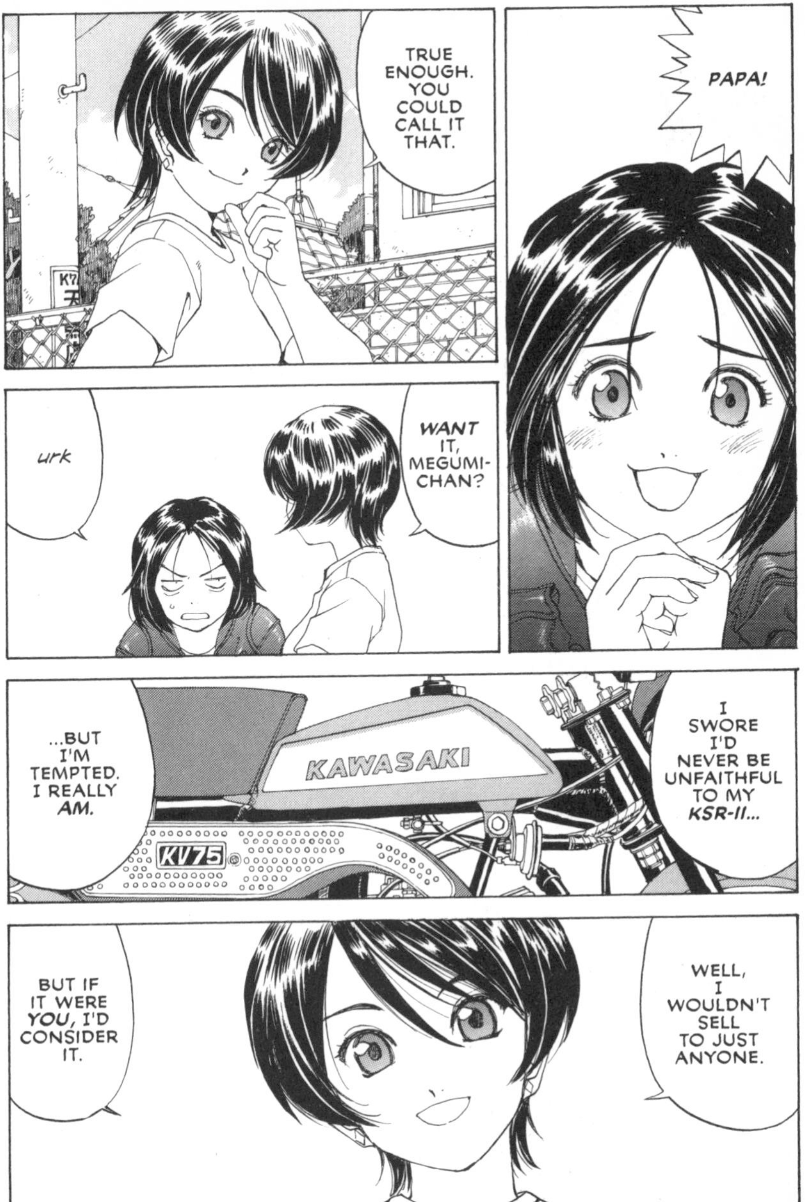
PAPA!
TRUE ENOUGH. YOU COULD CALL IT THAT.
WANT IT, MEGUMI-CHAN?
urk
I SWORE I'D NEVER BE UNFAITHFUL TO MY KSR-II...
...BUT I'M TEMPTED. I REALLY AM.
KAWASAKI
KV75
WELL, I WOULDN'T SELL TO JUST ANYONE.
BUT IF IT WERE YOU, I'D CONSIDER IT.

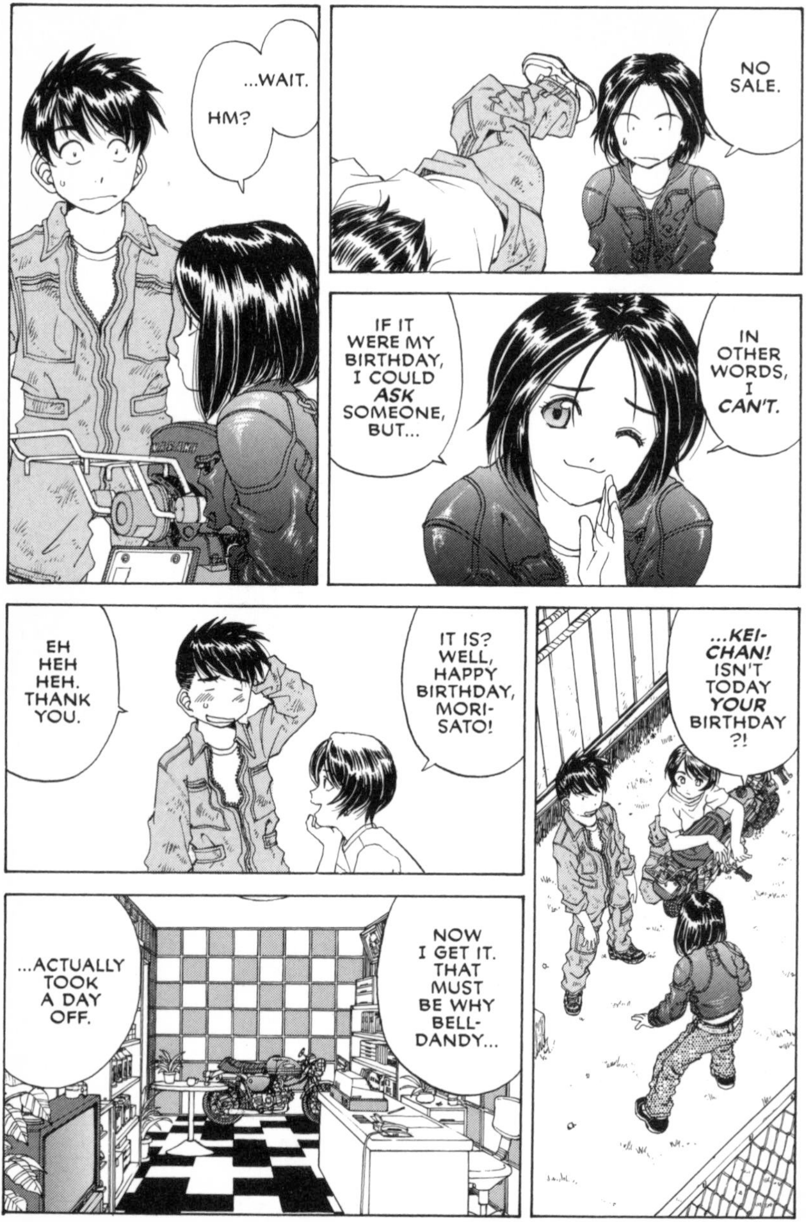
NO SALE.
IN OTHER WORDS, I *CAN'T.*
IF IT WERE MY BIRTHDAY, I COULD *ASK* SOMEONE, BUT...
...WAIT. HM?
...KEI-CHAN! ISN'T TODAY *YOUR* BIRTHDAY?!
IT IS? WELL, HAPPY BIRTHDAY, MORI-SATO!
EH HEH HEH. THANK YOU.
NOW I GET IT. THAT MUST BE WHY BELL-DANDY...
...ACTUALLY TOOK A DAY OFF.

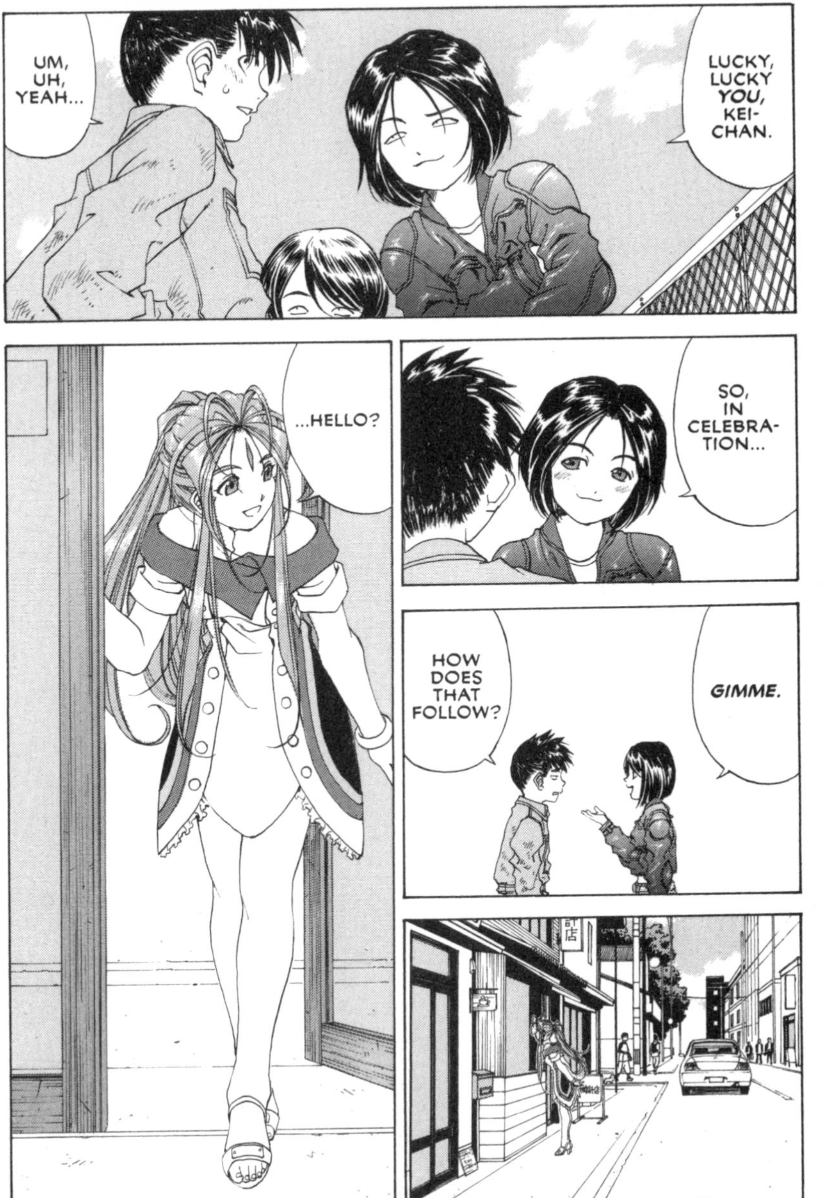
LUCKY, LUCKY *YOU*, KEI-CHAN.
UM, UH, YEAH...
SO, IN CELEBRATION...
GIMME.
HOW DOES THAT FOLLOW?
...HELLO?

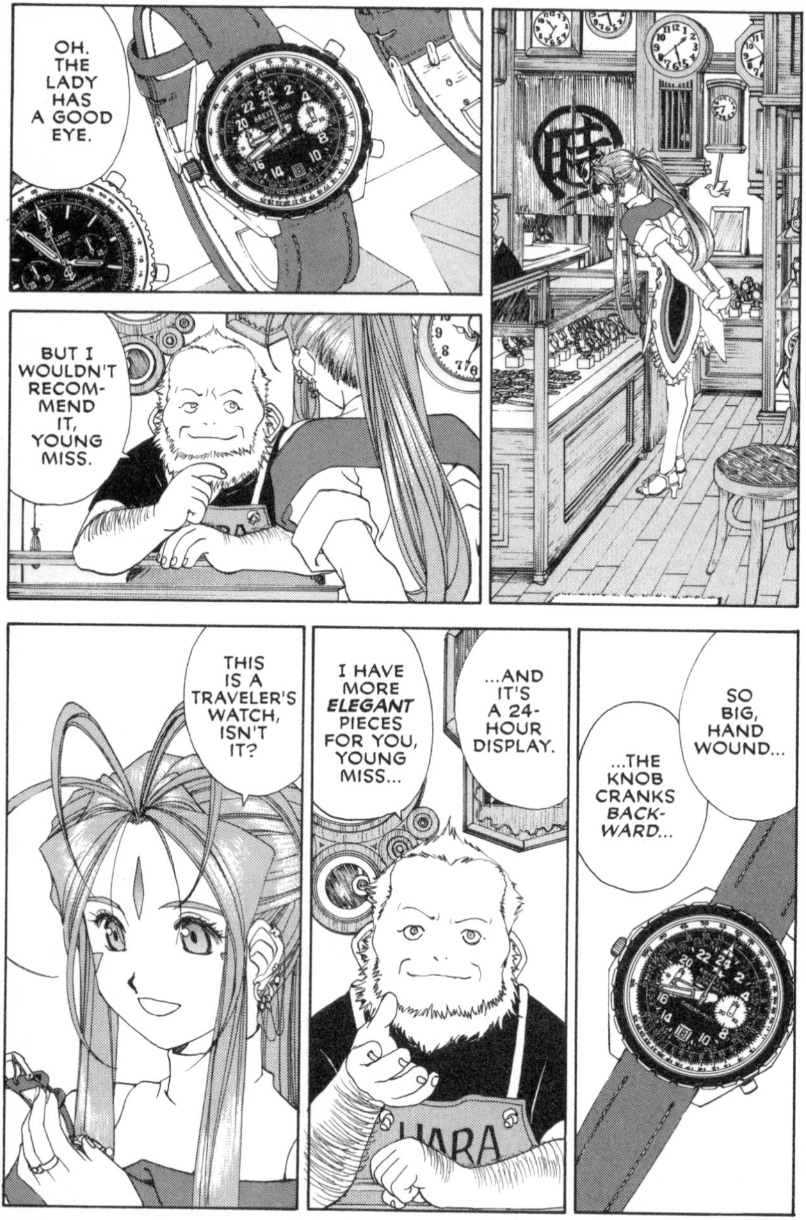
OH. THE LADY HAS A GOOD EYE.
BUT I WOULDN'T RECOMMEND IT, YOUNG MISS.
SO BIG, HAND WOUND...
...THE KNOB CRANKS *BACKWARD*...
...AND IT'S A 24-HOUR DISPLAY.
I HAVE MORE ***ELEGANT*** PIECES FOR YOU, YOUNG MISS...
HARA
THIS IS A TRAVELER'S WATCH, ISN'T IT?

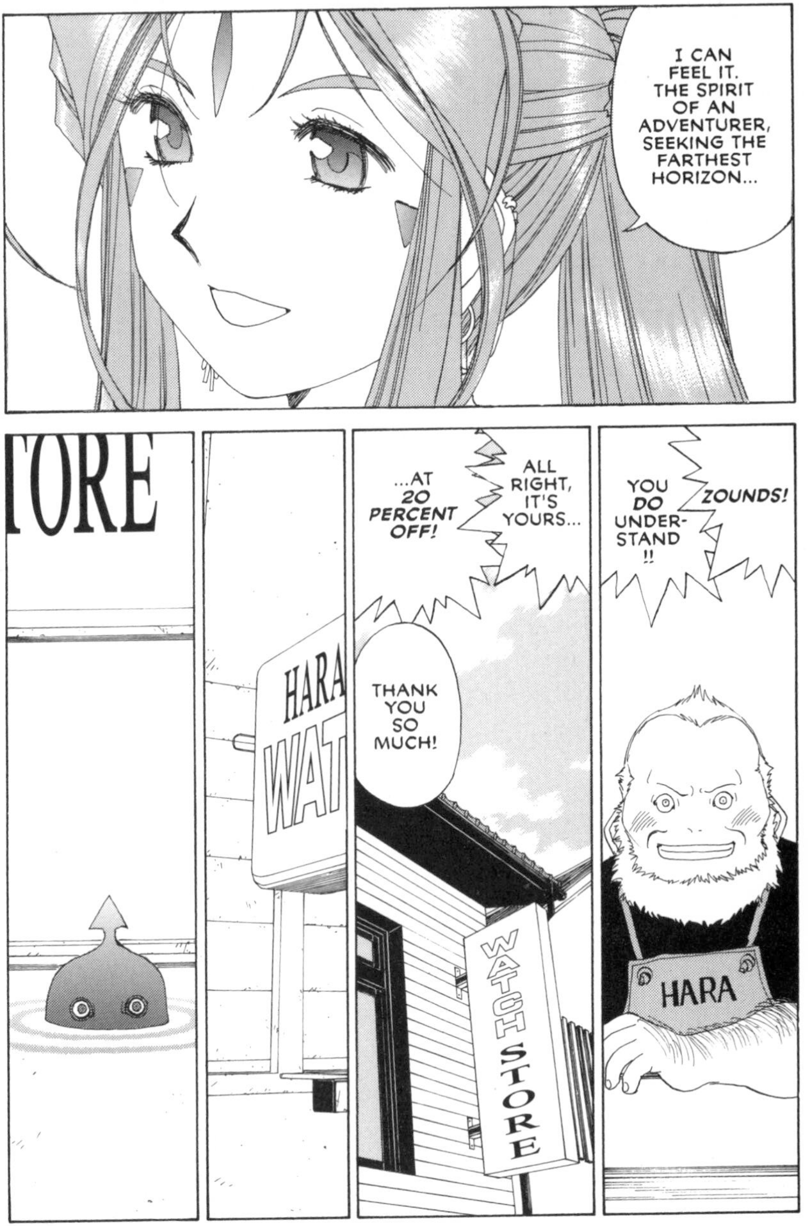
I CAN FEEL IT. THE SPIRIT OF AN ADVENTURER, SEEKING THE FARTHEST HORIZON...
ZOUNDS!
YOU DO UNDERSTAND!!
HARA
ALL RIGHT, IT'S YOURS...
...AT 20 PERCENT OFF!
THANK YOU SO MUCH!
WATCH STORE
HARA

CHAPTER 241

Birth!!

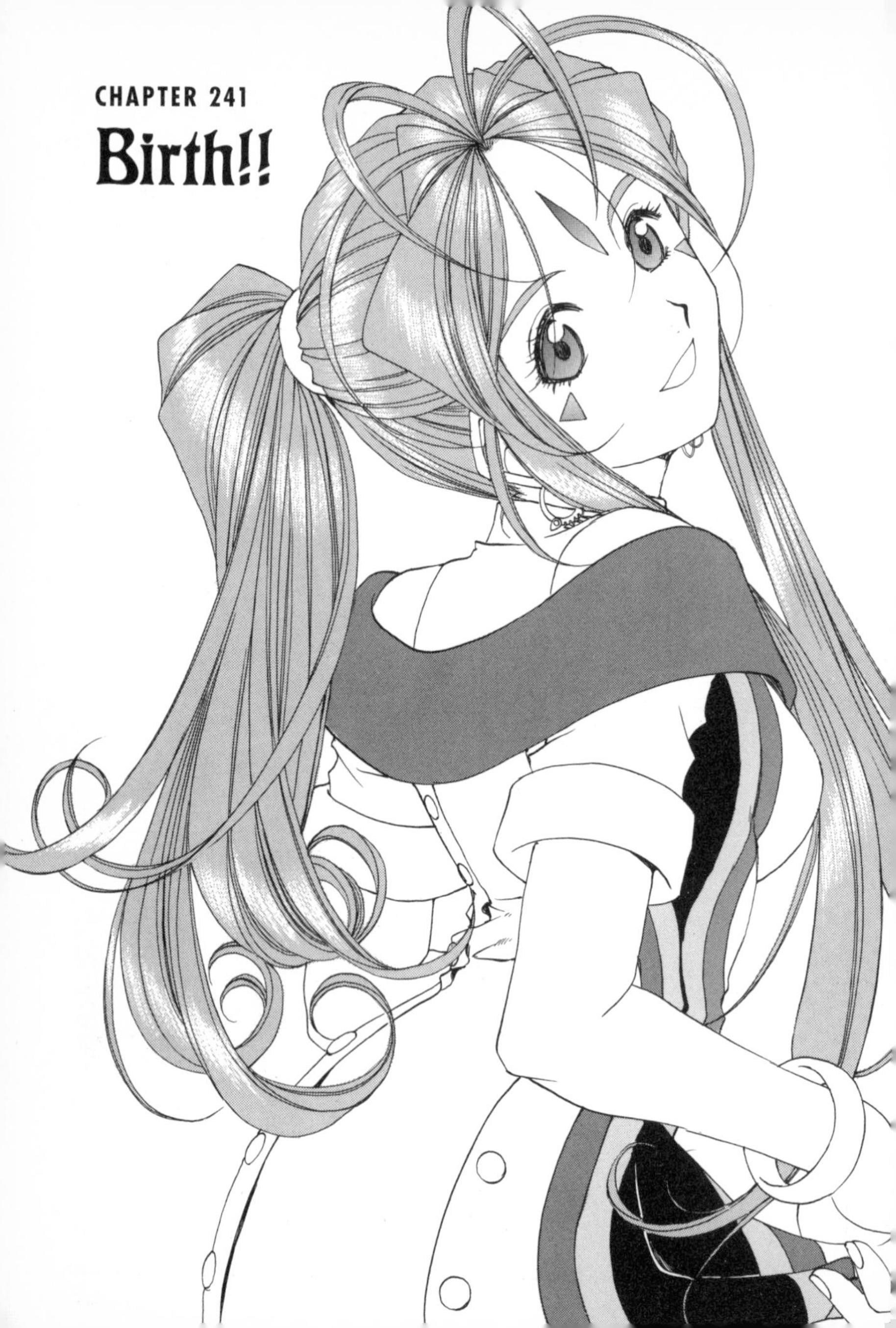

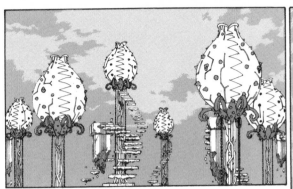

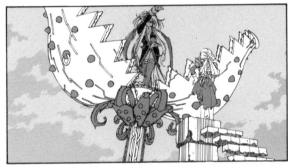

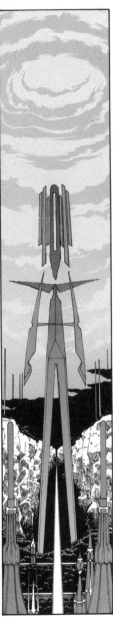

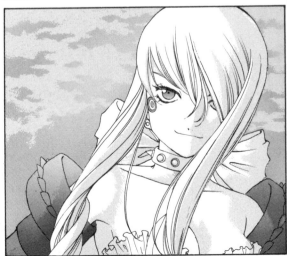

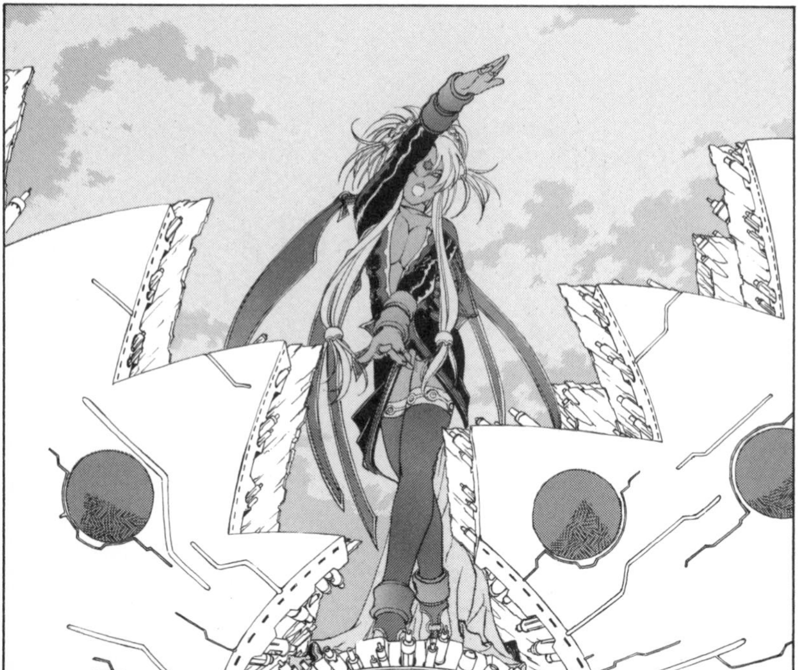

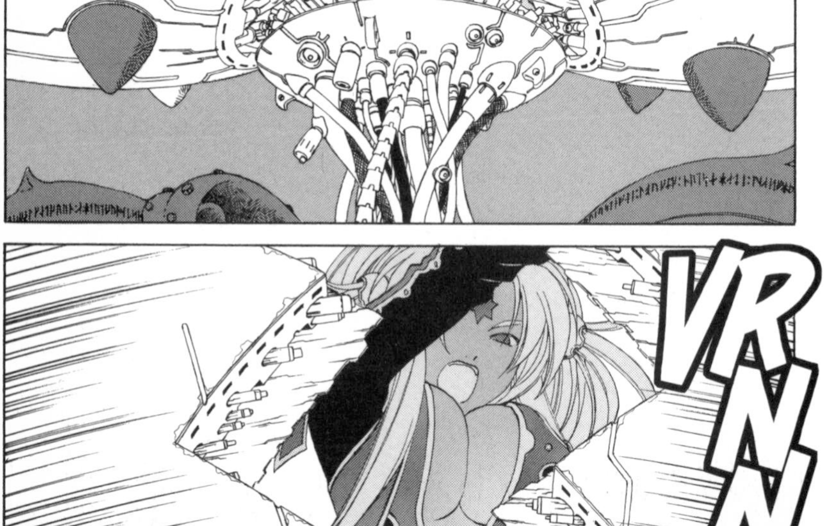
VRNN

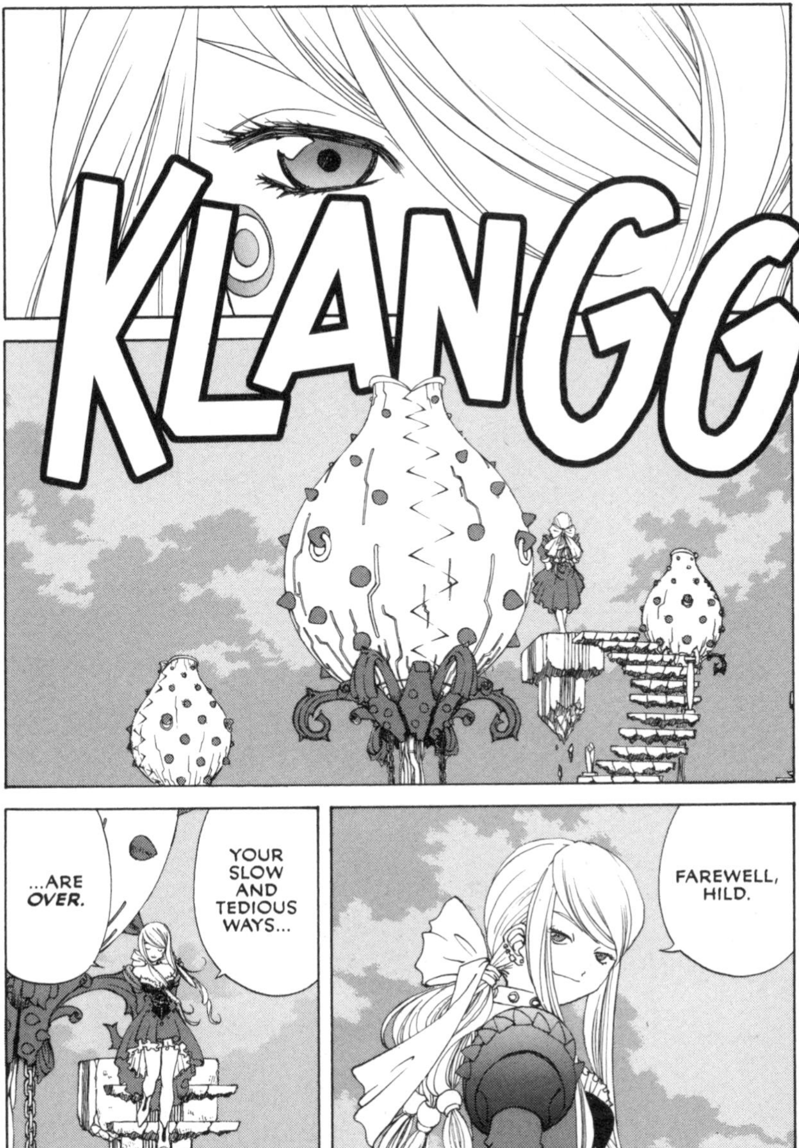
KLANGG
FAREWELL, HILD.
YOUR SLOW AND TEDIOUS WAYS...
...ARE *OVER.*

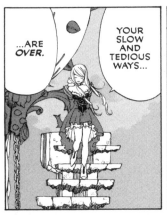

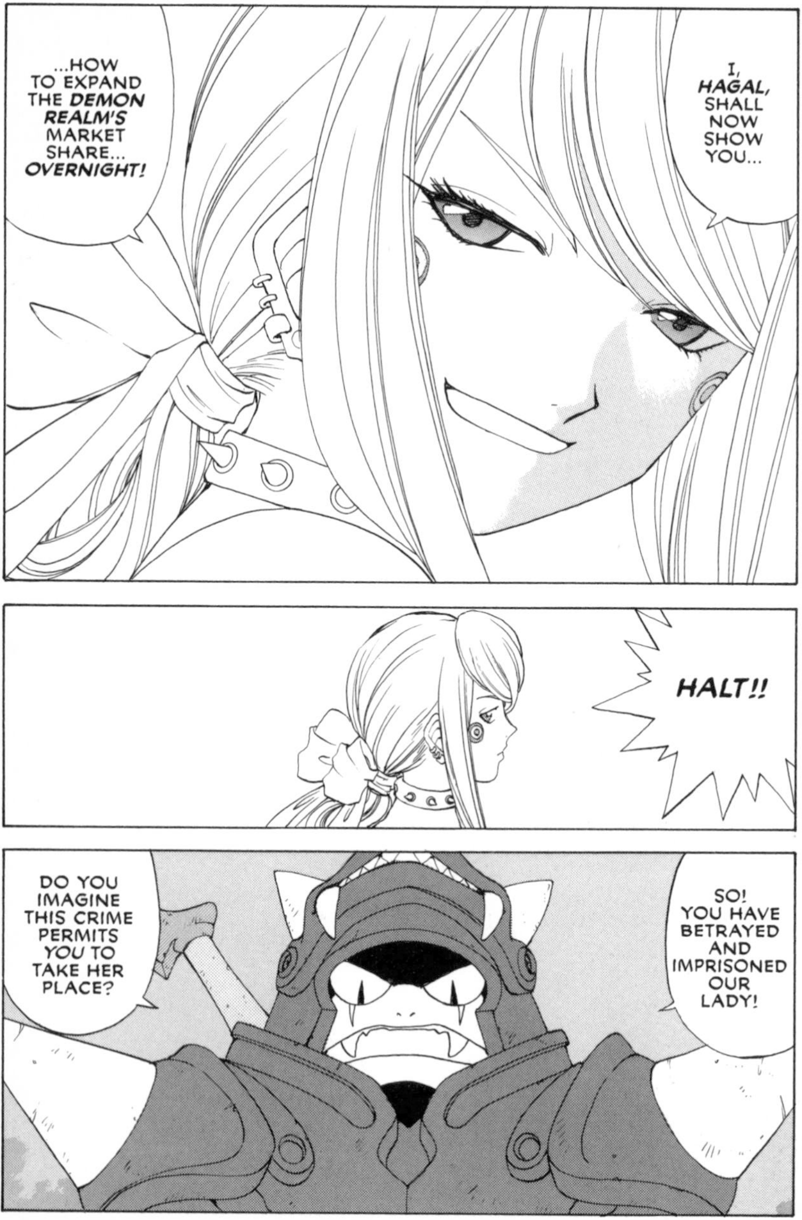
I, *HAGAL,* SHALL NOW SHOW YOU...
...HOW TO EXPAND THE *DEMON REALM'S* MARKET SHARE... *OVERNIGHT!*
HALT!!
SO! YOU HAVE BETRAYED AND IMPRISONED OUR LADY!
DO YOU IMAGINE THIS CRIME PERMITS *YOU* TO TAKE HER PLACE?

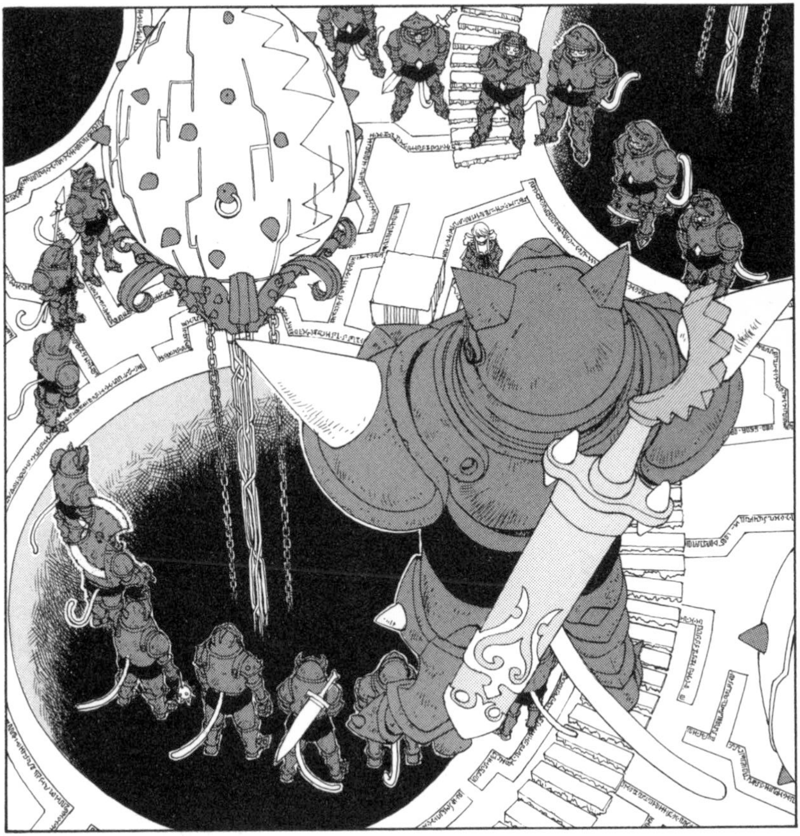

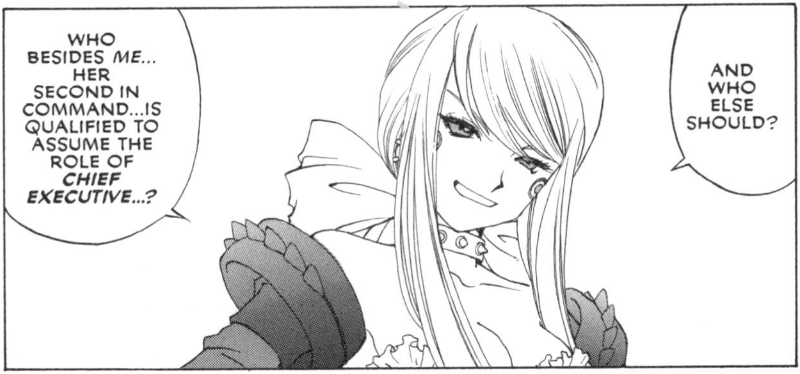
AND WHO ELSE SHOULD?
WHO BESIDES *ME*... HER SECOND IN COMMAND...IS QUALIFIED TO ASSUME THE ROLE OF ***CHIEF EXECUTIVE***...?

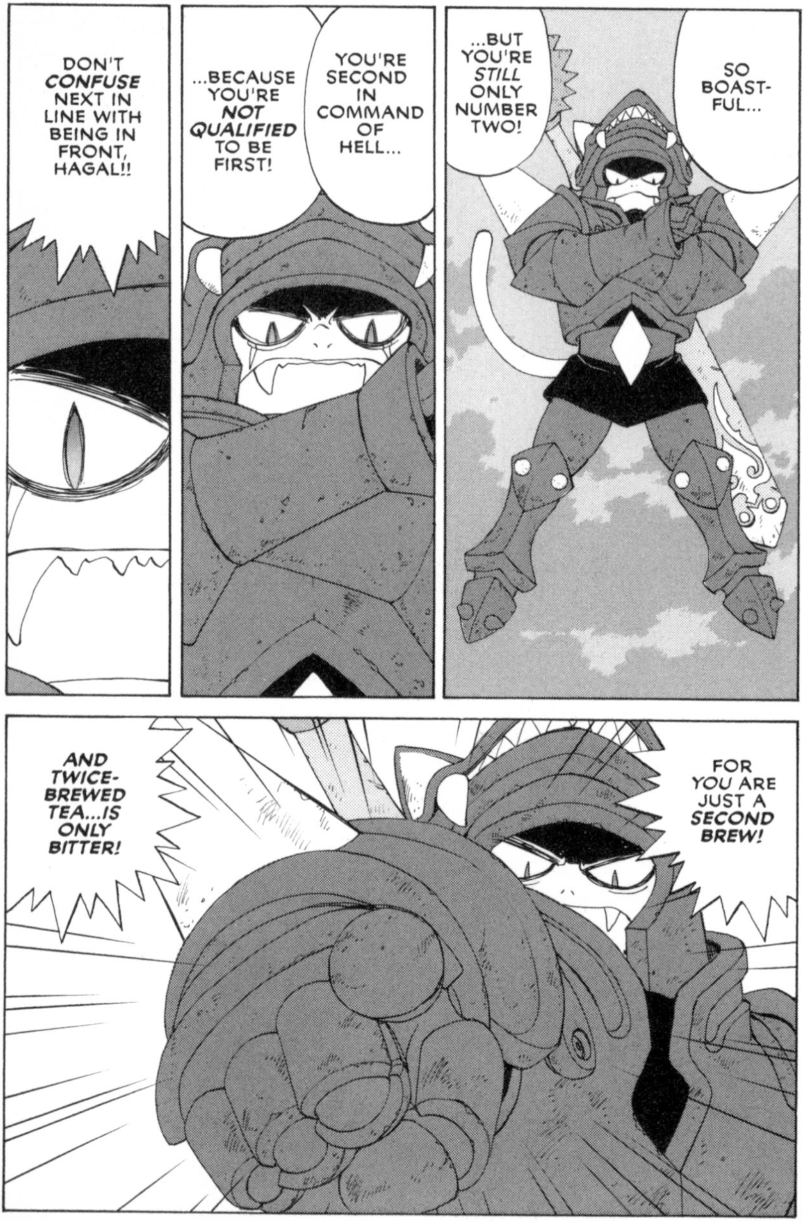
SO BOAST-FUL...
...BUT YOU'RE STILL ONLY NUMBER TWO!
YOU'RE SECOND IN COMMAND OF HELL...
...BECAUSE YOU'RE NOT QUALIFIED TO BE FIRST!
DON'T CONFUSE NEXT IN LINE WITH BEING IN FRONT, HAGAL!!
FOR YOU ARE JUST A SECOND BREW!
AND TWICE-BREWED TEA...IS ONLY BITTER!

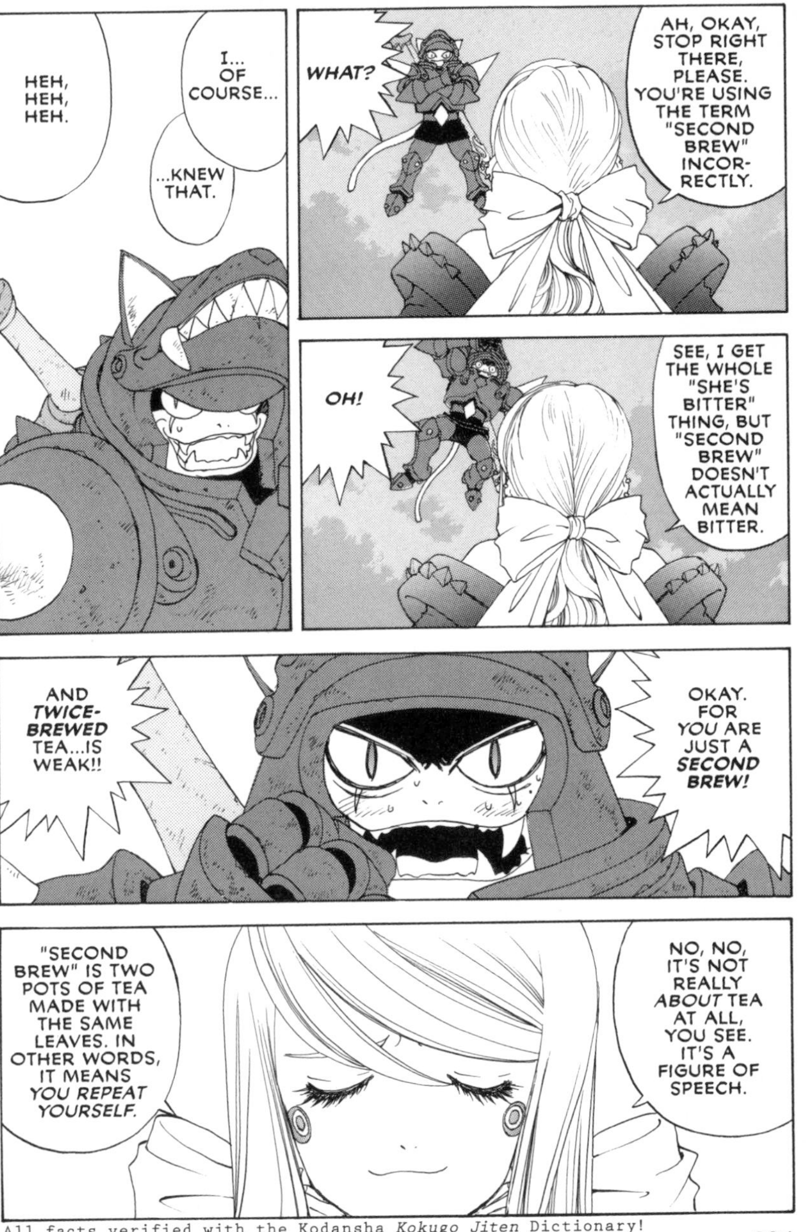
AH, OKAY, STOP RIGHT THERE, PLEASE. YOU'RE USING THE TERM "SECOND BREW" INCORRECTLY.
WHAT?
SEE, I GET THE WHOLE "SHE'S BITTER" THING, BUT "SECOND BREW" DOESN'T ACTUALLY MEAN BITTER.
OH!
I... OF COURSE...
...KNEW THAT.
HEH, HEH, HEH.
OKAY. FOR *YOU* ARE JUST A ***SECOND BREW!***
AND ***TWICE-BREWED*** TEA...IS WEAK!!
NO, NO, IT'S NOT REALLY *ABOUT* TEA AT ALL, YOU SEE. IT'S A FIGURE OF SPEECH.
"SECOND BREW" IS TWO POTS OF TEA MADE WITH THE SAME LEAVES. IN OTHER WORDS, IT MEANS *YOU REPEAT YOURSELF.*

All facts verified with the Kodansha *Kokugo Jiten* Dictionary!

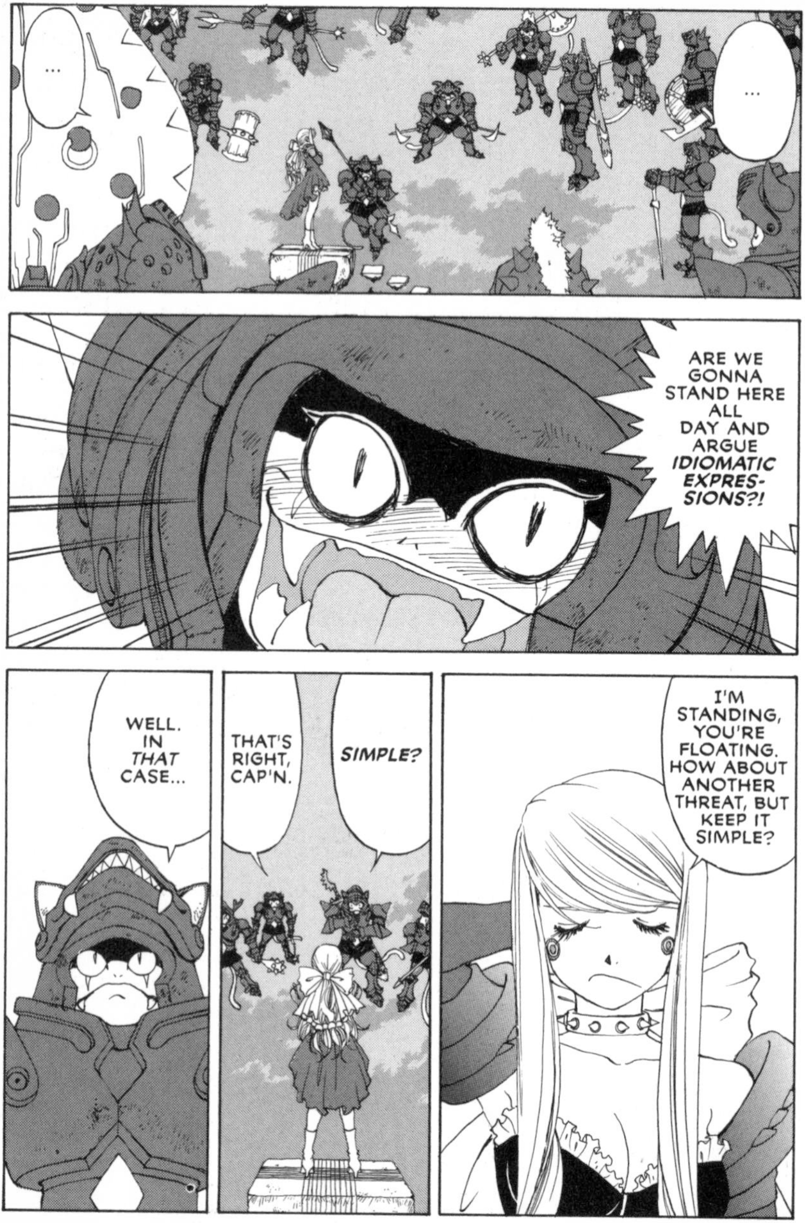
...
...
ARE WE GONNA STAND HERE ALL DAY AND ARGUE *IDIOMATIC EXPRESSIONS?!*
I'M STANDING, YOU'RE FLOATING. HOW ABOUT ANOTHER THREAT, BUT KEEP IT SIMPLE?
SIMPLE?
THAT'S RIGHT, CAP'N.
WELL. IN *THAT* CASE...

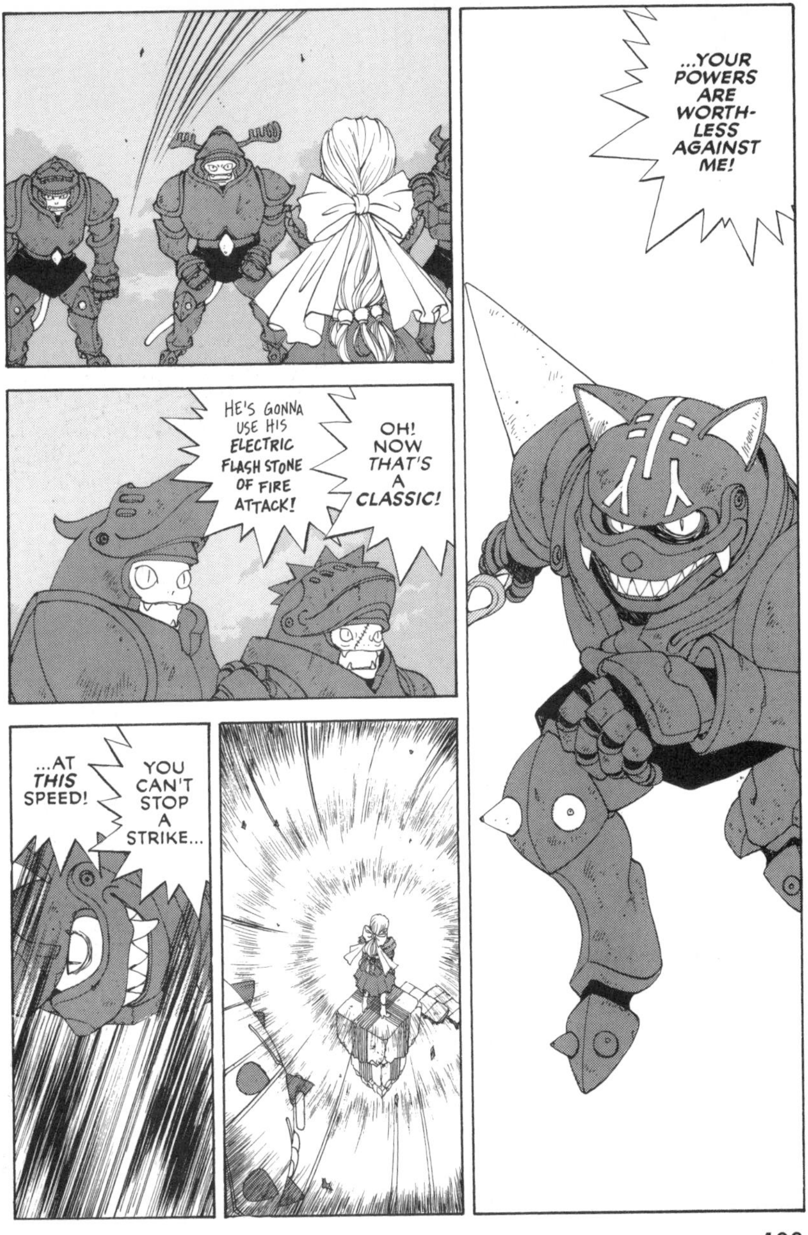
...YOUR POWERS ARE WORTH-LESS AGAINST ME!
HE'S GONNA USE HIS ELECTRIC FLASH STONE OF FIRE ATTACK!
OH! NOW THAT'S A CLASSIC!
YOU CAN'T STOP A STRIKE...
...AT THIS SPEED!

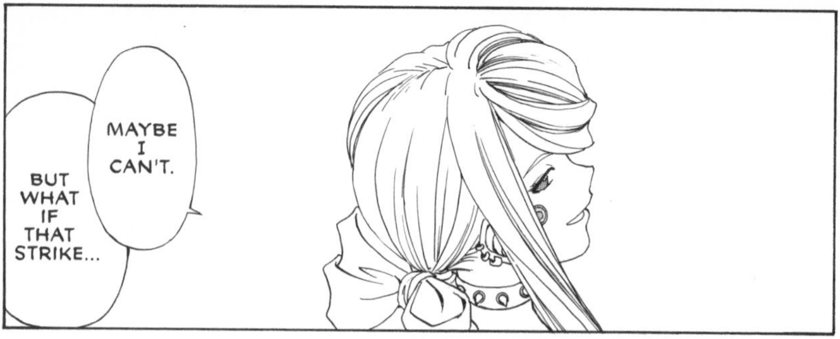
MAYBE I CAN'T.
BUT WHAT IF THAT STRIKE...

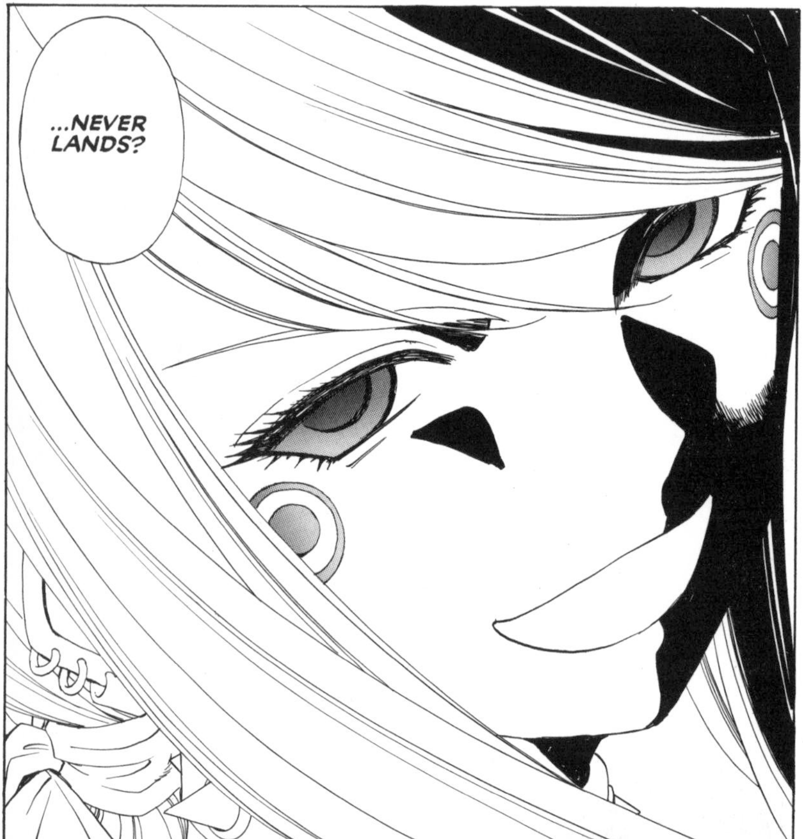
...NEVER LANDS?

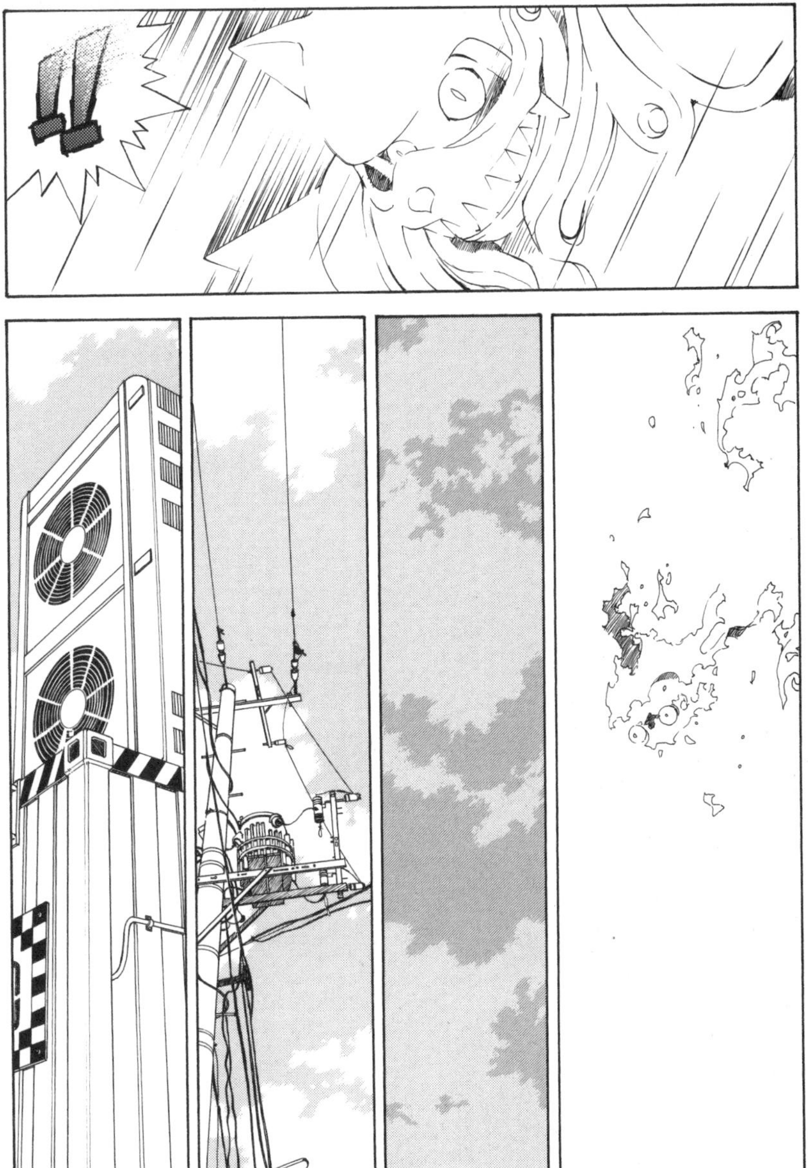

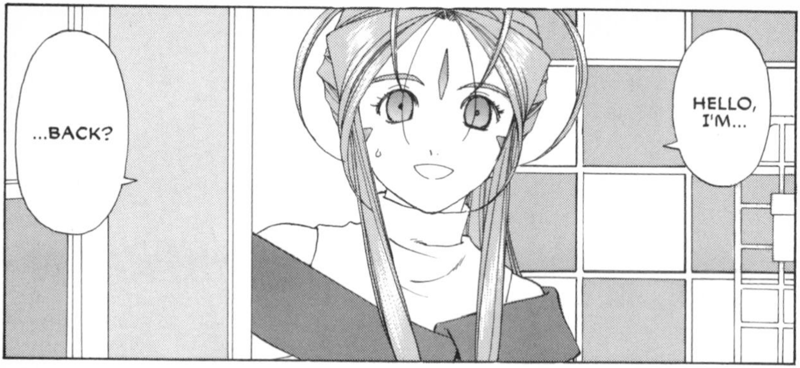
HELLO, I'M...
...BACK?

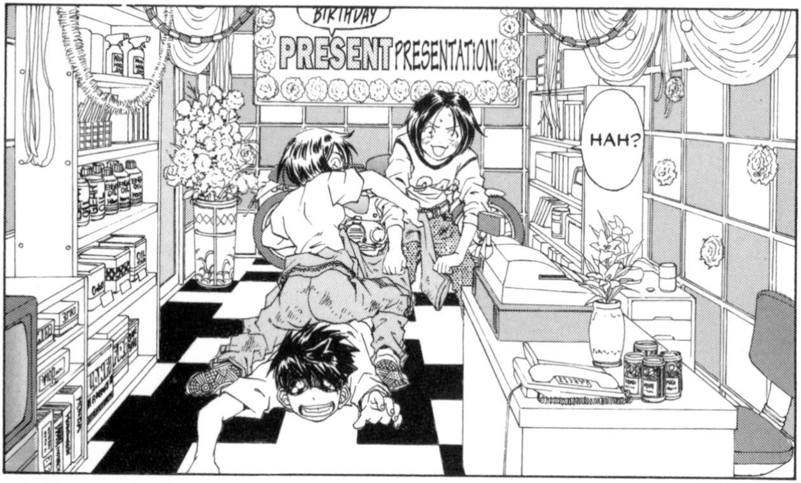
BIRTHDAY
PRESENT PRESENTATION!
HAH?

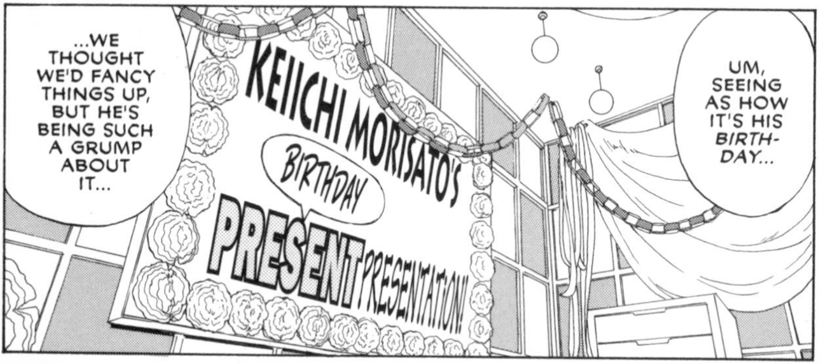
UM, SEEING AS HOW IT'S HIS *BIRTH-DAY*...
KEIICHI MORISATO'S
BIRTHDAY
PRESENT PRESENTATION!
...WE THOUGHT WE'D FANCY THINGS UP, BUT HE'S BEING SUCH A GRUMP ABOUT IT...

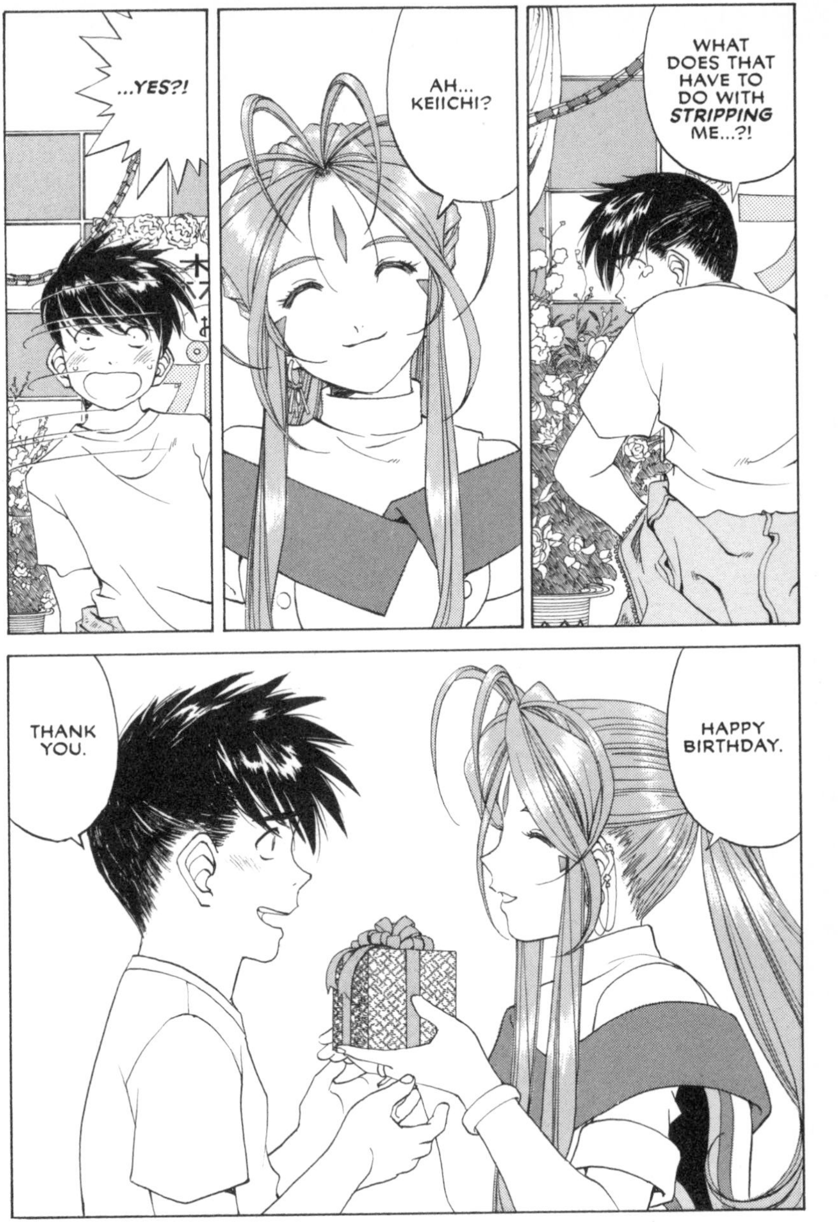
WHAT DOES THAT HAVE TO DO WITH *STRIPPING* ME...?!
AH... KEIICHI?
...YES?!
HAPPY BIRTHDAY.
THANK YOU.

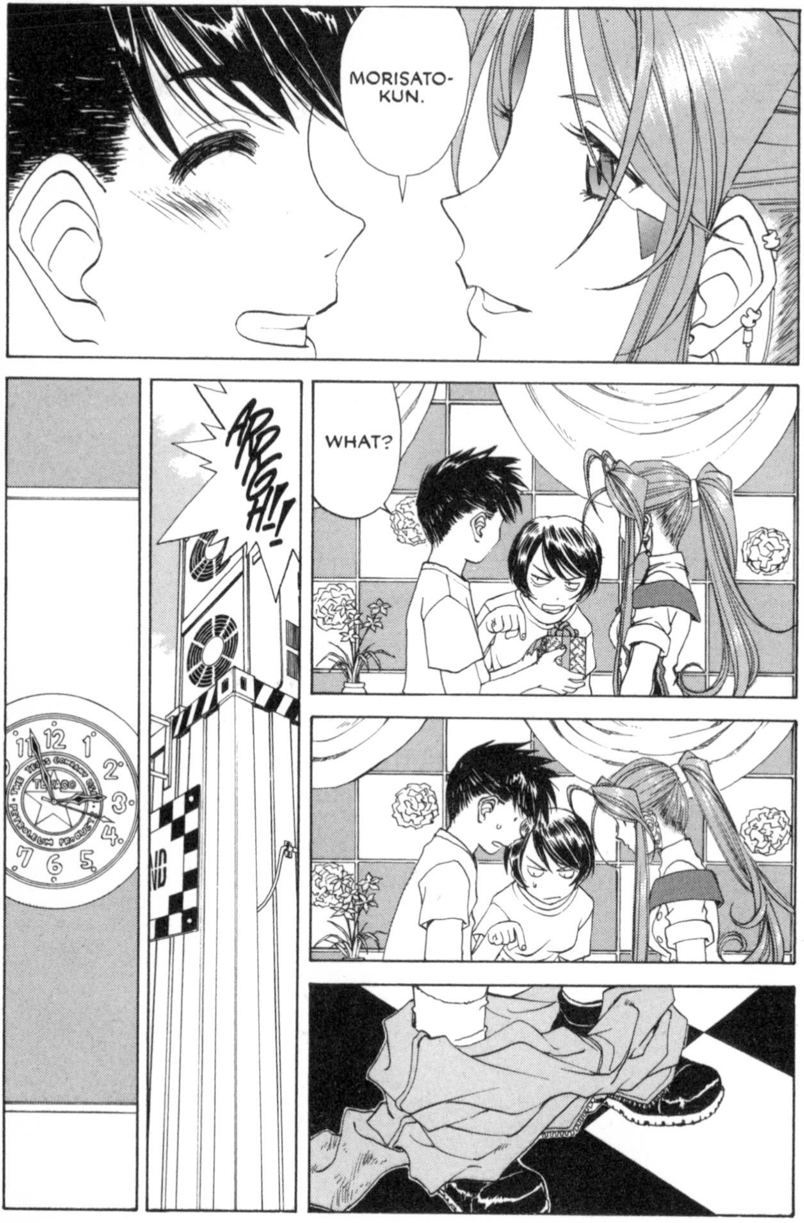
MORISATO-KUN.
WHAT?
ARRGH!!

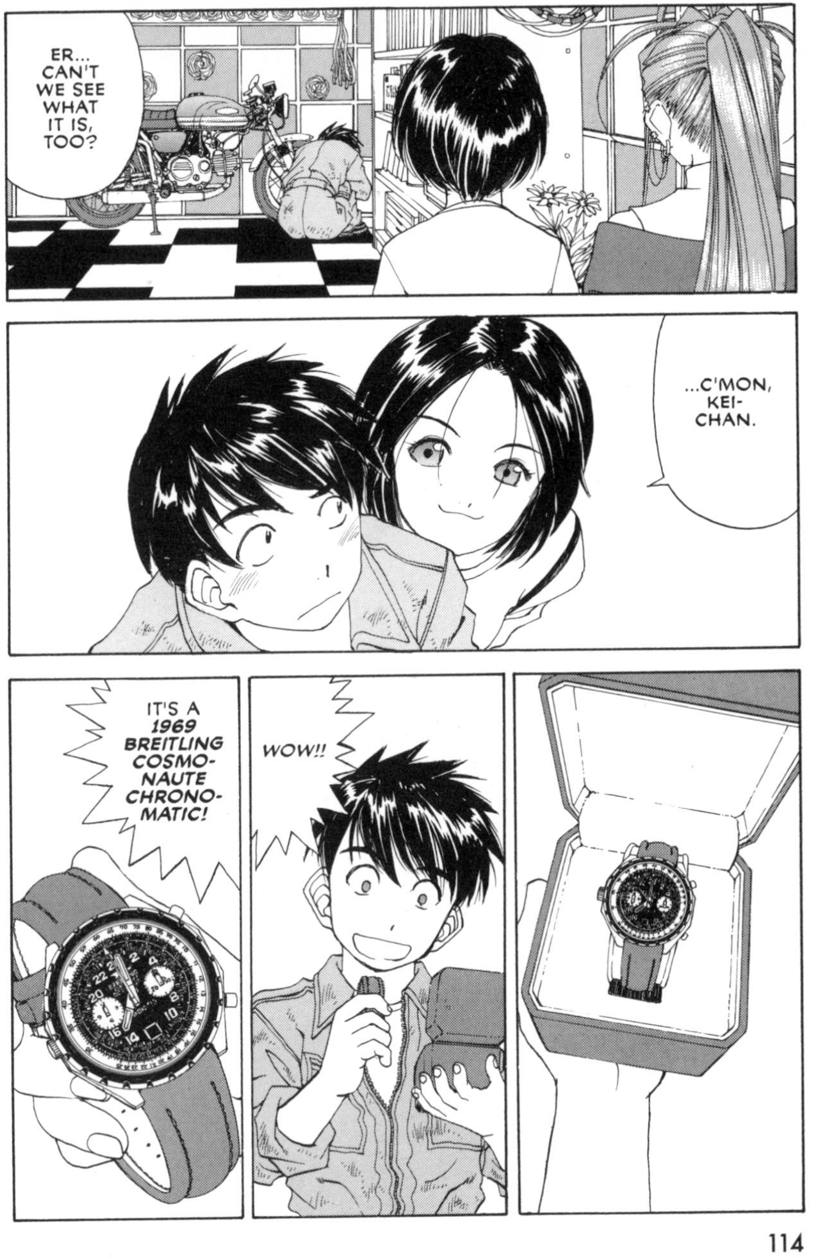
ER... CAN'T WE SEE WHAT IT IS, TOO?
...C'MON, KEI-CHAN.
WOW!!
IT'S A *1969* BREITLING COSMONAUTE CHRONOMATIC!

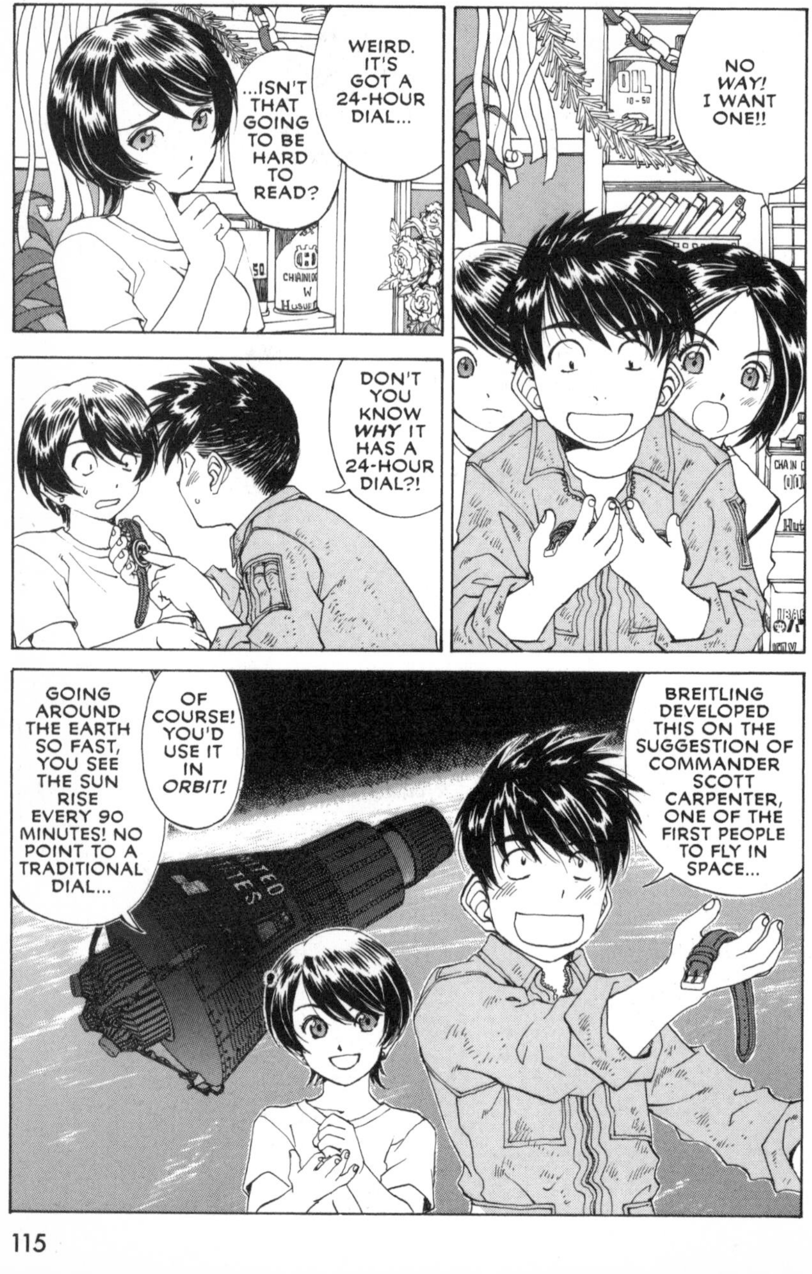
NO *WAY!* I WANT ONE!!
WEIRD. IT'S GOT A 24-HOUR DIAL...
...ISN'T THAT GOING TO BE HARD TO READ?
DON'T YOU KNOW *WHY* IT HAS A 24-HOUR DIAL?!
BREITLING DEVELOPED THIS ON THE SUGGESTION OF COMMANDER SCOTT CARPENTER, ONE OF THE FIRST PEOPLE TO FLY IN SPACE...
OF COURSE! YOU'D USE IT IN *ORBIT!*
GOING AROUND THE EARTH SO FAST, YOU SEE THE SUN RISE EVERY 90 MINUTES! NO POINT TO A TRADITIONAL DIAL...

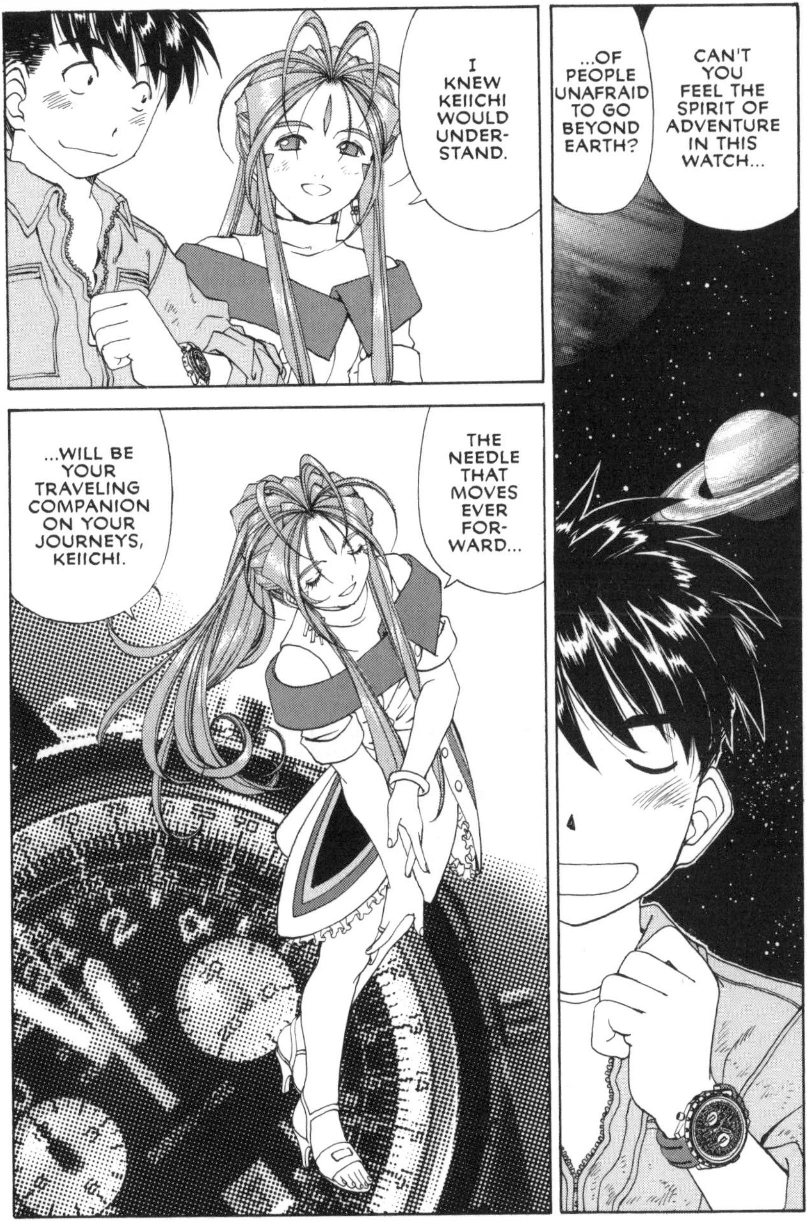
CAN'T YOU FEEL THE SPIRIT OF ADVENTURE IN THIS WATCH...
...OF PEOPLE UNAFRAID TO GO BEYOND EARTH?
I KNEW KEIICHI WOULD UNDER-STAND.
THE NEEDLE THAT MOVES EVER FOR-WARD...
...WILL BE YOUR TRAVELING COMPANION ON YOUR JOURNEYS, KEIICHI.

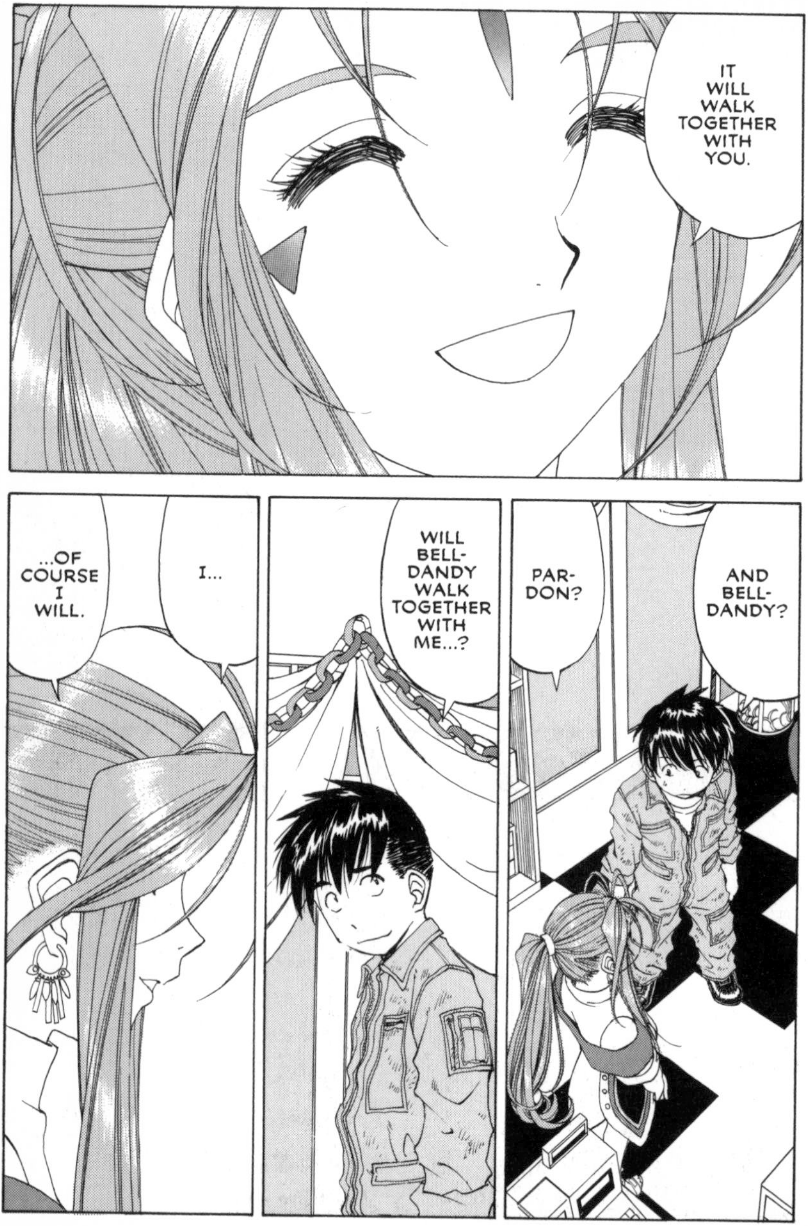
IT WILL WALK TOGETHER WITH YOU.
AND BELL-DANDY?
PAR-DON?
WILL BELL-DANDY WALK TOGETHER WITH ME...?
I...
...OF COURSE I WILL.

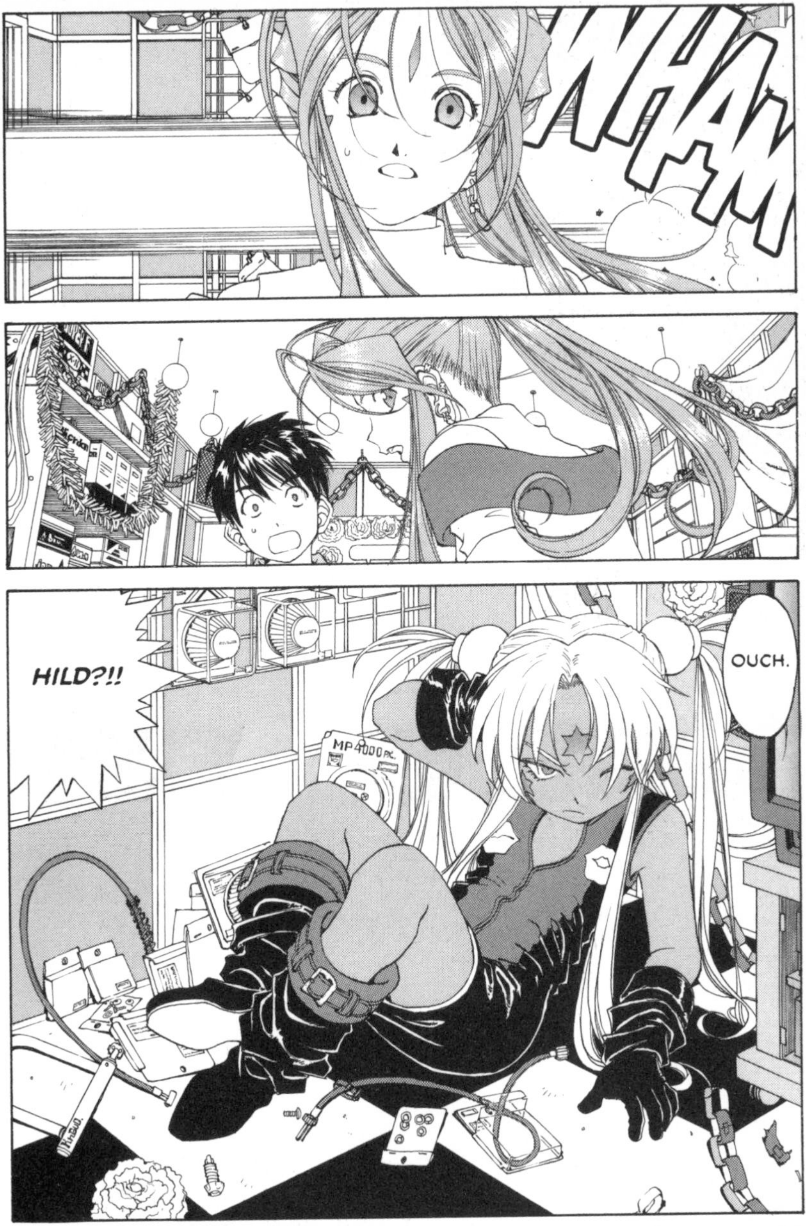
WHAM
OUCH.
HILD?!!

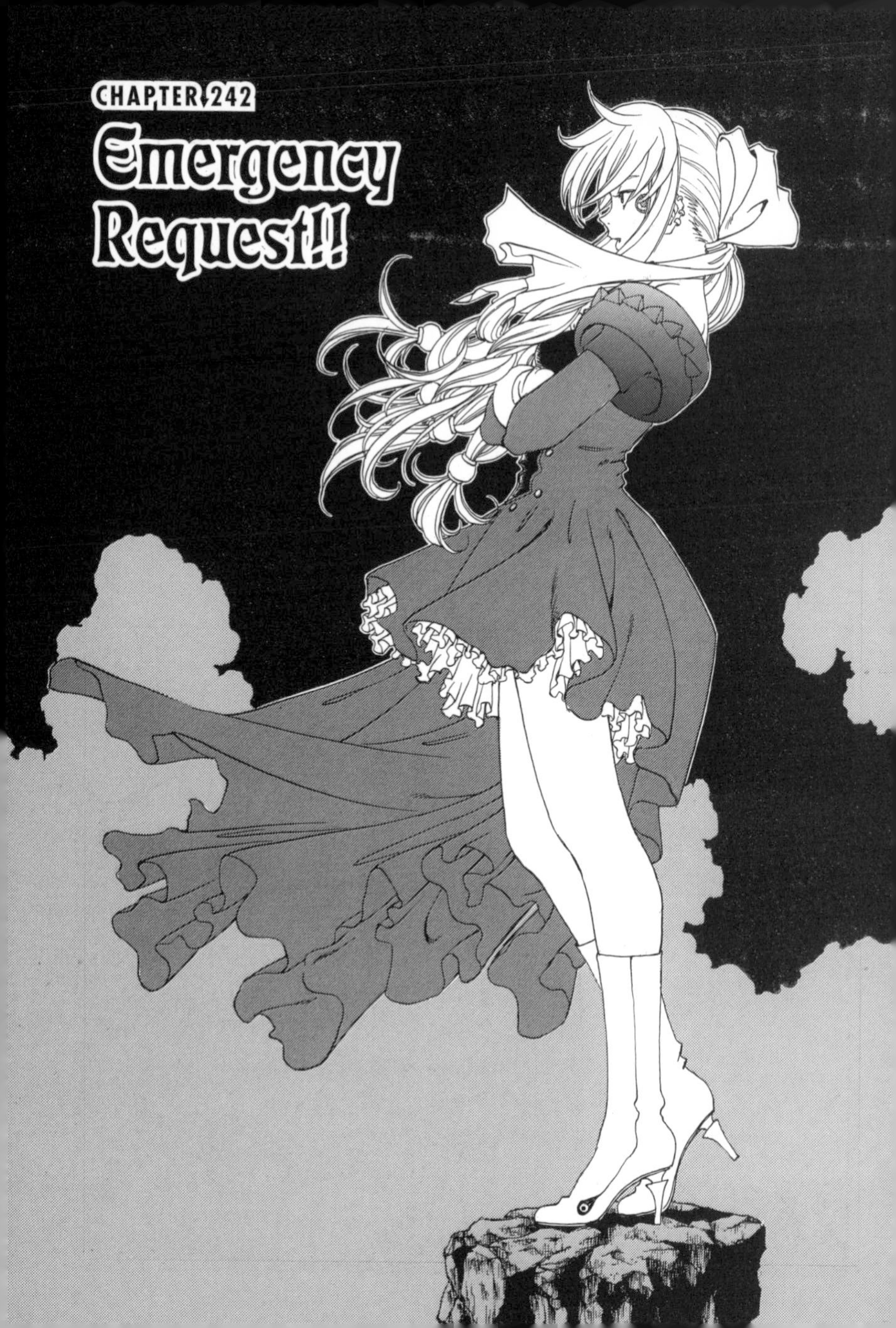
CHAPTER 242
Emergency Request!!

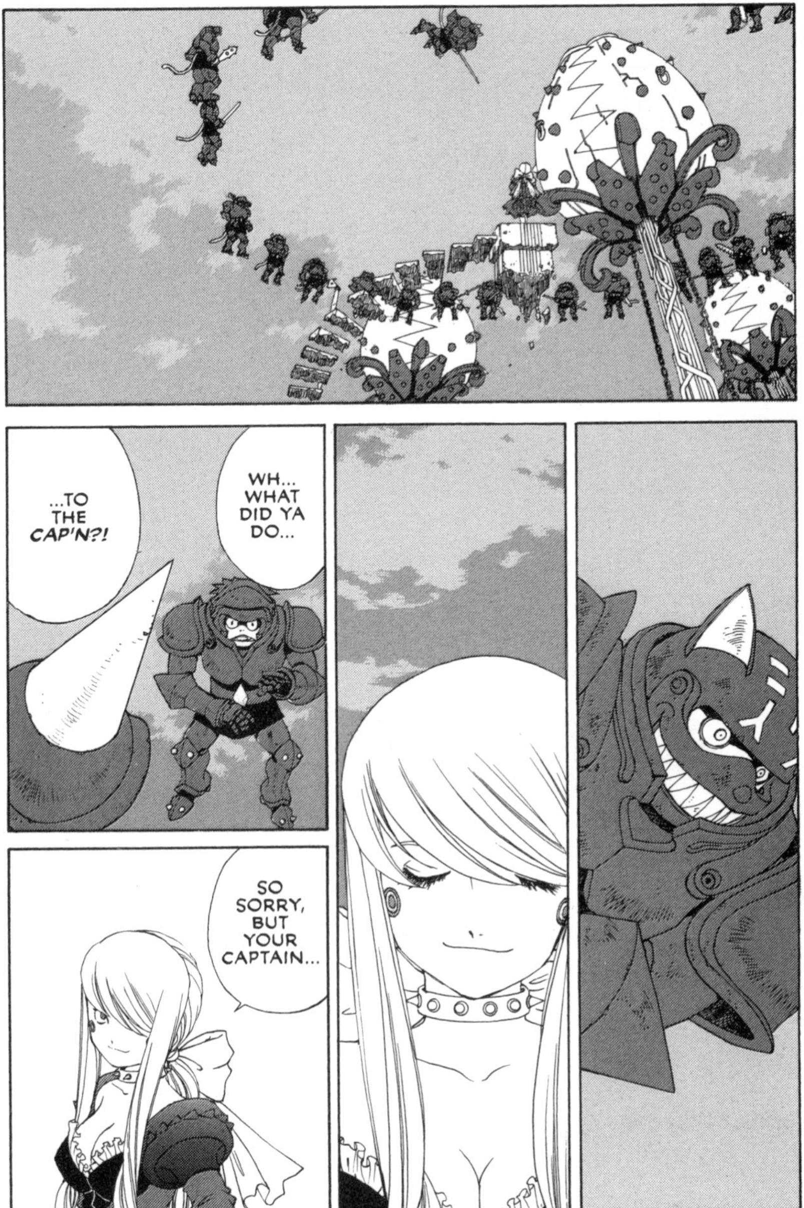
WH... WHAT DID YA DO...
...TO THE CAP'N?!
SO SORRY, BUT YOUR CAPTAIN...

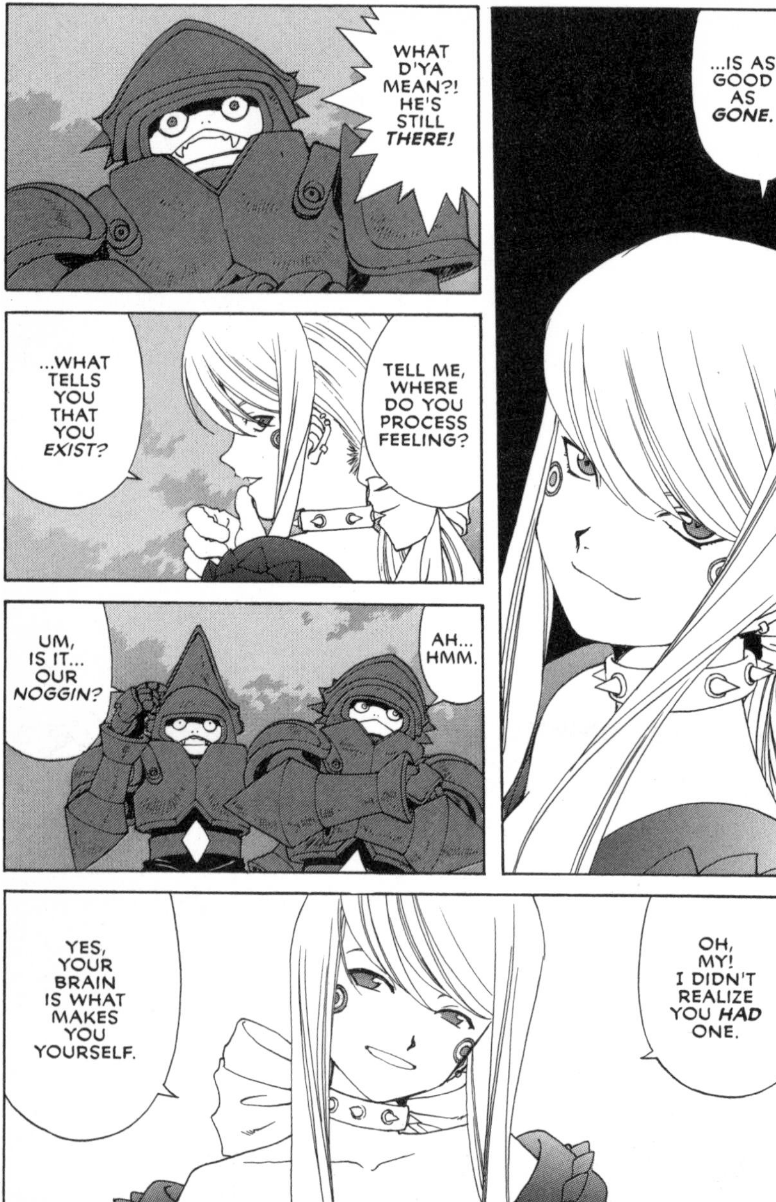
WHAT D'YA MEAN?! HE'S STILL *THERE!*
...WHAT TELLS YOU THAT YOU *EXIST?*
TELL ME, WHERE DO YOU PROCESS FEELING?
UM, IS IT... OUR *NOGGIN?*
AH... HMM.
...IS AS GOOD AS *GONE.*
YES, YOUR BRAIN IS WHAT MAKES YOU YOURSELF.
OH, MY! I DIDN'T REALIZE YOU *HAD* ONE.

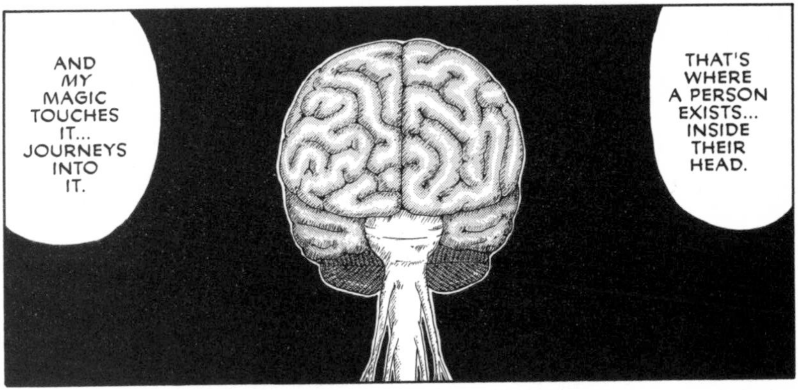
THAT'S WHERE A PERSON EXISTS... INSIDE THEIR HEAD.
AND *MY* MAGIC TOUCHES IT... JOURNEYS INTO IT.

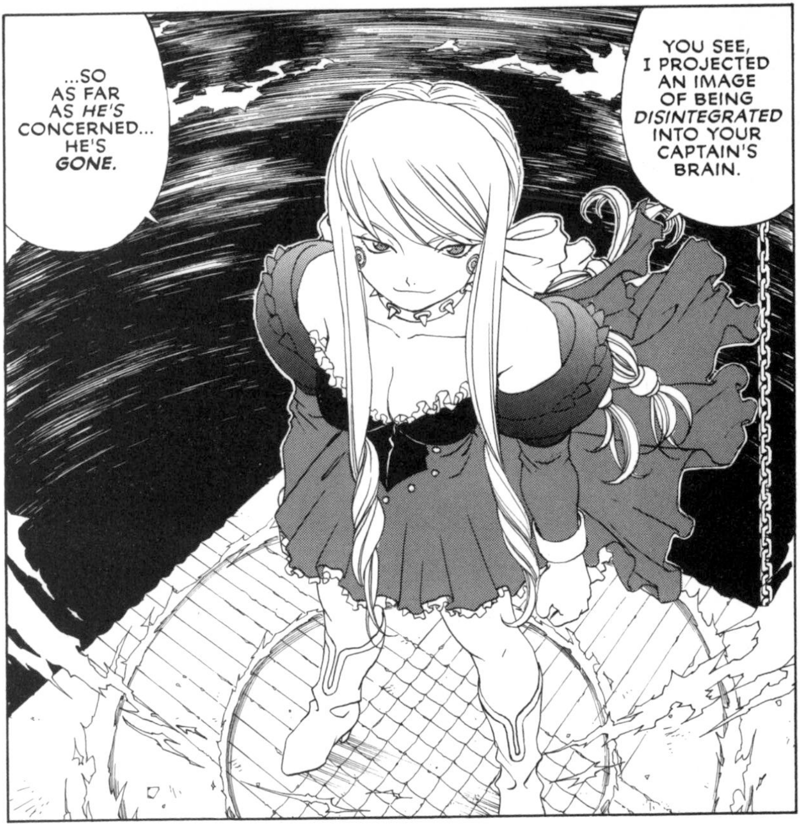
YOU SEE, I PROJECTED AN IMAGE OF BEING *DISINTEGRATED* INTO YOUR CAPTAIN'S BRAIN.
...SO AS FAR AS *HE'S* CONCERNED... HE'S ***GONE.***

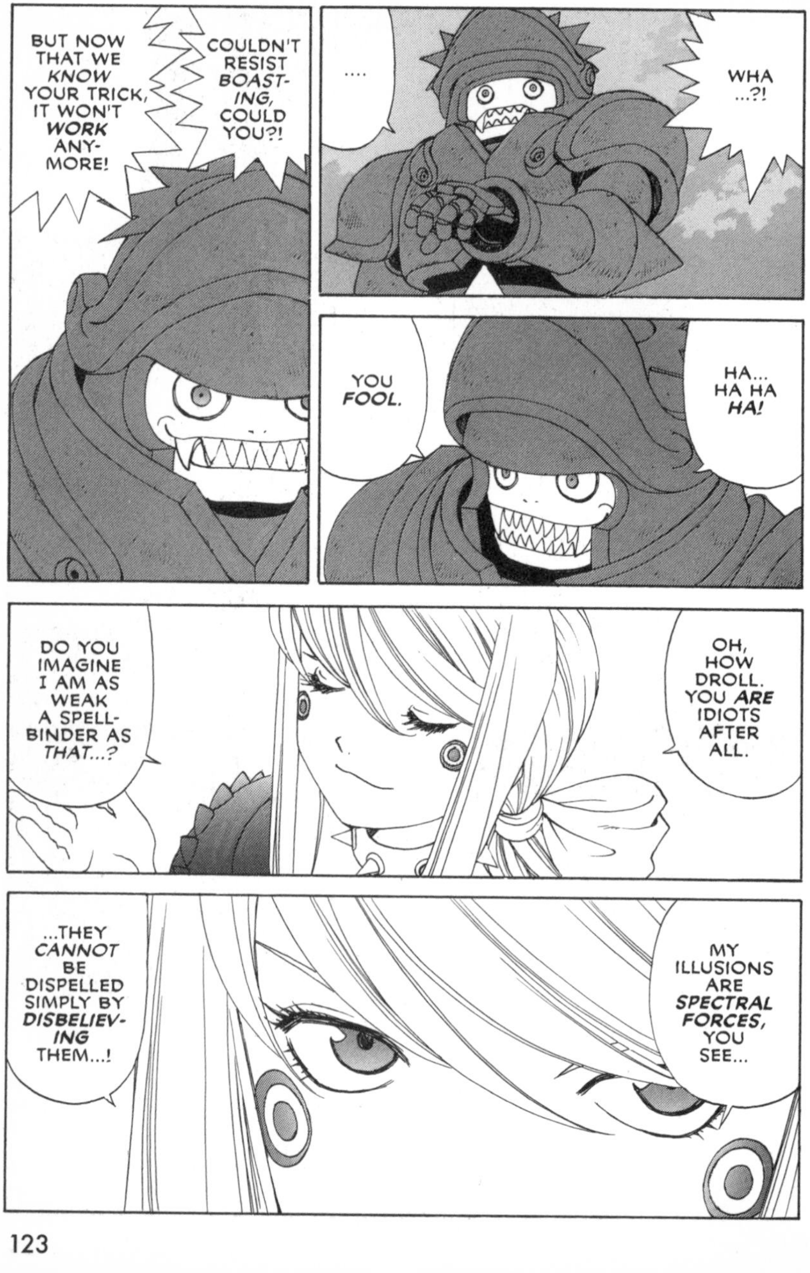
WHA ...?!
....
HA... HA HA *HA!*
YOU *FOOL.*
COULDN'T RESIST *BOASTING,* COULD YOU?!
BUT NOW THAT WE *KNOW* YOUR TRICK, IT WON'T *WORK* ANYMORE!
OH, HOW DROLL. YOU *ARE* IDIOTS AFTER ALL.
DO YOU IMAGINE I AM AS WEAK A SPELLBINDER AS *THAT...?*
MY ILLUSIONS ARE *SPECTRAL FORCES,* YOU SEE...
...THEY *CANNOT* BE DISPELLED SIMPLY BY *DISBELIEVING* THEM...!

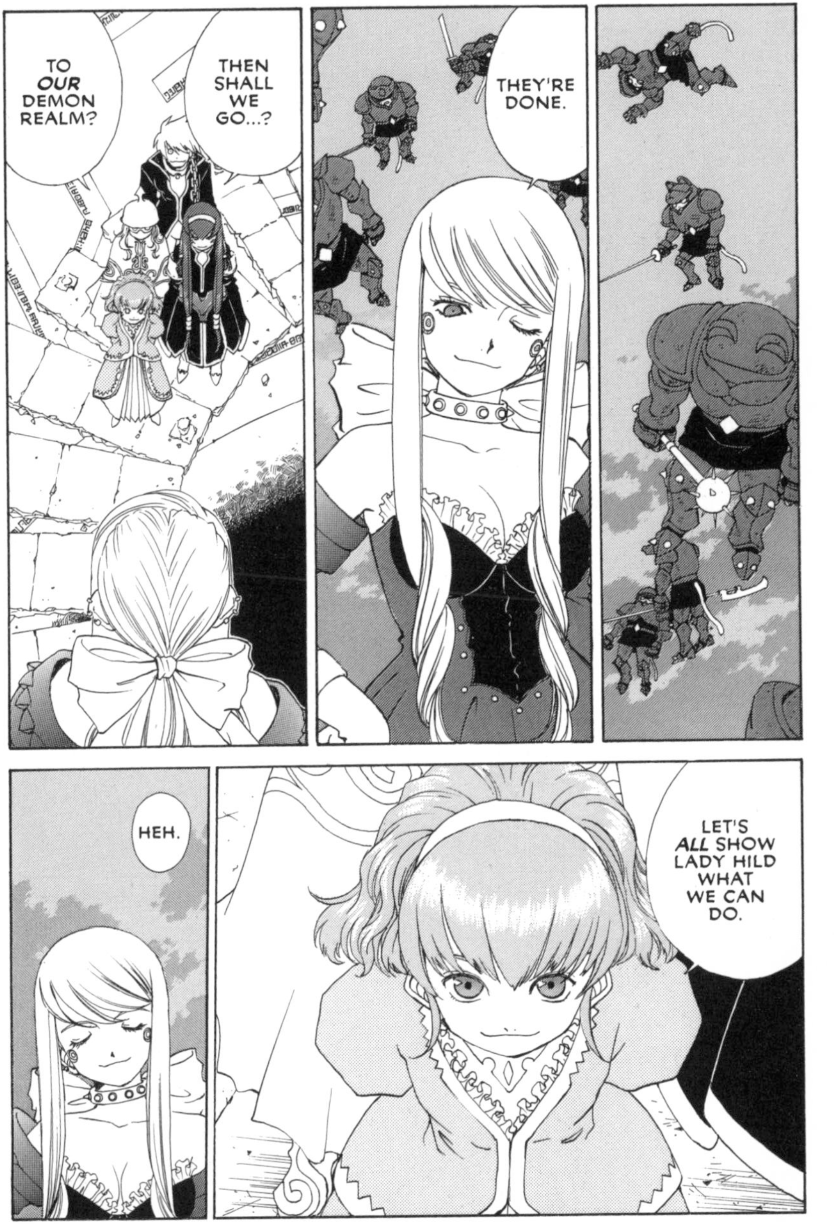
THEY'RE DONE.
THEN SHALL WE GO...?
TO *OUR* DEMON REALM?
LET'S *ALL* SHOW LADY HILD WHAT WE CAN DO.
HEH.

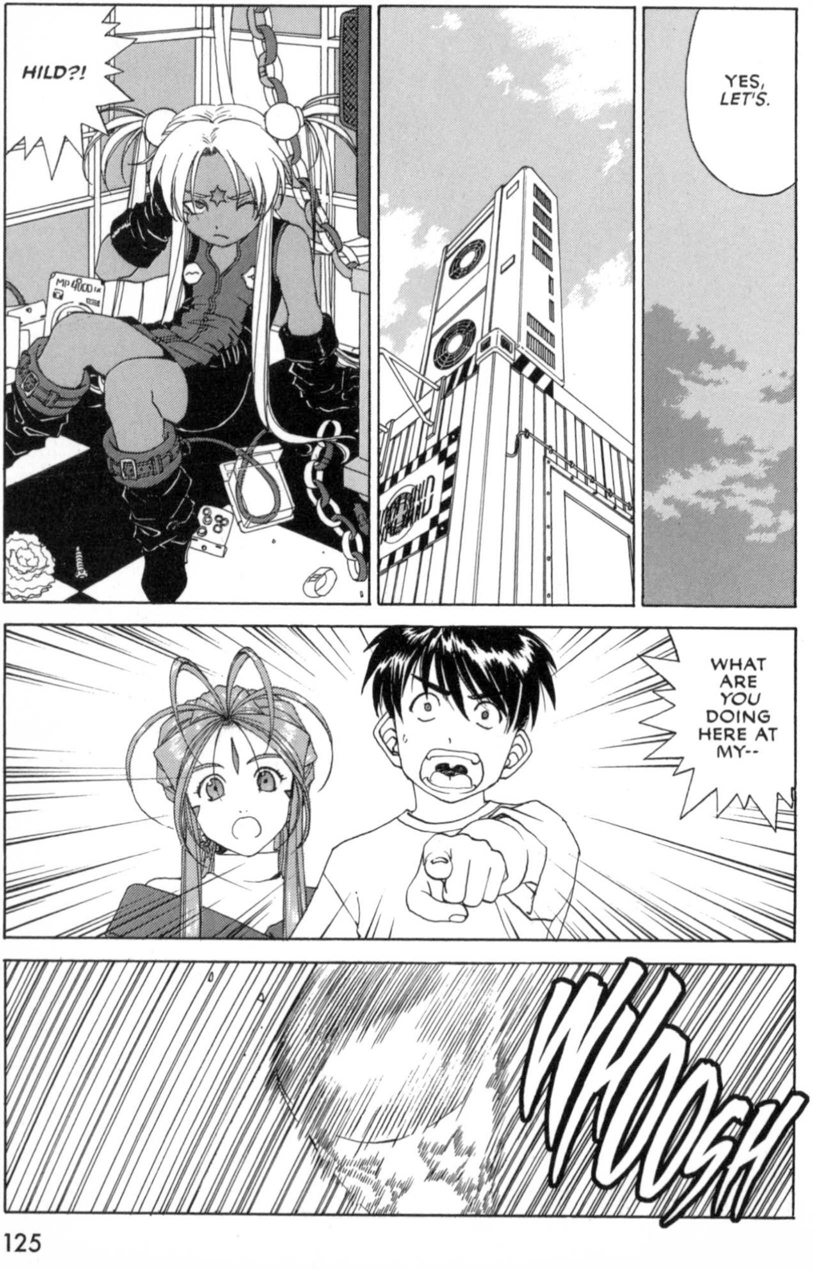
YES, LET'S.
HILD?!
WHAT ARE YOU DOING HERE AT MY--
WHOOSH

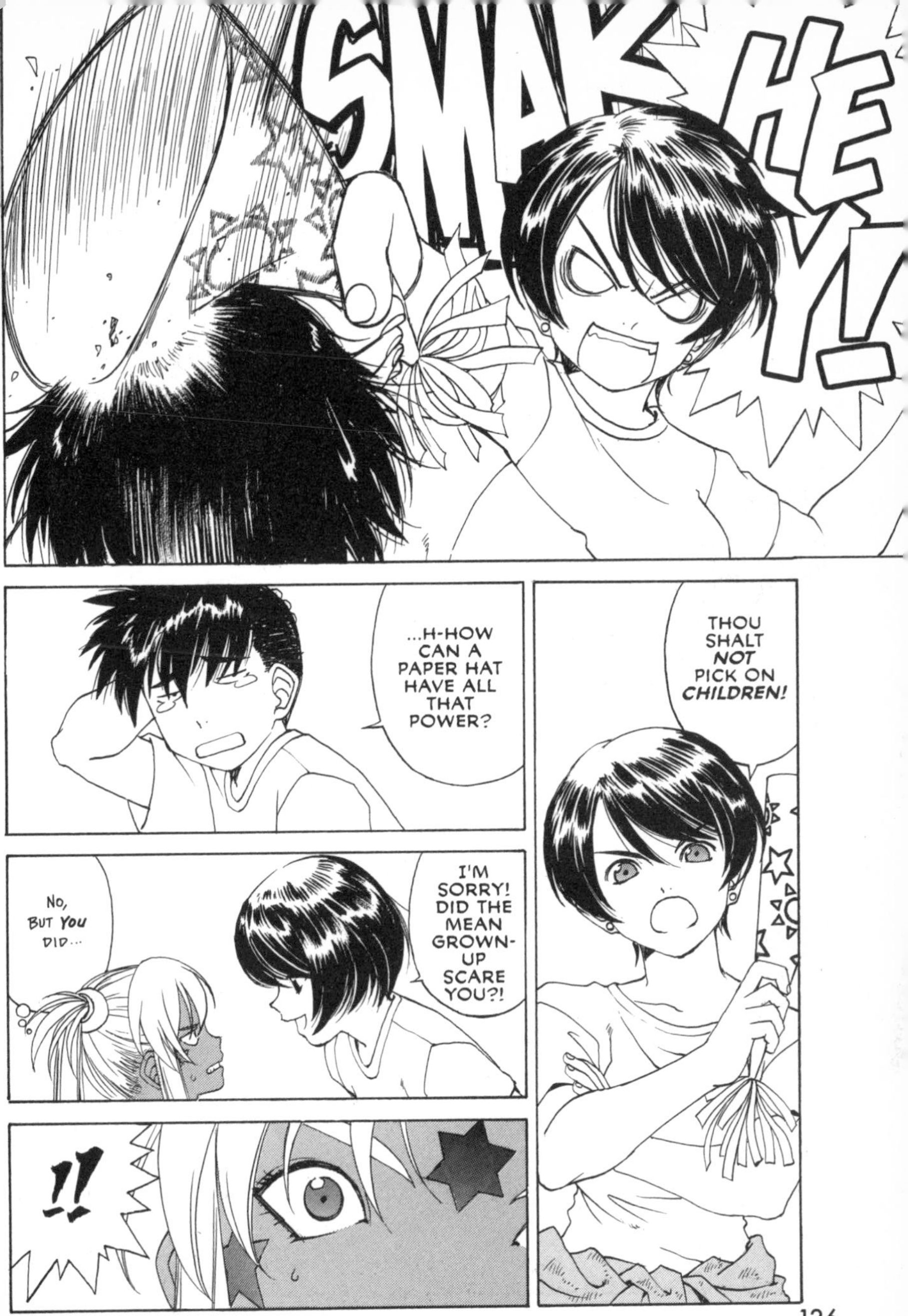
HEY!!
SMAK
THOU SHALT **NOT** PICK ON **CHILDREN!**
...H-HOW CAN A PAPER HAT HAVE ALL THAT POWER?
I'M SORRY! DID THE MEAN GROWN-UP SCARE YOU?!
No, but ***you*** did...
!!

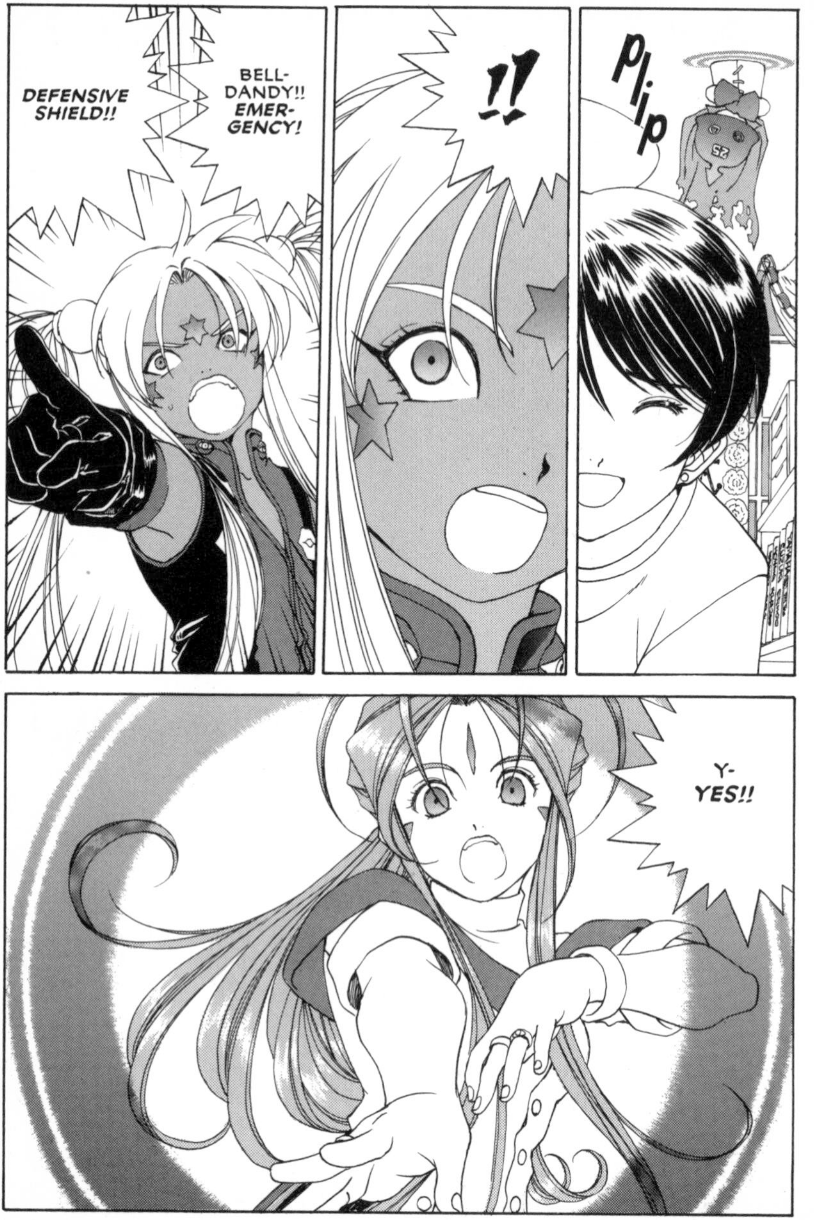
plip
!!
BELL-DANDY!! EMER-GENCY!
DEFENSIVE SHIELD!!
Y-YES!!

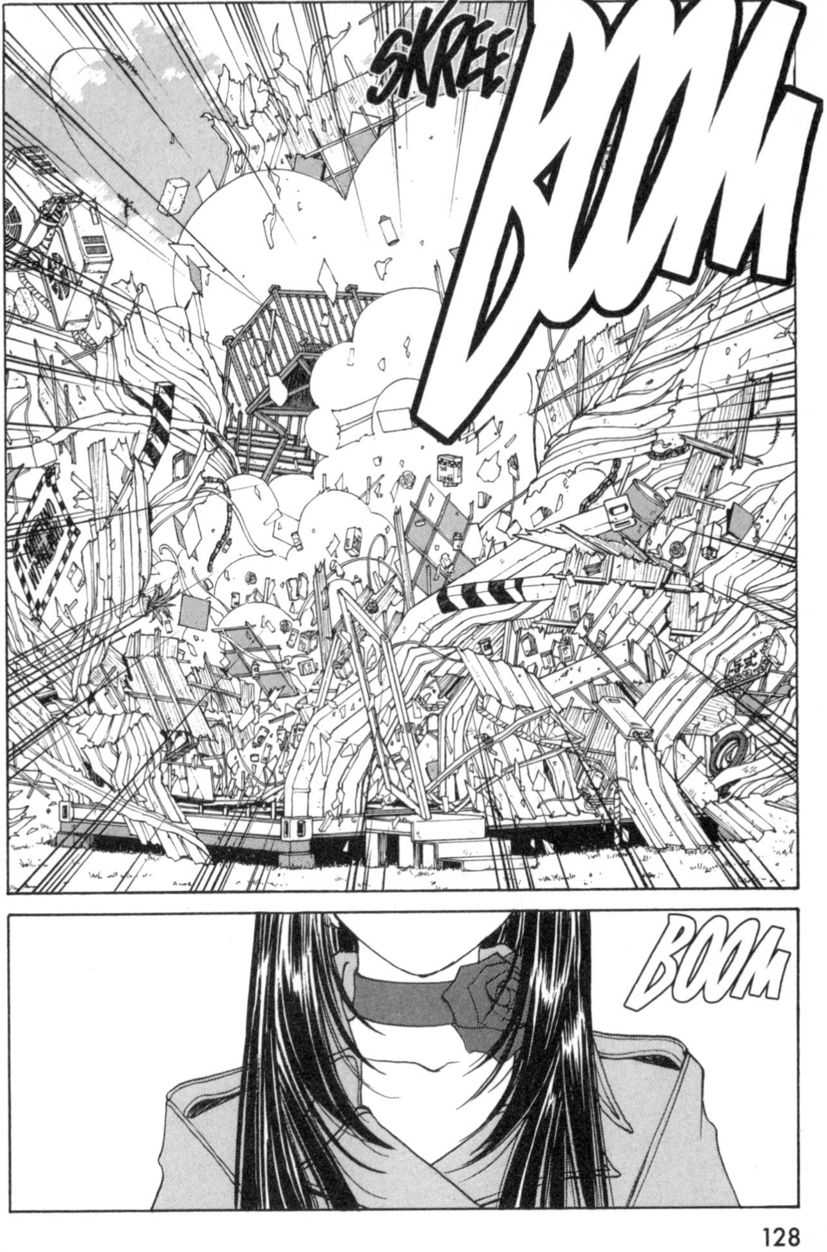
SKREE
BOOM
BOOM

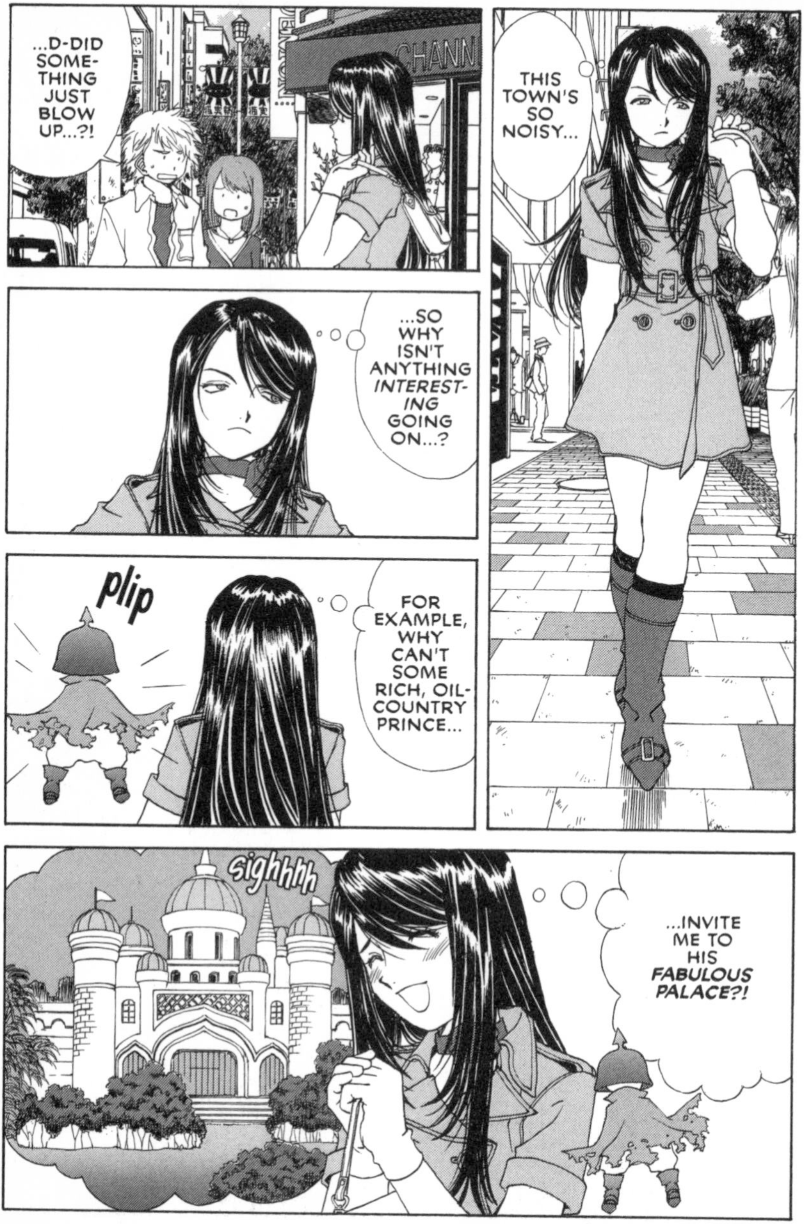
THIS TOWN'S SO NOISY...
...D-DID SOMETHING JUST BLOW UP...?!
...SO WHY ISN'T ANYTHING *INTERESTING* GOING ON...?
FOR EXAMPLE, WHY CAN'T SOME RICH, OIL-COUNTRY PRINCE...
plip
...INVITE ME TO HIS *FABULOUS PALACE*?!
sighhhh

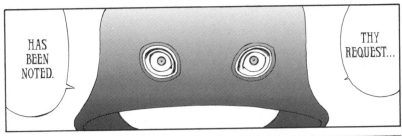

HAS BEEN NOTED.

THY REQUEST...

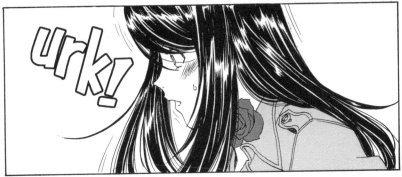

urk!

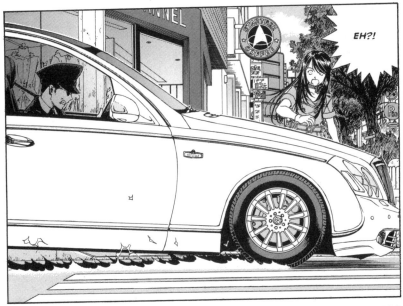

EH?!

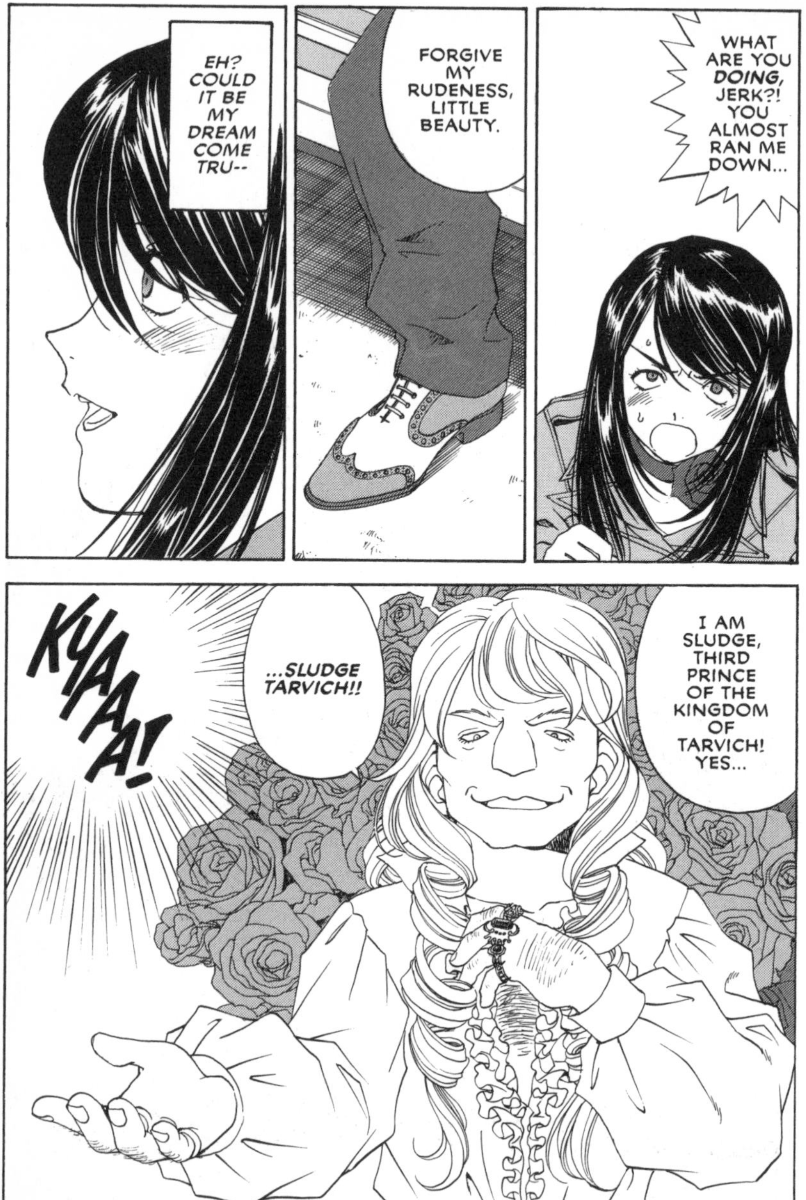
WHAT ARE YOU DOING, JERK?! YOU ALMOST RAN ME DOWN...
FORGIVE MY RUDENESS, LITTLE BEAUTY.
EH? COULD IT BE MY DREAM COME TRU--
I AM SLUDGE, THIRD PRINCE OF THE KINGDOM OF TARVICH! YES...
...SLUDGE TARVICH!!
KYAAAA!

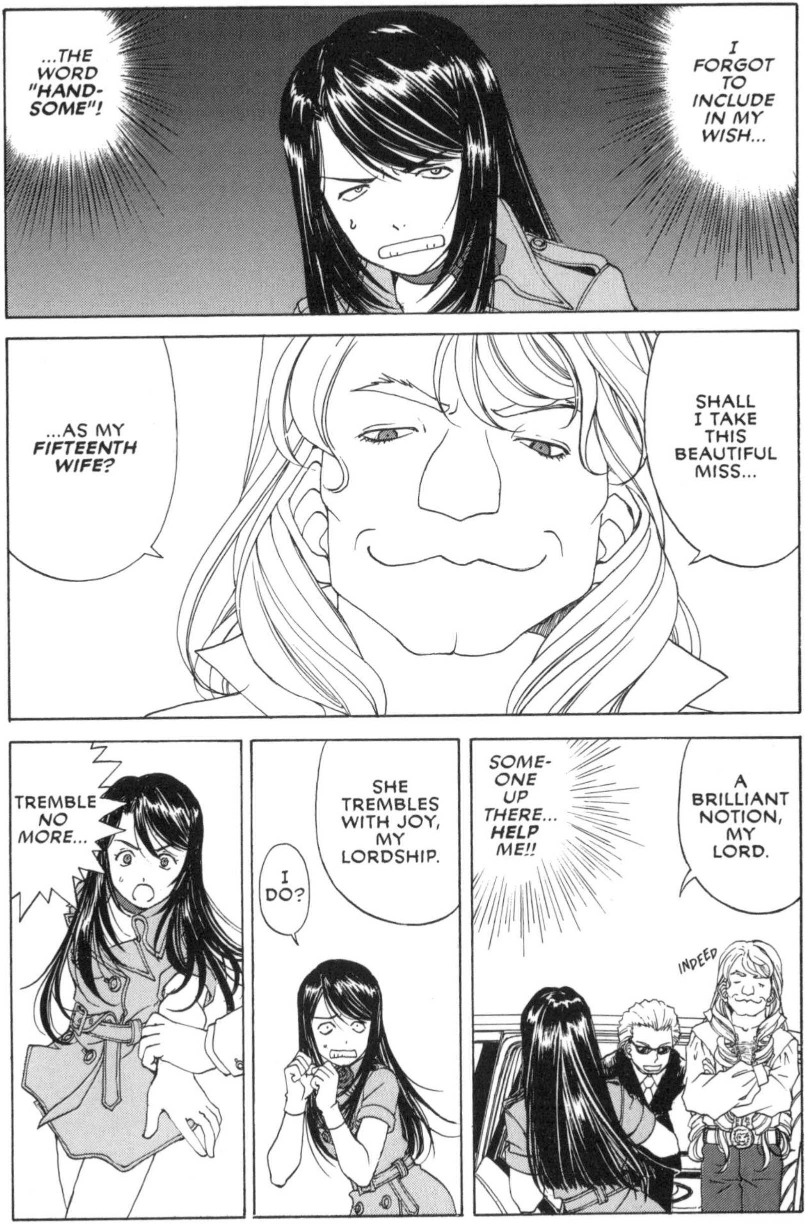
I FORGOT TO INCLUDE IN MY WISH...
...THE WORD "HAND-SOME"!
SHALL I TAKE THIS BEAUTIFUL MISS...
...AS MY FIFTEENTH WIFE?
A BRILLIANT NOTION, MY LORD.
INDEED
SOME-ONE UP THERE... HELP ME!!
SHE TREMBLES WITH JOY, MY LORDSHIP.
I DO?
TREMBLE NO MORE...

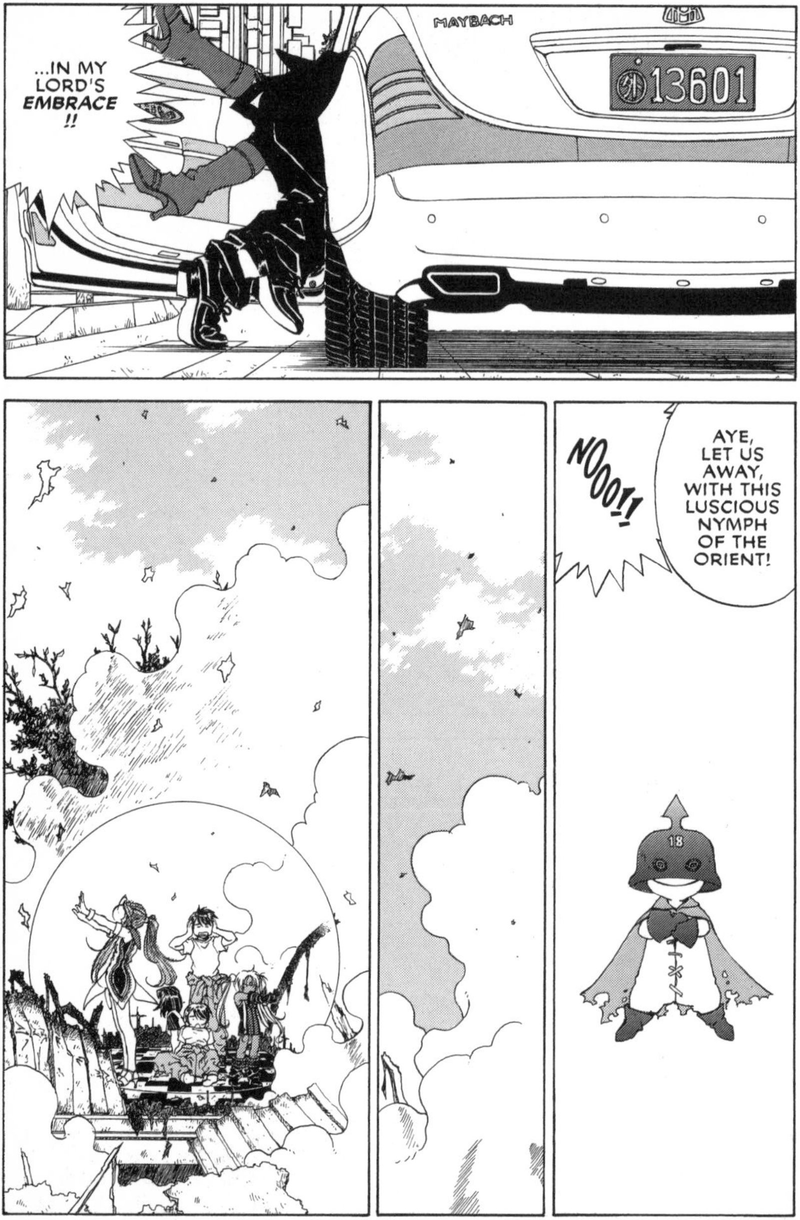
MAYBACH
13601
...IN MY LORD'S EMBRACE !!
AYE, LET US AWAY, WITH THIS LUSCIOUS NYMPH OF THE ORIENT!
NOOO!!
18

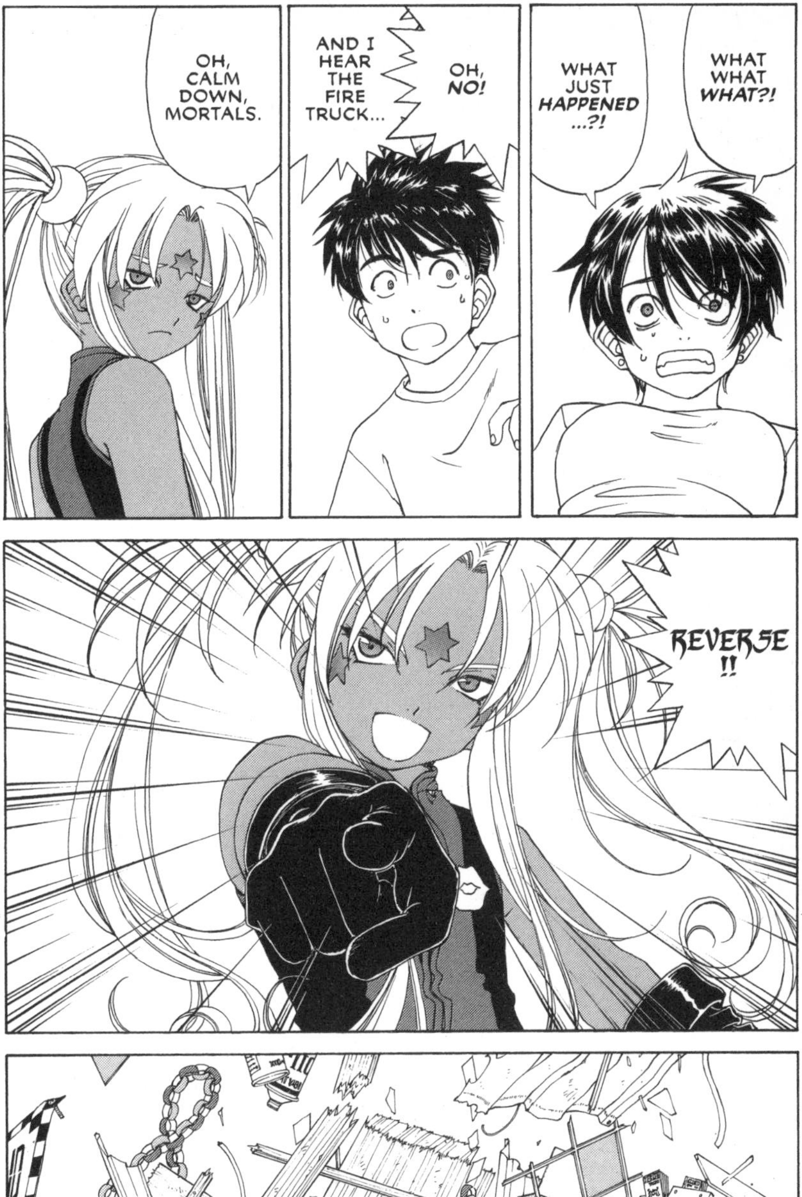
WHAT WHAT *WHAT?!*
WHAT JUST *HAPPENED* ...?!
OH, *NO!*
AND I HEAR THE FIRE TRUCK...
OH, CALM DOWN, MORTALS.
REVERSE !!

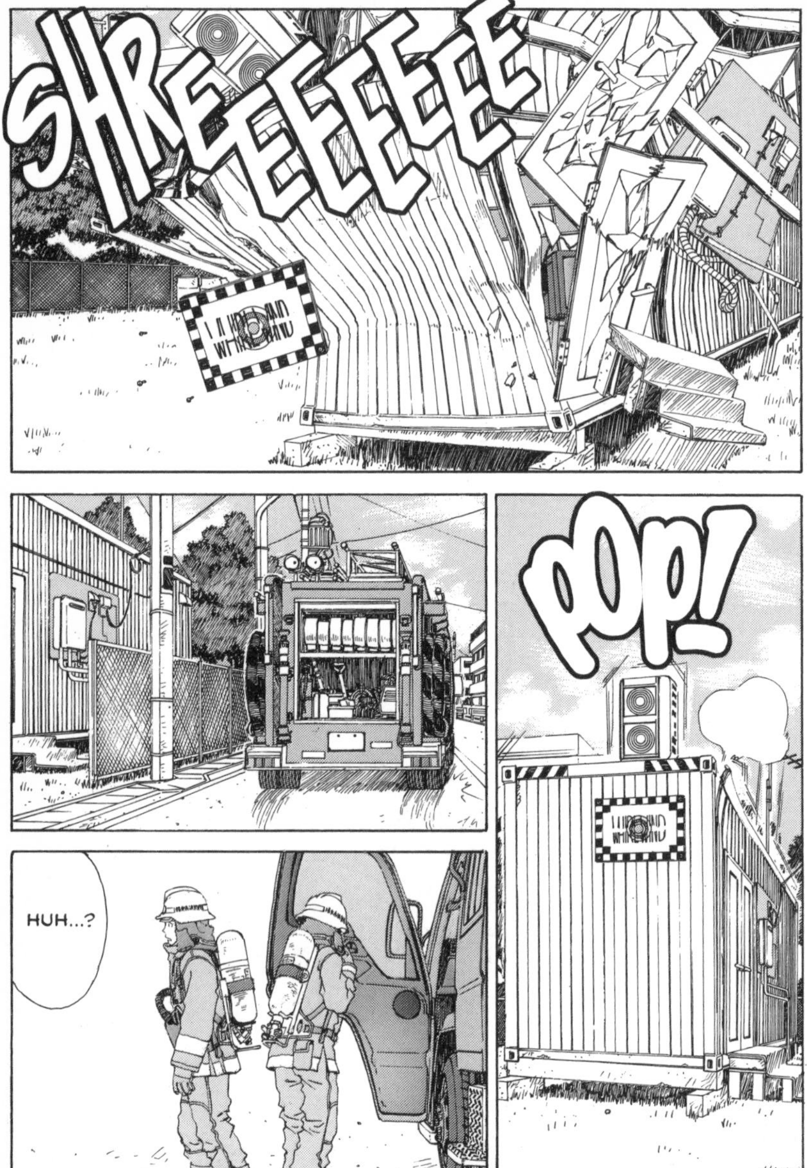
SHREEEEEEE
POP!
HUH...?

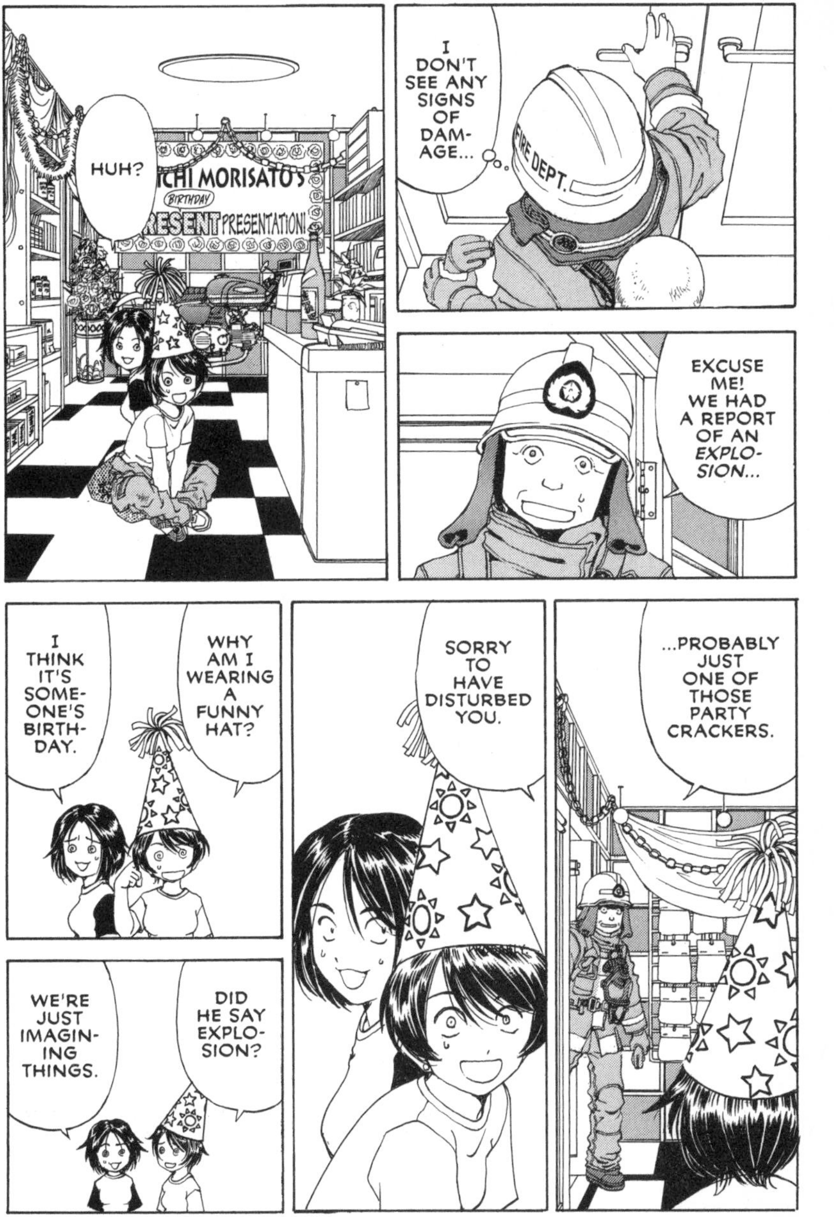
I DON'T SEE ANY SIGNS OF DAM-AGE...
FIRE DEPT.
EXCUSE ME! WE HAD A REPORT OF AN *EXPLOSION*...
HUH?
ICHI MORISATO'S
BIRTHDAY
RESENT PRESENTATION!
...PROBABLY JUST ONE OF THOSE PARTY CRACKERS.
SORRY TO HAVE DISTURBED YOU.
WHY AM I WEARING A FUNNY HAT?
I THINK IT'S SOME-ONE'S BIRTH-DAY.
DID HE SAY EXPLO-SION?
WE'RE JUST IMAGIN-ING THINGS.

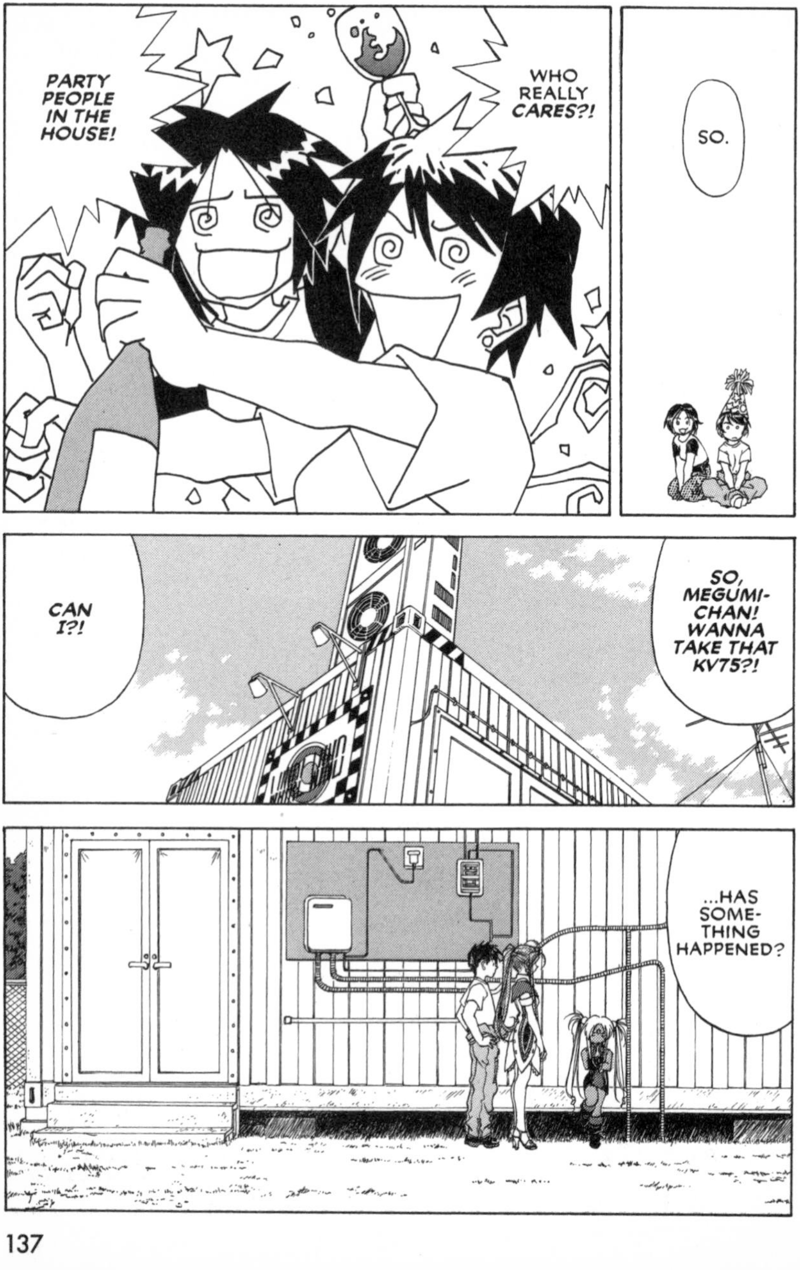
SO.
WHO REALLY CARES?!
PARTY PEOPLE IN THE HOUSE!
SO, MEGUMI-CHAN! WANNA TAKE THAT KV75?!
CAN I?!
...HAS SOME-THING HAPPENED?

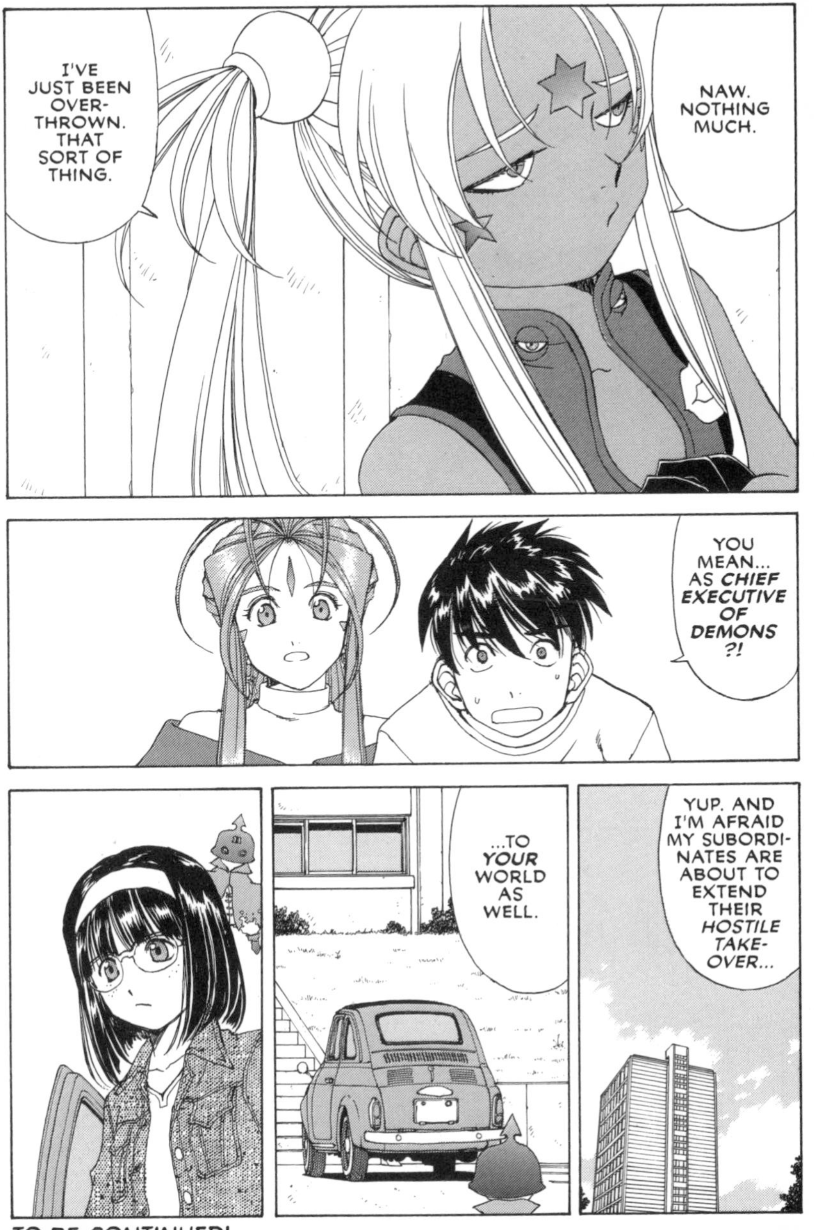
NAW. NOTHING MUCH.
I'VE JUST BEEN OVERTHROWN. THAT SORT OF THING.
YOU MEAN... AS *CHIEF EXECUTIVE OF DEMONS*?!
YUP. AND I'M AFRAID MY SUBORDINATES ARE ABOUT TO EXTEND THEIR *HOSTILE TAKEOVER*...
...TO *YOUR* WORLD AS WELL.

TO BE CONTINUED!

EDITOR
Carl Gustav Horn

EDITORIAL ASSISTANT
Annie Gullion

DESIGNER
Kat Larson

PUBLISHER
Mike Richardson

English-language version
produced by Dark Horse Comics

Published by Dark Horse Manga
A division of Dark Horse Comics, Inc.
10956 SE Main Street
Milwaukie, OR 97222
DarkHorse.com

To find a comics shop in your area,
call the Comic Shop Locator Service
toll-free at 1-888-266-4226

First edition: April 2011
ISBN 978-1-59582-711-1

1 3 5 7 9 10 8 6 4 2

Printed at Lebonfon Printing, Inc., Val-d'Or, QC, Canada

letters to the
ENCHANTRESS

10956 SE Main Street, Milwaukie, Oregon 97222
OMG@DarkHorse.com • DarkHorse.com

NOTE: Full addresses and e-mail addresses will not be printed, unless you ask! All fan artwork, letters, and e-mails submitted become the property of Dark Horse Comics.

I know I said this in vol. 37 ^_^ but as you know, we switch off every two months between another new (i.e., never before published in English) volume of *OMG!* such as this, and an "old" one—previous volumes of *OMG!* that we released years ago in flopped, Western-style versions, and are now redoing as unflopped, Japanese-style versions. The reason I'm bringing this up is because if you're wondering what's been happening to your letters and fan art (for which we are very grateful!) please check some of those recent "old" editions, such as vol. 16 and 17!

Just to keep you zinging through time like a pachinko ball (I don't know if there is an *Oh My Goddess!* pachinko game in Japan, but did you know it's common there to base them on anime and manga? Just the other day a new one came out based on *Maha go go go*, better known to us as *Speed Racer*! Now *that's* kicking it old school!), let's start with a little extra commentary about the December 1990 installment of *Oh My Goddess!* (chapter 24), which had to be cut from vol. 36 for length reasons. That's right, even our special features have special features!

The December 1990 issue of Afternoon also contained some color manga story pages

(you can see them at the beginning of vol. 4 of the Dark Horse edition). Unlike in the US, where it's common to have comics in color, in Japan it's highly unusual. There are a (very) few regular manga series that are in color, but they usually consist of short chapters—say, four or eight pages an issue; a current example is Seizou Watase's A Lion from the North, which runs in Afternoon's sister magazine, the weekly Morning (you may know it as the home of Takehiko Inoue's acclaimed samurai manga Vagabond).

More typically, though, the only time you see color manga pages used is as a kind of "teaser," to draw the attention of readers, especially in a manga's early days or when a new story arc begins, and on such occasions, the first four pages of the manga chapter might be in color—not much, but, of course, enough to make it stand out when most of the rest of the magazine is in black and white.

Fujishima used one page to show off how Urd and Belldandy were color coordinating their outfits, and this received an enthusiastic response from readers, especially two eighteen-year-old students from different parts of Japan who nevertheless expressed similar sentiments. Norio Takazawa of Chiba Prefecture said, "Belldandy looks so good in everything she wears. I wish we had a girl like her in our school," whereas "Yokkyun" from Hiroshima Prefecture said, "Belldandy's fashion was fabulous on this issue's color pages! I wish I could go to

a school festival with cute Belldandy and Urd there."

Fujishima replied, "I'm happy to hear that you liked her fashion. I wanted to improve her outfit even more. The next time I do a color page, I plan to show you a much, **much** more sophisticated design." The next time, by the way, was Skuld's debut in the April 1991 issue.

Okay, speaking of which, now let's go back (or forward) to Fujishima's comments from the spring and summer of 1991. But first, some errata: I don't think it was made clear in vol. 37, but Fujishima-sensei's comments about his Suzuki DR250 and Lotus Super 7 were not from the May 1991 issue of *Afternoon*, but the June issue. And where could that bring us but to the July 1991 issue of *Afternoon* (*Oh My Goddess!* Chapter 34). Van Halen's *For Unlawful Carnal Knowledge* was the number one album in the United States (Keiichi is a fan of Van Halen—see vol. 1, p. 138—so he might have gone out and bought that. It's not as if he has any other sort of carnal knowledge. Sorry, I was possessed by the unkind spirit of Urd there for a moment. Or maybe Peorth. Or Megumi. Come to think of it, any number of characters have remarked on his state), and just the month before, the first *Sonic the Hedgehog* game had come out from Sega ("SEGA!"). But that was of no concern to Mr. Fujishima, because . . .

"I finally bought a Super Famicom [what the Super Nintendo was called in Japan; you probably know this, but Famicom was short for "Family Computer," which is how Nintendo marketed the game console in Japan—as in, fun for the whole family] and am playing F-Zero. I heard a whisper on the wind that Namie Iwao [a fellow manga

creator who was something of a video-game expert; see the comments in vol. 34 on p. 138] can beat two minutes on the game. I can't do better than two minutes twenty seconds, even in practice mode. But can Iwao beat two minutes on the expert level? I'll try my best, too!" F-Zero was a racing game set in the twenty-sixth century, where contestants drove plasma-powered hover-cars for the entertainment of an intergalactic audience; it's no wonder it would appeal to a motorhead like Kosuke Fujishima. F-Zero made extensive use of so-called Mode 7 graphics, which created a pseudo 3-D effect through the constant rotating and scaling of the background. The game has had a number of sequels and spinoffs; you might have seen the anime version, F-Zero: GP Legend, which aired on FoxBox in 2005, before it was abruptly canceled.

In that same July 1991 issue of Afternoon, the probably-not-named-this-in-real-life Nakanoku Hokusai, a twenty-four-year-old professional (professional what, the reader doesn't say), remarked on the events of the previous chapter: "Just when I was thinking how cute Urd was when she got her license suspended, she turned into the 'Lord of Terror,' and . . . ha, ha! Ha, ha, ha . . . (laughter continues for two minutes)." Fujishima, who at that point owned five motorcyles and one car, confessed that the story was inspired in part by real life. "I've actually had my driver's license suspended twice, most recently three years ago, for speeding and several other violations. It's a sad memory for me, but I was able to reflect the experience in my work, so maybe it was useful after all."

Other readers were more interested in Urd's racy, rather than racing, appeal: Sonoji, a twenty-one-year-old student from

Hokkaido (Keiichi's home prefecture), said, "It's hard to let go of the sight of your beautiful legs peeking out from beneath the slits of your China dress," whereas twenty-year-old Yamanashi, who listed his (presumably) occupation as "sorcerer," continued this direct mode of address with, "Miss Urd, is it really 'Mistress Urd'?! From now on, are you going to stomp on men's bodies with your high heels?!" Fujishima replied on behalf of his fictional character, "I'm happy that a drawing I put a lot of effort into has won first place. I understand that some people felt it was 'S&M-ish,' but what I aimed for was precisely that 'S.' In fact, I really wanted to make it much more 'S' than it is, but I didn't have any background material on such matters. I don't think I'll find the will to acquire any in the future, either."

In the August 1991 issue (Oh My Goddess! Chapter 36), Fujishima recalled more innocent (?) pursuits, as his parents had just moved to a new house, and in doing so shipped all the plastic models he built in high school from his old room to his current residence. Fujishima-san went to high school in the late 1970s and early '80s, so the "G" character models he refers to are likely from Mobile Suit Gundam, whose original TV show and movies came out during that time. But we don't know what his 1/100 scale Tamiya (a famous Japanese model company; the Oh My Goddess! character is named for it) models were of, nor his 1/144 scale LS ones (LS being a modeler that went out of business in 1992), only that Fujishima was bewildered by the question, "What am I going to do with this pile?"

A thirty-five-year-old reader from Kanagawa Prefecture named Masaaki Susuki was troubled by the notion that Belldandy had a preference for long skirts, to which

the editor replied that Fujishima was still busy playing F-Zero and that he'd have to try and work the response in: "Just another eight seconds to cut off my time. I'm this close. Oh, I need to answer the letter, too. Well, how do you like the way her legs were revealed in chapter 36? If that was satisfactory, please let me know." The editor further related that Fujishima had managed to injure himself in an off-road bike accident the other day, noting that, "in some ways, he's a busy guy."

Remarking upon the nuclear submarine depicted in chapter 37 (September 1991), Fujishima said he used a model kit to research that, too, but burst out laughing at the spelling of the Japanese in the made-in-Hong-Kong kit's instructions, including, instead of "genshi-ryoku taabin" ("nuclear-powered turbine"), "genshi-ryoku-chiibin," which makes it sound really small and cute. Fujishima recommended people buy the kit just for the instructions, saying they were funnier than some manga. By the way, during his 2010 appearance at Anime Weekend Atlanta, the director of Appleseed and Halo Legends, Shinji Aramaki (who is only four years older than Fujishima), mentioned that one of the reasons anime shows used to have more mecha than they do now is that his generation were more likely to be model builders). The English-language editor notes that he remembers the funny English that used to be on import model instructions, and is amused to see that some came with funny Japanese, as well.

The Lord of Terror story arc suddenly introduced cosmic stakes to the Oh My Goddess! series, which had previously been more lighthearted (although, this being OMG!, it's not like things ever got 100 percent serious), and readers were thrown by the twists. A nineteen-year-old student from Saitama

Prefecture by the distinctive name of "I Saw Popeye!" lamented, "Ahhh! What's going to happen to Urd? And you've got God himself saying he's going to strike her down! I can't sleep thinking about it!" Fujishima reassured (?) the reader by saying, "I'm working on the script right now, but it looks like it's going to be a huge catastrophe. I'm scared to sleep, too! Please look forward to the goddesses running completely out of the control of the author."

As requested, plaudits poured in for the goddesses' gams (that's almost a Variety headline). Atsushi Mizuta, seventeen years old, from Ehime Prefecture, wrote in to say, "I was impressed by Belldandy's beautiful legs. But I guess things like this are so nice because they don't happen **so** often. Right . . . " A twenty-one-year-old reader from Aomori Prefecture was perhaps aptly named "Hee Hee," judging by the excited feedback of "Le . . . le . . . le . . . legs! Uhmmm . . . what should I do . . . ?! But I'm certainly happyyyy . . . " The editor noted that Fujishima himself was happy to have been able to draw so many legs, and thanked the readers for their "precious comments."

In the October 1991 issue of Afternoon (Oh My Goddess! Chapter 38), Fujishima found himself again concerned with beautiful lines, as he had just paid another visit to the famous Matsuda private collection of modern and historic Ferraris in Gotenba, and was delighted to see that it had acquired a Lamborghini Diablo as well—which had just come on the market in 1990 and was the first vehicle of that marque that could exceed 200 mph. "It was much more powerful in the flesh than in photographs," said Fujishima. "I wouldn't think of buying one, but a car with that mean look is quite nice, too." The English-language editor wonders if Fujishima-san was joking—or was Oh My Goddess! already that successful?—as the Diablo reportedly cost $240,000; with inflation, that'd be almost $390,000 today. The museum Fujishima visited back in 1991 is apparently no longer open; a single car from the collection (a 1963 Ferrari 250 GTO) recently sold at auction for $26 million!

A seventeen-year-old student from Mie Prefecture going by the name of "Kofuku wo yobu aoi kingyo" ("The blue goldfish of good fortune"), wrote into that issue to congratulate Fujishima-san on Oh My Goddess! finishing up its third year of publication. A foreign (?) student in Saitama Prefecture, twenty-two-year-old J. B. Keenan, was impatient, however: "I'm anxious to know what happens next in the Oh My Goddess! story line. One a month is a long time to wait."

Fujishima had thought things through, however. Contrasting with manga that have to be drawn one chapter a week (such as Naruto, Bleach, One Piece, etc., which appear in Japan's weekly Shonen Jump magazine), he said that drawing for a monthly magazine like Afternoon "lets me lead a full life," and he reflected how much faster his three years on Oh My Goddess! had gone by than high school, which in Japan, is also three years. "Please continue to savor the series as a monthly treat," said Fujishima-san. And with this volume's chapter 242, which appeared in Afternoon 206 months later, it looks like readers saw the wisdom of the creator! See you all in vol. 39!

—CGH

STOP!

This manga collection is translated into English, but arranged in right-to-left reading format to maintain the artwork's visual orientation as originally drawn and published in Japan. If you've never read comics this way before, take a look at the diagram below to give yourself an idea of how to go about it. Basically, you'll be starting in the upper right-hand corner, and will read each word balloon and panel moving right to left. It may take a little getting used to, but you should get the hang of it very quickly. Have fun! If this is the millionth manga you've read this way, never mind. ^_^

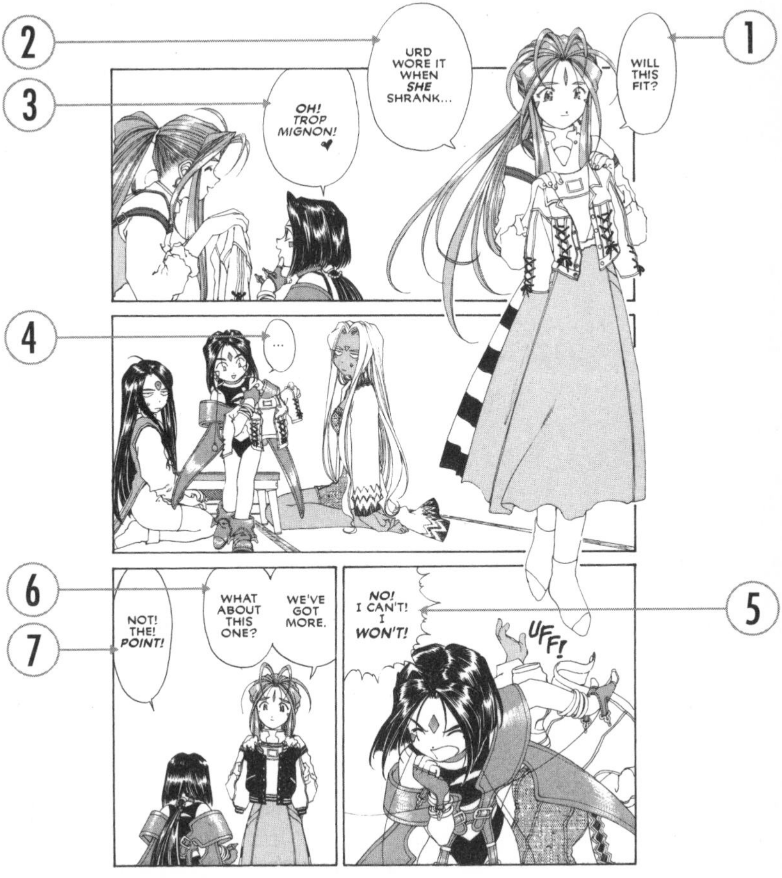
1
WILL THIS FIT?
2
URD WORE IT WHEN SHE SHRANK...
3
OH! TROP MIGNON!
4
...
5
NO! I CAN'T! I WON'T!
UFF!
6
WE'VE GOT MORE.
WHAT ABOUT THIS ONE?
7
NOT! THE! POINT!